GW00367866

Tristan's Shadow

Tristan's Shadow

SEXUALITY AND THE TOTAL WORK OF
ART AFTER WAGNER

Adrian Daub

The University of Chicago Press   CHICAGO & LONDON

ADRIAN DAUB is assistant professor of German studies at Stanford University.
He is the author of *Uncivil Unions: The Metaphysics of Marriage in German Idealism* and
Romanticism and of *Four-Handed Monsters: Four-Hand Piano Playing and the Making of
Nineteenth Century Domestic Culture.*

The University of Chicago Press, Chicago 60637
The University of Chicago Press, Ltd., London
© 2014 by The University of Chicago
All rights reserved. Published 2014.
Printed in the United States of America

23 22 21 20 19 18 17 16 15 14   1 2 3 4 5

ISBN-13: 978-0-226-08213-4 (cloth)
ISBN-13: 978-0-226-08227-1 (e-book)
DOI: 10.7208/chicago/9780226082271.001.0001

Library of Congress Cataloging-in-Publication Data
Daub, Adrian.
Tristan's shadow : sexuality and the total work of art
after Wagner / Adrian Daub.
pages cm
Includes bibliographical references and index.
ISBN 978-0-226-08213-4 (cloth : alk. paper) — ISBN 978-0-226-08227-1
(e-book) 1. Opera—19th century. 2. Wagner, Richard, 1813–1883—Influence.
3. Sex in opera.   I. Title.
ML1705.D383 2014
782.109'034—dc23
2013014689

♾ This paper meets the requirements of ANSI/NISO Z39.48–1992 (Permanence of Paper).

CONTENTS

ACKNOWLEDGMENTS

Although it is a book about the Gesamtkunstwerk, Tristan's Shadow came together in fits and starts, and as a result many forces, individuals, and institutions shaped its development and growth.

Over the years, the manuscript has benefitted from a number of careful and generous readers. Tom Grey and Stephen Hinton were instrumental in shaping the ideas contained in this book. Their comments and encouragement were essential to having the material assume the shape it has now. David Levin and Ryan Minor were invaluable in first responding to some of the book's individual chapters and then guiding me through the process of tying them all together.

Since this is a book about opera composers who have largely gone from being celebrities to being entirely marginal in the opera canon, much valuable insight into the overall shape of the project came from people outside music. The members of the Junior Faculty Reading Group in the DLCL, Martón Dornbach, Marisa Galvez, Héctor Hoyos, Nariman Skakov, Lisa Surwillo, and Laura Wittman were essential in giving me an early sense why a general academic reader might care about this largely forgotten set of operas. Kara Levy was not only a fantastic editor in the early going of the project, but she also provided invaluable advice on how to make the book accessible to those not steeped in the subject matter.

An internal faculty fellowship at the Stanford Humanities Center gave me the opportunity to heavily revise the final manuscript. I am indebted to the other fellows at the center for many a valuable suggestion in the final stages of composition.

At the University of Chicago Press, Doug Mitchell and Tim McGovern expertly steered the manuscript through the vicissitudes of the review process and provided valuable guidance to reworking it. I am glad I was able to say thank you to Doug by introducing him to the work of Alexander Zemlinsky. Susan Karani copyedited the manuscript with great care and palpable enthusiasm for the subject matter.

Chapter 1 was previously published in *Nineteenth Century Music* 32, no. 2 (pp. 160–77), chapter 3 was previously published in *Opera Quarterly* 25, nos. 3–4 (pp. 230–46), parts of chapter 7 were published in *Opera Quarterly* 26, no. 4 (pp. 526–51), and portions of chapter 5 appeared in *Cambridge Opera Journal* and the *Companion to Walter Benjamin*, edited by Rolf Goebel and published by Camden House. I thank these publications for the permission to reprint. This book is dedicated to my father, who introduced me to the world of Richard Wagner.

Tristan's Shadow: The Fate of Sexual Difference in Opera

This book presents a story of aesthetics and opera. It will be about actual operas, how they were written, composed, and performed, but its primary concern will be what composers thought they were doing when composing operas—what they imagined the opera form entailed, what problems it posed, and what promises it held beyond the walls of the opera house. As a result, the shadow it traces is not that cast by Wagner's innovations in compositional technique, or in new musical logics that emerged in his wake; it is the shadow of a particular ideology of the operatic, what could be asked of the form, and what needed to be asked of it. *Tristan*'s shadow persists at the border between music and philosophy, between actual operas on the one hand and the more theoretical demands and desiderata of operatic aesthetics on the other.

Somewhat counterintuitively, *Tristan and Isolde* constitutes the middle point of this book's narrative, even though all of these chapters consider works written after its 1865 premiere. My argument is that *Tristan* was able to cast the long shadow it did in operatic aesthetics because of the way it combined earlier topoi, specifically theories about love and theories about the unification of the arts. These constituted the powerful light source that enabled *Tristan* to cast its shadow. Conversely, its legacy proved so troubling for the composers of the late nineteenth and early twentieth century because of contradictions and misgivings that became fully explicit only in the 1920s, in the so-called opera crisis (*Opernkrise*).

The following chapters connect three moments, each about a half century apart, and argue that they together illuminate a peculiar, and peculiarly German, path of operatic aesthetics. Significantly, the first of these three stages hardly had anything to do with opera. About a half century before *Tristan*'s 1865 premiere, the German Romantics furnished the philosophical vocabulary Wagner would later bring to bear on opera. They applied this in two central respects—their philosophies of eros, and their critiques of the separation of the arts. Wagner's speculations about the nature of the erotic and Wagner's theories of the Gesamtkunstwerk are confraternal twins born of German Romanticism and Idealism. Wagner's seminal contribution to opera aesthetics was the realization that the erotic and the total work of art were linked, could be linked, or had to be linked in and through opera. This also entailed a move to an opera that understood itself as a carrier of an implicit or explicit philosophical program—that understood itself in terms of a philosophy of history and a theory of modernity.

Whether Wagner ever succeeded in actually realizing these outsized ambitions has been hotly debated ever since. Are his operas really "total works of art"? Did he mean for them to be? How distinctive is his musical drama; how enduring its legacy in operatic practice? What was never in doubt was that these ambitions loomed large for composers looking to follow in his footsteps. In 1924 Kurt Weill would write that the "artwork of equal rights between word, music and scene, . . . through *Tristan* held the world of opera production in its thrall for fifty years."[1] And Weill's fifty years was, if anything, putting it conservatively. The decisive legacy he impressed upon his successors was that opera needed to reflect on issues of philosophy, of history, and of its own location within a broader project of modernity. This book tells the story of how opera composers who were influenced by Wagner, or otherwise labored in his shadow, grappled with the expanded role the *Meister* had assigned to opera. It is an intellectual history rather than a musical one, dealing with how musicians responded to a theory that was no longer just about aesthetics, but about politics, society, and history.

Fifty years after *Tristan*, post-1918 Germany found itself racked by a full-blown *Opernkrise* concerning the very viability of the form. It brought to a head the sense of unease Wagner's heirs—ardent followers and skeptical fellow travelers alike—had felt for the better part of the preceding decades. The anxieties that erupted in a pervasive sense of crisis after the Great War disrupted the infrastructure of Germany's music world, and they had built and intensified ever since Wagner—some even seemed to animate Wagner's operas themselves. Many of Wagner's most eminent followers (Franz Schreker, Hans Pfitzner, Richard Strauss) got involved in the torrential outpour of pamphlets and articles, as did the music critics and historians (Paul Bekker, for instance, and Richard Batka) who had rushed to declare them Wagner's legitimate heirs.

Then there were the composers of the younger generation, like Kurt Weill, who did not think there was a "crisis" of *opera* at all—just a crisis of Wagner-style opera. This book posits that Weill was correct, and that many of the problems that came to a head in the *Opernkrise* were uniquely associated with Wagner's legacy in German opera.

Tristan's Shadow follows a generation of composers who found themselves caught between these two poles: the overweening demands implied in Wagnerian musical aesthetics; and the creeping sense that an *Opernkrise* was brewing, that the form itself might be superannuated, and incapable or undeserving of reform. While Wagner's legacy fanned out well beyond the borders of the German-speaking world, influencing musicians, poets, and dramatists like Charles Baudelaire, Claude Debussy, and Alexander Scriabin, this constellation of opposing demands was the unique lot of Wagner's successors in Germany. The German "special path" in opera in the second half of the nineteenth century ran between the rock of German Romanticism's outsized demands on the form and the hard place of a pervasive sense that opera could only fall short of that demand.

OPERA AND SEXUALITY AFTER WAGNER

At first glance, it is anything but obvious that either Wagner's erotics or Wagner's concept of the Gesamtkunstwerk are somehow special in the history of opera. Fascination with the erotic seems as old as opera itself. Forms, styles, and movements come and go—but the erotic plot remains by and large a constant preoccupation. And opera constitutively undertakes the combination of different media. Since its beginnings in the late 1500s, it has reflected on what it means to do so. That does not mean, however, that at every point in the tradition opera found or was looking for the same thing when it turned to eroticism. This extends not only to the philosophical or ideological conceptions of love that asserted themselves in marriage plots, love duets, or love deaths in opera. It also extends to the role these plots, duets, and deaths played in the formal constitution of opera as such. At times, love may have provided simply a compelling topic for opera; at others, the way characters interacted erotically dictated, or otherwise stood in dialogue with, those features that were taken to be characteristic of opera as form.

In December 1858, Richard Wagner wrote a letter to the philosopher Arthur Schopenhauer. Wagner had first encountered Schopenhauer's magnum opus *The World as Will and Representation* in 1854, and it had made a powerful impression on him. By the time his friend Georg Herwegh gave him the book,

Wagner had already written several of the operas that would make him famous. But the letter speaks volumes about Wagner's relationship to philosophy, and to the erotic, even before he encountered the thought of Schopenhauer, which would go on to crucially inform the erotics of Wagner's later oeuvre, especially the *Ring Cycle*.

While he decided not to send the letter, he described its intent to Mathilde Wesendonck, wife of his friend, the silk merchant Otto Wesendonck, and likely his lover. The letter fragment contained annotations on a particular passage from Schopenhauer's book, but then quickly went on to propose a modification of Schopenhauer's theory of the will. In the passage, Schopenhauer questions why star-crossed lovers would take their lives. Why annihilate the self, rather than go to extremes to defend their little slice of salvation? Schopenhauer had written the passage more than a decade and a half ago; Wagner had read it four years prior. But it is clear why it drew his interest now: not only was his private life a shambles, with the composer torn between his wife, Minna, and Mathilde (he in fact wrote the letter with a gilded pen given to him by the latter), but he was also writing a work about the very situation that Schopenhauer was scratching his head over—the story of *Tristan und Isolde*, who find salvation in a loving death.

But Wagner was interested in more than just informing the curmudgeon and misogynist Schopenhauer about just how little he understood what unhappy love felt like. Schopenhauer's book concludes on a decidedly pessimistic note—only resignation in the face of the inevitable frustration of the will, the negation of all willing, can bring the human being to peace. In his letter, Wagner makes a modest proposal: what if we understand "the predisposition for sexual love as a path of salvation, towards self-knowledge and self-denial of the will—and not just the individual will"?[2] In other words, Wagner proposed that erotic love could bring the will to rest in another human being, thus permitting a reconciliation of our striving without the need for resignation.

Wagner's argument remained a fragment, just as the letter proposing it remained unsent. There is little contained in Wagner's claims in the fragment that one cannot draw from his operas. But what is nevertheless remarkable is that Wagner felt compelled to write this letter in the first place. After all Wagner uses a two-page fan letter to essentially rewrite Schopenhauer's entire book. The small alteration he proposes in the theory of what he, like Schopenhauer, calls "the metaphysics of sexual love," amounts to a one hundred and eighty degree turn of Schopenhauer's entire thousand-page-plus tome!

The episode may be unremarkable in itself, insofar as it points to the well-attested conclusion that Wagner may have had a somewhat inflated sense of self. Beyond that, however, the fact that Wagner felt compelled to pontificate on the finer points of metaphysics with a master like Schopenhauer suggests that he to some extent considered Schopenhauer a peer. They were both philosophical thinkers, and at least when it came to human sexuality, Wagner was, or so he supposed, well positioned to offer friendly advice to a senior colleague.

More to the point, Wagner's letter claims to communicate an *Anschauung*, which is usually rendered as "intuition," but in this case is probably something closer to an experimental "observation." It is unlikely that even a man as indiscreet as Wagner would be adducing his travails with Minna, Wesendonck, and soon Cosima as his evidence in an argument about metaphysics. No, the "observation" Wagner thought he could offer to the master thinker in Frankfurt was gleaned during the writing of *Tristan*. Not only, then, does Wagner place himself implicitly on a level playing field with a titan of German philosophy; he also turns to his opera as a theoretical text. For Wagner, *Tristan* can respond to, and even critique, *The World as Will and Representation*.

This is an anomaly in the history of music. Whether or not we take seriously Wagner's self-conception as a philosopher of sorts, albeit a philosopher by other means, it is important that he conceived of himself that way—and that his admirers, including many composers, often did too. Of course, Wagner felt compelled to pontificate on any number of topics, tossing out in his pamphlets, articles, and missives ideas on art, politics, religion, race, history, and sex, "whenever the impulse struck"[3]—ideas that were sometimes charming in their eclecticism, sometimes amateurish, and sometimes nothing short of monstrous. But, given his range, it is significant that when Wagner felt the urge to offer friendly advice to Schopenhauer, his intervention had to do with the status of the erotic in philosophy.

The spell by which Wagner ensorcelled his century has often been cast in erotic language, and for good reason. The plots of his operas seemed to deal with the erotic in new ways; the intense chromaticism, the luxuriant, yearning tempi of his music, and the constant deferral of harmonic resolution smacked to his contemporaries of a barely sublimated eroticism. What made Wagner unusual, however, was that he coupled these technical innovations with explicit speculations about the nature of sexuality.

This, again, represents an anomaly in the history of music. When Paul Robinson, in *Opera and Ideas*, sought to make a case for the intellectual history of opera, he hedged on the directness of the connection, positing that "the process by which an idea moves from one medium to another is . . . virtually impossible to follow."[4] And similarly, when scholars like Lawrence Kramer, Michel Poizat, and Elisabeth Bronfen make a case for erotic or eroticized categories in opera (such as hysteria), they think that opera is drawn to the erotic by a kind of psychic kinship, or an elective affinity.[5] Or they, like Slavoj Žižek, regard the opera house as an anatomic theater in which theories of the psyche, of drives and subjectivity can be tested, in which "the move from Montiverdi to Gluck's *Orpheus* corresponds to the move from Descartes to Kant."[6]

As Wagner's letter to Schopenhauer makes clear, his relationships to the history of ideas and to the erotic exceed such affinities. He understands his operas as philosophical interventions, and he thinks of the erotic as a privileged locus for such intervention. And in his writings he attempts to outline the reasons he has for doing this. They may not be good reasons, or strike us as sound today—but they created a compelling imperative for his reception and for his successors. For at least a time, operatic sex after Wagner became a matter of philosophy.

Throughout the nineteenth century there had been a school of grand metaphysical speculation about the nature of sexuality. By 1840, one could find these kinds of grand theories about the species, the nature of erotic attraction, and the nature of the bonds it instituted in the novels and stories of Romantic writers and in the philosophy of Arthur Schopenhauer, the Hegelians, and Søren Kierkegaard. By 1880 it had largely been consigned to the opera stage. Literature by and large trafficked in emphatically "realist" love stories, or love stories that eschewed the metaphysical for a more concretely modern setting; philosophy increasingly refused to deal with sex at all, leaving it to biology, sociology, psychology, and any number of emergent individual sciences. In articulating his own philosophy of love and desire, Wagner drew on the heyday of metaphysical speculation about sex, rather than on the thought on the subject that dominated his own day. If anything, Wagner raised the erotic to a higher power than those thinkers who had influenced him.

Wagner had come of age at a time when Romanticism's hold over German literature was beginning to wane, but he spent much of his youth reading (and in some cases meeting) the poets of Romanticism, and he came into his own as a composer among Romanticism's critics and would-be liquidators. He cobbled together a philosophical system from the remains of German Idealism (incorporating above all the thought of Ludwig Feuerbach), traces of which remained constants in his thought even after he discovered the philosophy of Arthur Schopenhauer in the 1850s. Through these influences, Romantic and Idealist conceptions of love and the sexes, far grander than the pictures emerging from sexology, sociology, and psychology in Wagner's own time, made their way into Wagner's operas.

The central idea of Wagner's theory of the erotic is the one that motivated his attempt at helping out Schopenhauer. Wagner, as Martin Gregor-Dellin has noted, transposed Schopenhauer's concept of the will into the concept of sexual love, "drawing out the erotic component of [Schopenhauer's] philosophy of will and making it absolute."[7] He posited love as a "means of salvation" in two ways. In the first place it constituted the primary means of overcoming our individual alienation and self-enclosure. It is love, he writes, "that drives the subject beyond itself and forces that subject to connect with another."[8] Unlike in Schopenhauer, love for Wagner can push beyond the representation of individuality; it is an instinct toward transcendence. Secondly, love represents a way of freeing ourselves from legislating structures that lord over the individual and compel his life without him having any say in it. In *Opera and Drama*, Wagner characterizes love as "the salvation without which force is brutality, and freedom is pure randomness," and contrasts it with love that is "taught and forced upon us from above."[9] Love thus undoes a subject-object distinction that has become totalized, with the autistic subject in one corner and the overwhelming force of the objective world in the other.

The idea that humanity is beset by absolutized oppositions that require mediation is one Wagner drew from Hegel and his followers. Most important and direct among his sources was Ludwig Feuerbach.[10] But the idea that love consisted of recognizing the self in an object, and thus a bridging of a dualism between the subject and its object supposedly characteristic of Enlightenment thought, had been a mainstay of German philosophy for the decades on either side of the turn of the nineteenth century; however garrulous and opinionated the thinkers of Romanticism and Idealism were, from Friedrich Schiller to the brothers Schlegel all the way to Hegel and his students, they all agreed on this point. Significantly, it fell out of fashion in seminar room and lecture hall around the same time that Wagner brought it into the opera house.[11] The fact that he pledged fealty to Schopenhauer in doing so, while in fact Schopenhauer's metaphysics of sexual love amounted to a contemptuous rejection of this kind of fetishism of recognition, desire, and love, gives us a sense of just how happy Wagner was to graft incompatible philosophical influences onto one another in the service of his idée fixe.

But Wagner's debt to recent philosophy did not stop at this idea of love as salvation or of true freedom. He was just as clearly indebted to the metaphysics of unification around the turn of the nineteenth century. Under the influence of Neoplatonist revivals in the eighteenth century, thinkers like Novalis (Friedrich von Hardenberg), Friedrich Schlegel, Franz von Baader, and Friedrich

Hölderlin embraced the Platonic idea of eros as a complete merging with the other, a restoration of a unity rent asunder either by historical forces or by the forces of human sexuality itself.

Around the turn of the nineteenth century, the transition from a more unified or organic form of life, to the reified life in which men and women found themselves isolated and alone, in need of reunification, was understood in the terms furnished by Rousseau—that is to say, as a historical process. Rousseau, Hölderlin, Schiller, Hegel, Schelling, and Baader all posited that the more unified world was not (just) a hope for the future, or a point of critique for the present—it had actually existed in time, whether this be a prelapsarian age, a state of nature, ancient Greece, or the Middle Ages.

Wagner doesn't ever explicitly invoke those narratives, but it is important that they subtend the "Romanticism of alienation" that powers Wagner's erotic philosophy. This matters because the idea that an older, more organic state of affairs has become lost in the civilizing process forms a largely unelaborated foundation of both Wagner's music and his musical aesthetics. Consider the rapturous unification of Siegfried and Brünnhilde at the end of *Siegfried*, which brings together two individuals pulled apart by an arbitrary paternal decree. The scene begins with a moment of recognition—that is to say, of difference: Siegfried, unaccustomed to the female form, has assumed he is waking a man, but then recoils in terror when he realizes that "that is no man!"

As the two work themselves into a musical frenzy, the process of unification goes well beyond recognition: "Do you not see me? / How my gaze devours you, / does it not blind you?" Brünnhilde asks, and Siegfried rhapsodizes how "my breast beats / desirously in yours." Just as in Tristan and Isolde's erotic exchanges, grammar breaks down, but more importantly so does corporeal identity. His heart can beat in her chest, his seeing can blind him, blood seems to circulate from one body to the other, again and again they invoke the language of ingestion. Brünnhilde and Siegfried are no longer two entities in dialogue—they become one organism: "He is eternal to me / is for me always, / Inheritance and self / one and all / glowing love / laughing death." The Romantic naturalist and philosopher Franz von Baader had once suggested that lovers embrace because they seek to extend their ribcages around the other, merging their two bodies into one—Siegfried and Brünnhilde seem intent on putting Baader's idea into practice.

The fact that merging the two transgresses against any number of divine injunctions (to say nothing of the incest taboo) points to another feature of Wagner's philosophy of the erotic. True love for Wagner has the structure that Denis de Rougemont has identified with the medieval concept of passion—that is to say, it is necessarily transgressive and tends toward self-destructiveness.[12] Tristan and Isolde commit adultery; so do Siegmund and Sieglinde. Lohengrin's love for Elsa is doomed by the fact that her love compels her to put into words what she is by decree prohibited from putting into words. "Is this merely love?" Elsa asks: "What shall I call / this word, inexpressibly divine / as your name—that I, alas, may never know?" Her desire reaches beyond "mere" love, and wishes to penetrate into a divine sphere that she knows will annul their union.

Love in Wagner is anarchic. It refuses to recognize the strictures of custom or decree, and even when it recognizes them, as in the case of Elsa, it cannot help itself and breaks every law and commandment anyway. True love, for Wagner, "springs from unalienated, real human nature,"[13] and corrodes anything tradition, morals, or power would contrive to put in its way. Put differently, love asserts its *autonomy* from the larger structures of society, of morality, and even of history. When *Götterdämmerung* opens, Wotan's spear has been shattered; the god himself hides away in Valhalla. The old world order is no more, and it is up to Siegfried to create a new one. But instead the curtain rises to reveal him and Brünnhilde emerging from a "rocky bower," where they've spent the night in connubial bliss by the fire. The way the opera's prologue juxtaposes their postcoital glow with the Norns' gloomy world-historical premonitions epitomizes just how irresponsible love is in Wagner, just how little it allows itself to be subordinated to other concerns.

This autonomy of the erotic, an autonomy bordering on anarchism, constitutes perhaps Wagner's most easily identifiable borrowing from German Romanticism. The idea that love emancipated the couple from the wanton dictates of convention and religion was an article of faith among the German Romantics, one that Wagner appears to have internalized at a very young age. It animates *Das Liebesverbot*, composed in 1834 by a twenty-one-year-old Wagner, and seems to have been the focus of Wagner's very first foray into the form—a fragment called *Die Hochzeit*, written when Wagner was nineteen. His discovery of Feuerbach only served to confirm his belief in the rule-transcending power of love. The original final monologue Wagner wrote for Brünnhilde in *Götterdämmerung* was an explicit précis of Feuerbach's thought on the matter, celebrating a world "without rulers," "treaties," or "customs," and instead governed only by love.

As the end of *Götterdämmerung* makes clear, Wagner attaches a great deal of political importance to the concept of love. The man who read Schopenhauer and sought to correct his resignation by reference to love was a revolutionary in exile, and his frustrated political hopes were largely displaced into the erotic realm. Here, too, texts from a half century prior appear to have been Wagner's guide—particularly, Friedrich Schiller's letters *Über die ästhetische Erziehung des Menschen* (*On the Aesthetic Education of Man*, 1795). In the final letter of his treatise, Schiller had argued that, by giving in to love, rather than appetite or social dictate, the men and women of his era were taking their first tentative steps toward an "aesthetic state" that would no longer be ruled by the social division of labor, but rather be unified and "harmonic."[14]

The idea that eroticism between individuals can structure an entire state, most evident perhaps in the plot of *Lohengrin*, actually runs through all of Wagner's oeuvre: In *Die Feen*, Wagner's first completed opera, marriage between a fairy and a human helps Wagner articulate the relationship between aristocracy and bourgeoisie.[15] In *Lohengrin*, the fate of the Kingdom of Brabant, and indeed that of the Holy Roman Empire and Western Christendom, comes to depend on the events in the marriage bed of Elsa and her nameless knight. When the city of Nuremberg transitions from a state dictated by tradition, codes and (aesthetic) form, to one governed democratically by spontaneity and love in *Die Meistersinger von Nürnberg*, this transition occurs by means of aesthetic education.[16]

As Laurence Dreyfus has pointed out, given this grab bag of influences, and Wagner's flightiness in combining them, the theory outlined above did not turn out to be particularly good philosophy, though it made for "astonishingly wonderful opera."[17] The individual philosophemes assimilated by Wagner were not his lasting legacy, however; rather, Wagner brought to opera a style of grand speculation about the erotic that had previously characterized Romantic poetry and Idealist philosophy. It was not Wagner's answers to these questions that turned out particularly influential (though they made their effects felt as well), but rather the kinds of questions about the nature of sex he wanted opera to address, and those aspects of opera he turned to to address them.

The composers laboring in *Tristan*'s shadow encountered Wagner not just through his music, but also through his thought. When Richard Strauss, who had been raised in a strictly anti-Wagnerian household, experienced what he would later call his "conversion," it was not by attending an opera performance, or reading a score. It was when his friend and mentor Alexander Ritter introduced him to Wagner's writings and to Schopenhauer.[18] The composers of the era (and most certainly the critics of the era) experienced Wagner as a "philosophizing musician," as the critic Rudolf Louis put it, alongside the "music-making philosophers," like Nietzsche and Herbart.[19] Whatever they thought of Wagner's philosophical efforts, they knew that the most influential opera composer in several generations had made opera the direct carrier of a philosophy of love—a fact they had to reckon with one way or another.

In the course of its migration from the lecture hall to the opera house, sex attained a different status in opera, a status that it maintained among Wagner's uneasy heirs for almost a half century after the *Meister*'s death. Sex ceased to function as a plot point or motor; instead, the plot itself became a kind of experimental design in an investigation into the nature of sex and desire. In the operas of Franz Schreker, for instance, the action no longer depends on interpersonal relationships. Rather, the plot unfolds entirely at the instigation of a figure of erotic desire: a character hears a "distant sound" and sets the plot in motion in going after it; a character seeks to shield himself from his own abject ugliness by building an isle of joy; a character seeks to escape the family curse that drives him to rape. Eugen d'Albert begins one opera with a married couple in which the husband is ugly and the wife conveniently blind, and then lets their prestabilized harmony unravel. In *Feuersnot* (1901), Richard Strauss's librettist Ernst von Wolzogen arranges the world of the opera around a young maiden losing her virginity. Wagner's son Siegfried devotes an entire opera to almost sociological variations on the theme of adultery, while Franz Schmidt's opera *Fredegundis* is organized entirely around the erotic allure of its title character's red hair. Erotic attraction and repulsion move from being mere plot devices to being the plot.

If opera became a preferred petri dish for outsized speculation on the nature of sexuality, this was not owed only to the arcane preoccupations of composers and librettists, or to Wagnerian idiosyncrasies passed down to his heirs. Rather, there were formal qualities of opera—that is to say, qualities that attended to opera in general—that made it such a perfect anatomic theater of desire. Those qualities were shaped and brought into sharp relief by Wagner. This study posits that there is a logic to the entwinement of these two fields, opera and sexuality, at this precise point in history—that it was necessitated by a concern with totality that attained renewed importance in aesthetics in the wake of Wagner and with the advent of modernism. At a time when opera was supposed to transport a philosophy of art and history, eroticism provided a straightforward way of untangling opera's post-Wagnerian philosophical underpinnings, but of doing so sensuously rather than philosophically.

SEX AND THE GESAMTKUNSTWERK

There was another field where Wagner had a similar impact on aesthetics well beyond music or opera, where Wagner was present not just as a practitioner, but as a theorist and even philosopher. His grand speculations on the nature of desire are inextricably linked to an aesthetic project, the Gesamtkunstwerk. Although the idea of the total work of art has often been reduced to a mere synchronization of different media, it was in truth highly speculative, both in terms of the reasons that made it necessary and the social and political effects Wagner ascribed to it. The Gesamtkunstwerk was not just intended to bring together the separate arts; it was meant to address the reasons for and the effects of their separation. Wagner's operatic aesthetic thus depended on the erotic philosophy he drew from men like Schiller, Hegel, Feuerbach, and Schopenhauer. The logic of desire and repulsion, of inclusion and exclusion on which Wagner's erotics depend, finds its expression in the Gesamtkunstwerk. When Wagner changed the status of sex in the opera house, he changed it in tandem with the opera form itself.

The Gesamtkunstwerk has often been understood as an intervention into debates about performance techniques and technologies, or at most about the status of opera in society more generally. And indeed it initially emerged as such an intervention, though Wagner meant for it to be much more than that. Wagner came of age in the world of the theater—fatherless at an early age, he had been surrounded by older siblings, relatives and friends of his parents who worked as actors, writers, and directors, either professionally or as amateurs.[20] His work at opera houses in Magdeburg, Riga, and Dresden quickly brought the ambitious young man into conflict with the limitations which money, time and professionalism placed on operatic performance. Wagner's autobiography *Mein Leben* relates a number of encounters with the work of other composers, dramatists, and poets which *ex negativo* shaped his own nascent aesthetic project. Most of Wagner's irritations in these episodes revolve around a mismatch or mésalliance of opera's constituent media. Wagner faults Karl Gutzkow for using the orchestra only for "melodrama"; Heinrich Laube's attempt to dragoon Wagner into writing music for his libretti sharpened the young composer's sense that he was the best judge of what words should go with his music.

But when Wagner got around to articulating his operatic aesthetics in the following decades, such pragmatic considerations were for him only symptoms of a much larger philosophical question. Behind the messy jostling for control over a necessarily collaborative and contentious communal production like the opera, Wagner espied a historical problematic, one that opera exemplified and might help resolve. This historical problematic coincided to a remarkable degree with the central tenets of Wagner's erotic philosophy: the arts were to be brought together in order to address the social alienation of modern man; their fusion would reunite the subject with its cosmos, and would separate the total work of art from the compartmentalized and anomic everyday world. This reunification would necessarily have political consequences. Like the German Romantics, Wagner suggested that the arts had once been unified, but had become undone under certain historical pressures. An "organic" unity of the arts—that is to say, one that was more than just a wanton combination of discrete parts—depended on an "organic" state. Modernity had effected a compartmentalization and atomization of different, largely autonomous spheres of life (one of them being art). In such a "mechanical" state, the "organic" unity of the arts had to come asunder, but restoring it somehow might be able to revolutionize that state, to make it less mechanical and more organic.

Das Kunstwerk der Zukunft and other writings of the 1850s were supposed to propose a theory that combined Wagner's dramaturgic instincts about the interrelation of different agents in opera with this more systematic background. *Das Kunstwerk der Zukunft*, dedicated to Feuerbach and heavily indebted to the philosophy of history of the turn of the nineteenth century, proposes that the arts that were unified in Greek religious rites came apart as the influence of this religion weakened. What ailed opera, then, was the result of the gradual sliding apart of music, dance, and drama, and their antagonistic relationship to one another. Where *Oper und Drama* outlined in some detail how the project of "music drama" might address this sliding apart, *Das Kunstwerk der Zukunft* also showed that previous attempts to reunite the separate arts had failed by having one art colonize the other, or by being too deferential to one art's particular and limited logic. To describe the attempt to transcend their egoism and self-enclosure, Wagner again and again turned to the concept of love. For this reason he reserved particular vituperation, for any attempts to sanctify as necessary the separateness of the arts—the tendency to treat them "absolutely" rather than relationally. As we shall see in chapter 1, the tendency toward contented separation and refusal of larger relationships is presented throughout Wagner's writings and operas as a kind of erotic-aesthetic impotence and bad faith.

While Wagner, and certainly his followers, usually tended to use the term "absolute" disparagingly, at other times Wagner's own use of the term "absolute music" is somewhat suppler. *Das Kunstwerk der Zukunft* describes Beethoven as the heroic sailor who navigated "the boundless sea of absolute music to its limits," and who discovered "new, unknown shores" that no longer divide "the old continents," but rather "*connect* them for the newborn, [beatific], artistic humanity of the future."[21] Many observers have correctly located the echoes of Feuerbach's thought in this and similar statements, but they have erred in assuming that Wagner is making Feuerbach's critique of the "absolute" his own.[22] Rather, Wagner here juxtaposes a kind of "bad infinity" (as Hegel would put it) that is "beyond" the particular determinations of sensuous reality (the "boundless sea of absolute music") with a kind of infinite that subtends and brings together the particular "continents." How else to make sense of Wagner's insistence that Beethoven somehow found "limits" in a "boundless" sea?

Wagner's passage draws on Feuerbach in a different way: "absolute music" is absolute in being nonrelational, abstract. Beethoven's version of it, on the other hand, makes possible relationships between different media, such as the final movement of Beethoven's *Ninth Symphony*. For the Wagner of the late 1840s and early 1850s, this movement seems to mark the logical endpoint of "absolute music." If, as Wagner's friend Theodor Uhlig wrote in the *Neue Zeitschrift für Musik* in 1851, the problem with absolute music was that it was "necessarily infinite in expression,"[23] then that judgment stood in tension with Wagner's own use of the word *infinite*. Even before encountering the thought of Schopenhauer, Wagner wrote in 1841 "that what music expresses is eternal, infinite and ideal."[24] This kind of all-subtending infinitude was often associated with the erotic—Wagner writes of the "infinitely feminine woman [*unendlich weibliche Weib*]," the infinity of "passion, love and yearning in themselves."[25]

If "infinity" thus both represents the shortcoming of absolute music and furnishes the means by which it can be transcended, this is because, as Sanna Pederson has noted, Uhlig's restatement is a "typical, anti-Romantic indictment of music,"[26] while Wagner's relationship to Romanticism was far more ambivalent. Uhlig died in 1853, just as Wagner, egged on by his friend Georg Herwegh, began exploring the thought of Arthur Schopenhauer. In Schopenhauer's vision of music as the expression of the noumenal will, Wagner found both confirmation of his previous repudiation of the German Idealist "Absolute," and a theory of an all-pervading *hen kai pan* indebted to German Romanticism.

Wagnerian eroticism and the Gesamtkunstwerk are fraternal twins born of German Romanticism. Wagner had inherited from the German Romantics a metaphysics of sex that treated love as a kind of unification with the cosmos; he combined this metaphysics of erotic unification with the long-standing call for the reunification of the separate arts heard since the turn of the nineteenth century.[27] As Matthew Wilson Smith has shown, what has made Wagner's conception so appealing, so seductive, and yet so threatening to subsequent generations of musicians, artists, architects, and writers was that it participated dialectically in the central problematics of modernity. It was a move against the autonomy of art (insofar as it insisted that art should and could organize life), and it was a forceful reassertion of that autonomy (preventing art's integration into the anomie and instrumental rationality of modern life). It was antibourgeois (at its simplest, the total work of art was intended to counteract the division of labor), and yet seems deeply indebted to bourgeois values and commodity culture. It was revolutionary—not for nothing did Wagner arrive at his definitive ideas about integrating the arts during his years of exile after the failed Dresden uprising of 1849. And it was reactionary, insofar as it aimed at the restoration of an "organic" state that seemed to have little to do with our modern way of life.

During the period in which Wagner developed his aesthetic program, the concept of love was bound up in much the same dialectic. Early Romanticism had turned erotic love into a battering ram against the status quo; later Romanticism deployed it as a replacement for politics, a form of accommodation with the state of things. In the works of Schiller, the Romantics, and even Schopenhauer, there was a pervasive sense that love, just like art, was moving toward commodification. Wagner's philosophical predecessors and guides tended to view both love and art through the lens of what Peter Furth has called the "Romanticism of alienation,"[28] according to which any given particulars were once unified organically, but have come apart into alien and alienated atoms in the modern world. Wagner fully embraced these positions in both fields, and, with his characteristic knack for syncretic thinking, linked the two—the reified artwork and reified sexual relationship were not accidentally similar, but rather intrinsically linked.

It was only consistent, then, that in his art Wagner sought to undo both of these at once. At the conclusion of *Tristan and Isolde*, a dying Tristan waits for his love, whose arrival is to be heralded by a shepherd's pipe. Tristan expires with Isolde's name on his lips, and when she is roused from his side she sings of Tristan as though he were standing before her, dying (or at least losing consciousness) at the end of her aria. The scene not only radically reduces the number of characters in the opera, but it also pares down the plot to its most elemental form. This is why the scene has often (and erroneously) been called the *Liebestod*: Wagner strips away layer after layer of operatic accoutrement until literally nothing but love and death are left. Since Tristan is present only in Isolde's mind (and as a dead body on the ground), love and death seem to outlast even the people doing the loving and dying. As Wagner had written in 1841, music "does not speak of the love, the yearning of this or that individual in this or that situation, but passion, love, yearning in themselves."[29] In Wagner's operas attraction and longing never seem to rise psychologically from within the characters; those emotions take hold of them from the outside like fate. The love potions that so frequently recur in Wagner's operas are not creaky plot devices—they are rather indexes for how the erotic buffets these characters without regard for their individual projects and motivations.

The end of *Tristan und Isolde* demotes the titular lovers to bystanders to their own love and death, in no small part thanks to the music, which takes the lovers' dying breaths and preserves them, divested of bodily specificity. As the drama becomes more concentrated, the music moves from the diegetic (the shepherd's pipe) and the recognizably operatic "number" to a musical soliloquy that subjects the voice to the sonority of the orchestra. At one point, Isolde thinks she sees dead Tristan draw a breath: "Don't you see . . . how wondrously mild sweet breath escapes his lips?" The audience does not see any evidence for this breath, but it gets to hear it: a *vibrato* in the strings takes over for Tristan's lungs. Perhaps it isn't Tristan who has breathed, but only the orchestra. Isolde's final words, "drowning, sinking, unconscious, utmost rapture," describe a divestiture of self, an erotic merging with a larger whole akin to what Freud called the "oceanic feeling" of the Death Drive. At the same time, she almost seems to provide an explicit gloss on the musical logic of the scene: her voice is submerged and drowns in the music, her grammar breaks down, and the one-word rhymes create the impression of a discourse that divests itself of its linguistic character, and becomes simply music.[30] As she becomes "unconscious" and approaches transfiguration (Wagner's moniker for this scene), the subjectivity of her voice diffuses into the melodious ocean of instrumental music.[31]

Michel Poizat has shown that the orchestra takes over for the voice in these final pages of *Tristan* at the point "where it can go no further."[32] As Isolde and Tristan are at last united in death, the medium of that unification is the orchestra. Their voices shed the shackles of individuation and embodiment and join an all-encompassing ether, an ether that transcends all particularity and thus also all sexuality. As Jean-Jacques Nattiez has put it, *Tristan* closes with a double moment of androgyny: as male and female unite in a final embrace, "the female spirit of music dictates to the poet-composer . . . what plot he has to construct and what music he has to write."[33] Tristan's and Isolde's deaths constitute the convergence point of the sexes and the convergence point of the arts. They are no longer dialoguing or synchronized particulars; they seem to have returned to a state prior to differentiation, where a vibrato and a breath, sound and language, or, as Friedrich Kittler has put it, "noise" (*Rauschen*) and musical notes are no longer, or perhaps not yet distinct.[34]

The erotic scene of longing and death thus constitutes an allegory of the relationship between "music drama's" constituent units (e.g., drama and poem).
Just like the individuals named Tristan and Isolde, they have to transcend
themselves, give themselves over to another constituent (music), to achieve
apotheosis. Wagner here perfectly melds two ideas he drew from his eclectic
background in metaphysics and aesthetics: that sex works away the particularity of the lovers and reduces them to mere epiphenomena of their own love;
and that the separation of the different arts represents a historical problem
that requires overcoming. The absolute unification represented by the "love-
death" is identical to the advent of the total work of art, a music that seems
to shed the voices that sing it, and the plot and words that attach to it. Theodor Adorno called such moments phantasmagoria: moments in which music
seems to exist independent of individuals, or, on more materialist terms, seems
to exist independent of musicians.

Consider for example the first presentation of the grail in *Parsifal*: the Bayreuth instrumentalists, safely stowed away in their lowered orchestra pit; the
singers onstage as mute spectators; the ostensible hero of the story in the same
position as the operagoer, standing and gaping at a mystical ritual on a stage.
From the dome of the opera house, disembodied voices drift down; from below the stage the booming voice of Titurel beckons. This is music that appears uncaused by human throat or hand, but instead as manna from heaven.
But religion is only one of the spheres Wagner cannibalized to allegorize his
aesthetic ambitions. In *Parsifal*, it is salvation that provides the analogue for
the rapturous coming into being of the Gesamtkunstwerk; in *Tristan* and elsewhere it is salvation through sex. In *Das Kunstwerk der Zukunft*, Wagner wrote
that "just as man can sink himself into the nature of woman through love, . . .
so each of the individual arts can find itself in the complete, and fully liberated
work of art."[35]

The disappearance of vocal/erotic individuality in *Tristan*'s final bars constitutes what Freud would have called the "primal scene" of the history traced
in this book: in *Tristan*'s climactic scenes, sexual specificity and aesthetic
particularity fall away at the same moment. The aesthetic totalization of the
Gesamtkunstwerk, which goes well beyond the mere synching of media toward a wholesale indifferentiation under the aegis of music, is placed in direct
analogy to the resolution of the erotic plot at the end of *Tristan*. Behind this
analogy stand a conception of unified work of art on the one hand, and a conception of the erotic that understands sex as a return to an absolute on the
other. Together, these two conceptions would haunt those composers trying
to write opera after *Tristan* for at least a half century.

The relationship of music and drama was what Wagner thought made his operatic oeuvre distinctive; he pursued it in two rather separate arenas, and Wagnerians and Wagner critics alike have struggled for over a century and a half to understand how they relate. Wagner pursued a new relationship between music and drama firstly as practitioner—that is to say, composer, poet, and dramaturge—but he also interrogated the same relationship philosophically, seeking to embed his aesthetic choices in a broader theory of society, politics, and history. As Matthew Wilson Smith has remarked, Wagner's operatic practice has tempted critics to emphasize the techniques and technologies of performance (from compositional techniques, to staging, to the mechanics of the "Wagner curtain" and Bayreuth's steam machine), and to dismiss Wagner's more ambitious theoretical underpinnings as so much metaphysical window dressing. Alternatively, scholars have acted as though Wagner's operas were faithful realizations of his concept of Gesamtkunstwerk. This study pursues a strange development that this dichotomization has tended to obscure: the fact that Wagner's aesthetics had an afterlife independent of what his actual operas actually accomplished. After Wagner the cosmic unity, the restoration of Greek totality, the possible reversion of the mechanistic state into an organic one, haunted composers not because Wagner had somehow realized them (we would know if he had); it haunted them as a possibility, as a terrifyingly wide and ambitious frame of reference. Just writing an opera was dangerous business in *Tristan*'s shadow, and Wagner's heirs had to work up the courage to do so again.

SEXUALITY AND CONSCIOUSNESS

What Wagner drew from the modish but idiosyncratic ideas of Schopenhauer's writings, his would-be successors could draw simply from the zeitgeist. By the time Wagner died, the idea that sexuality was an all-explaining absolute of which all particulars were simply appearances had taken hold in the wider culture—Darwin, eugenics, race theory, and the first stirrings of psychoanalysis and empirical psychology all had a part in this renaissance. The idea of the absolute nature of love and the epiphenomenal character of the particular proved very useful to an art form that had to redefine itself under the impression of Wagner: If there was a new demand placed on the coherence of the different constituents of the opera form, and if that coherence ultimately pointed toward a philosophy of history, then how better to make sensible opera's important new mission than through a field like the erotic, which was subject to the same historic development? The erstwhile unity of the erotic, after all, had sundered in modernity just as the individual arts had—why not reunite both at once?

The commonsense picture of the sexual relationship Schopenhauer held up for ridicule thus became a powerful allegory for the increasing separation of opera's constitutive media. In modernity, Wagner had argued, bourgeois conceptions of marital law had eclipsed the all-unifying mysteries of love through its "marriages of convenience calculated to [procure] property and riches,"[36] just as the arts, unified among the Greeks, had slid apart. While Wagner's cultural critique of sexuality does not fixate on the Greeks, the idea that the greatness of Greek art had its source in Greek eroticism had taken root in German thinking ever since Johann Joachim Winckelmann (1717–68), whose work Wagner was well acquainted with. For Winckelmann, Greek art was inimitable because the peculiar erotics that had underpinned it had been displaced by Christianity. This was what Wagner's onetime admirer Nietzsche regarded as the chief promise of the work of art proposed by Wagner: it restored aspects both of Greek eroticism and Greek religion (those aspects he termed "Dionysian"), both eclipsed by Christian morality.

Just as Wagner did, Nietzsche understood that the Gesamtkunstwerk was not the first attempt at a restoration of Greek plenitude, but he thought it was far more successful than previous attempts. For Nietzsche, a botched attempt at restoration constituted opera's birth defect: when the *Camera de' Bardi* sought to self-consciously revive antique drama, they "cut out or crippled the roots of what had once been an unconscious art, growing spontaneously from the life of a people." At the movement of its birth, opera already lagged behind its project of recuperating a more holistic integration of different arts; the world that would have permitted such integration organically had vanished. Nietzsche's criticism points to a standard thought in the Romanticism of alienation—any attempt to consciously fuse what was unconsciously one and the same in antiquity could only be mendacious. Having to be conscious of the demand that the arts should be integrated means we are no longer able to "truly" integrate them: "What we call opera today, the travesty of the ancient music drama, came about only through a direct aping of antiquity: without the unconscious power of a natural drive, constituted according to an abstract theory, it has become an artificially generated homunculus."[37]

This view of consciousness and unconsciousness resonated uncannily with a pervasive view of sexuality after Schopenhauer and Romanticism. From Schelling via Schopenhauer to Darwin and Freud, the existence of an unconscious became a lodestar of nineteenth-century thought about gender and sexuality. Whether they gave it a pessimistic spin (à la Schopenhauer), or a downright utopian one (à la the early Romantics), it became a common assumption that in erotic attraction neither party could ever be fully cognizant of what was really going on—the will or the absolute asserting its powers in and through the individuals. For both Schopenhauer and the Romantics, this meant that erotic unions that were brought together too consciously— for reasons of economy, dynasty, convenience, etc.—were phony homunculi in the vein of Nietzsche's characterization of the modern opera. This was a line of argument that Wagner, with some unsavory admixtures from mid-nineteenth-century racism, fully endorsed. In both sex and opera, then, authentic unity could come about only if it was preconscious—only if it didn't need to be brought about laboriously, but sprang into existence spontaneously and to some extent unconsciously. As Wagner remarked in *Das Kunstwerk der Zukunft*, "The Will toward a common work of art [*gemeinsamen Kunstwerke*] arises in each art unconsciously and automatically [*unwillkürlich, unbewusst, von selbst*]." *Unwillkürlich* literally means that the impulse is not subject to choice, to either doing something or preferring not to. The will toward the common work of art springs from us before we know it. Once we're conscious of it, it becomes a matter of *Willkür* and therefore inauthentic.

Both Romantic/Schopenhauerian views of sex, and the theory of the opera as a reconstitution of antique forms of intermediality, depended on the unity being prior to the particulars that face us in everyday experience. Opera could unconsciously unify different media because those media had originally been one to begin with, but had drifted apart with time. Similarly, if one asked Schopenhauer, Tieck, or Fichte, the oneness that lovers felt when they were attracted to each other was owed to the fact that the lovers were originally one anyway, and had decomposed into individuals only subsequently. Only the shared *hypokaimenon* enabled the kind of unconscious and automatic unity sought by Wagner in both sexuality and artwork; and opera's *hypokaimenon* became important precisely at the moment at which sexuality was offered as such an all-subtending absolute.

As Gary Tomlinson has proposed, opera reflects notions of selfhood pervasive at a particular moment.[38] In the case of Wagner, this reflection was itself philosophically licensed: individual and species related in much the same way that individual media attained their quiddity only by reference to an overarching totality. Just as the "Romanticism of alienation" understood modern sexuality as a decline from earlier amorous practices, so did modernity put particular pressures and demands on the unification of media in opera. When the critic Leopold Schmidt reviewed the opera *Notre Dame*, based on Hugo's novel and composed by Franz Schmidt (no relation to Leopold), he praised Schmidt's musical idiom, but remarked on a more general difficulty: "One feels the ambivalence between the demands of this kind of text and the essence of this totally authentic musician."[39] For the critic Schmidt, then, this "kind of text," the novel, existed far apart from opera, separated by the kind of "ocean" Wagner himself had described. Opera could not tell the stories novels could—if it tried, it would tear itself apart trying to reconcile the "demands of this kind of text" and those of "authentic music."

If some critics became more restrictive in their assessment of what stories opera could and could not tell, suggesting that certain limitations could not be overcome by the totalization of the work of art, new forms emerged that promised to unify different arts more effectively and more *à la mode* than opera could—above all was cinema. As early as 1917, the critic Hermann Haefker proclaimed the cinema as the true Gesamtkunstwerk.[40] As Jeremy Tambling has noted, early film stood in a "parasitic relation to opera,"[41] appropriating its techniques and melodramatic tone. Increasingly, this parasitism served to cast into doubt the viability of opera itself. D'Albert's operas, for instance, were increasingly disparaged as "tasteless cinema thrillers"[42] that appealed only to "the cinematic public of our time."[43] For these critics, opera that didn't live up to the high standards set by Wagner was mass entertainment and thus better left to the cinema than to the opera house.[44]

"WAS IST NUN MIT DER OPER?"

If Wagner misread Schopenhauer, the Romantics were his likely influence; but through them he was being diverted by one of the oldest voices of Western thinking about sex—Plato. Wagner's reading of Schopenhauer brings out another aspect of the sexual relationship, one deriving ultimately from Plato—that sexual complementarity doesn't just create a bigger, better, or more complete being; it produces a *complete* being *tout court*. For Aristophanes, the unification of lovers in sex recreates an original plenitude.

It is quite clear that this places a peculiar demand on opera, one that had not been implicit in earlier schemes to unite or unify the arts. Such attempts, such as the musically organized paintings of Moritz von Schwind or the musical ekphrases of Liszt's *Années de Pèlerinage*, sought to bring together a discrete number of separate arts, or else sought to enlarge one art to encompass others. The demand of the Gesamtkunstwerk, by dint of its Romantic provenance, goes further and points ultimately toward the cosmic: not only are its constituent media supposed to be better or more completely integrated, but they are to some extent supposed to exhaust the possible, to furnish a totality of sense and meaning, or restore one that was historically lost. This is why earlier attempts at "total" works of art were not possessed of what Adorno has called Wagner's "allergy against the particular."[45]

But the question of alienation from an original plenitude applied to opera in yet another way: the worry that Northern (and in particular German) audiences were alienated from the opera unfolding on the stage had been a concern at least since Goethe, who reported back from Italy that "here the people are the basis on which everything rests. The audience plays along, the crowd becomes merged with the theater into one whole."[46] Compare this with Wagner's own characterization of the Italian operagoer over a half century later: "There gathered an audience which passed its evenings in amusement; part of this amusement was formed by the music sung upon the stage, to which one listened from time to time in pauses of the conversation."[47] Italy becomes both the model for a theater that bridges the chasm between audience and spectacle (hence the mania for Mediterranean settings and *verismo* around the turn of the century), and the specter of what happens if their unification isn't pursued with sufficient seriousness. In each case, the opera becomes a microcosm for society more generally—an opera house riven by alienation indicates a society characterized by the same.[48]

What Goethe claimed happens spontaneously in the Italian *opera buffa* becomes a moralized demand in Wagner. The self-consciousness Goethe had felt before the spontaneity of the Italian *commedia* was only intensified after Wagner; what had seemed to Goethe a mere Nordic unease became, after Wagner, a moral failing. As Wagner puts it apropos of the art of acting, "strictly speaking, art ceases to be art at that point where it enters the reflecting consciousness as art."[49] The Italian audiences could enjoy their entertainments unreflectively; their Nordic cousins encountered them perforce reflectively. The "mutual divestment of self [*gegenseitige Selbstentäußerung*]" that took place between the Italian or French performers and their audience gave way to a pinched and self-conscious effort to enjoy something that was in fact contrary to one's own national essence. This is why, starting in the 1850s, Wagner agitated for what he called an *Originaltheater*—first in Zürich, then in the form of a Goethe foundation in Weimar, and finally in the shape of the Bayreuth festival. As Wagner's son-in-law Houston Stewart Chamberlain put it, this "Originaltheater" was intended to "give [the German people] a dramatic form that arose organically from its own original development."[50]

"Originaltheater" was explicitly conceived as an antidote to the destructive influence of modernity on the kind of "mutual divestment" that alone marks genuine theater. In the modern theater the "audience is as much conscious of itself [as audience] as the actor is in the thrall of his . . . own personality, just as though he were outside the theater."[51] The question of whether opera was still possible as a form at all was made, if anything, more urgent by the immense demands Wagner's conception placed on it. To be sure, most of the composers who followed him rejected details or even the totality of Wagner's conception. But the awareness that such demands of totality, of quasi-religious ritual, of unification of the arts *could* be made of opera was never far from their own attempts.

When critics accused d'Albert of writing "cinema thrillers" rather than true operas, when Max Nordau thought Wagnerian opera led to nervous "degeneration," they were pointing to defects in the aesthetic object, but they also implied that these operas' audiences approached them in a fundamentally inappropriate way. Not only was opera changing for the worse, but audiences had changed in fundamental ways that made opera unintelligible to them. Weissmann thought that the modern inability to produce and consume opera the way their forebears did was owed to objective factors: his diagnosis is animated by an—albeit obscure and careless—cognitive theory, but fundamentally Weissmann thinks that it is our "nerves" and their relationship to the human spirit that have undergone a transformation, which in turn has robbed musical, and in particular operatic, listening and composition of its erstwhile naturalness. The music of this "world crisis" may be able to lay hold of "previously unknown stimuli [*Reize*]" from time to time, but it "searches yearningly for a new totality [*Geschlossenheit*]."[52]

But even those music critics who didn't come to opera with vitalistic or biologistic categories wondered about which modern audiences were still the right ones for the form. In a 1924 article, the music critic Paul Bekker pointed to the enormous imaginative investment that opera demanded of its audience: opera is that "transitory moment in which the stage life stands as the only truly existing, built of cardboard, painted in colors one shouldn't look at in the bright light of day, carried by sounds set down in the score really only as a stopgap measure, mimed and sung by people whose real existence is only a vegetating between two scenes."[53] Bekker's description intimates just how difficult and how fleeting that "transitory moment" may be. Writing at a time when cinema, to say nothing of panoramas, dioramas, and the like had set new standards of seamless and immersive spectacle, Bekker seems keenly aware that opera's effects simply could not keep up. The ritual of sung dialogue, the Germanic costumes, the staid customs unchanged for decades, all gave the opera something hopelessly superannuated.

As Bekker puts it in another article, "What to do now about opera? [*Was ist nun mit der Oper?*]" In its awkward mixture of the musical, the dramatic, and the balletic, "is it a paradox which we cannot really take seriously?" Or is it that we can *no longer* take this strange mongrelized form seriously in the cold, clean space delimited by modernity? "Is opera a representative social pursuit [*Gesellschaftsangelegenheit*] of a past age, which we kept alive by sheer force of thoughtless habit?"[54] If the erotic suggested the possibility, and even the imperative, of a preconscious unity, critics like Bekker suggested that such preconscious may no longer be available to modern audiences, or at least no longer available in the opera house. Around the same time, Adolf Weissmann framed Bekker's question more bleakly yet: "Opera is not dead, but the creative powers of this art form have weakened."[55]

Bekker's worries about the form's superannuation are value-neutral. But Wagner himself knew no such neutrality. In fact, he understood the failure of opera's spell not as a possible verdict on the medium; he understood it as a moral verdict on the audience. This concern is allegorized in his last opera, *Parsifal*. In the opera's first act, young and ignorant Parsifal witnesses the grail ritual. He is ushered into the grail sanctum by Gurnemanz, who is subjecting him to a moral test: Can he empathize with the arcane ritual he sees before himself? Can he feel *Mitleid*, com-passion? "Do you understand what you saw here?" Parsifal of course fails this test, and a disappointed Gurnemanz tells him, "You are after all but a fool / be gone, be on your way." *Parsifal* the opera thus presents an allegory of opera's demand on its audience, where Parsifal the man represents the opera audience, and the religious ritual represents the performance onstage. But the demand Gurnemanz places on Parsifal—the demand Wagner places on his audience—the demand to *believe* the ritual, to have the pain onstage become one's own pain, is a *moral* demand. Parsifal is a worse person for failing to empathize; at least at this point in his trajectory, there is something wrong with him as an audience member.

Thomas Mann's 1906 short story "Wälsungenblut" is on its face a rather pointed satire of Wagner's ambitions. But the way Mann lapses at crucial points into precisely the categories Wagner relied on makes clear just how hard it was around 1900 for a German opera lover to dissociate fully from Wagner's aesthetics, even if one treated Wagner's actual music with a good deal of irony. At the climax of the story, the twin protagonists, Siegmund and Sieglinde Aarenhold, attend a performance of *Die Walküre*. Mann treats his reader to an in-depth description of the opera's first scene, which features Siegmund and Sieglinde's famous namesakes—a description that oscillates between moments of rapt immersion in the stage action, and jarring moments of sudden distance.

The story is narrated beat by beat, breathlessly, as though it were not familiar to either the reader or the twins. But, again and again, the representational nature of the performance intervenes and interferes in the reader's enjoyment (and, one has to assume, the twins' as well). One moment, we are treated to a languorous account of the onstage action, framed in such romantic hues that whoever narrates it, is perhaps too wrapped up in what is happening onstage. But in between, the narrator obsessively points to Siegmund's "rosy, fleshy" arms, and important steps in their romance are precipitated by looks at the conductor in his pit. "Siegmund" and Sieglinde" onstage are at times the Valsung twins, at others two underpaid actors forging about on a stage made of papier-mâché and cardboard. Each time, of course, the Aarenhold twins themselves change status as well: in moments of rapt attention they watch their perfect analogues play out their own desires—they are the opera's ideal audience. At other times, when they see only fleshy arms and panicked looks at the conductor, they seem like precisely the wrong audience—too knowing, too detached, too ironic. With eagle-eyed precision they espy errant details that destroy the illusion.

In what is perhaps the most telling moment, the narrator, clearly relating the Aarenhold twins' perception of the scene, tells us how "happy they were together that the heavy oaf [Hunding] had been bested, and their eyes had the same way of narrowing when they smiled." In the German, as in the English, it becomes for a moment difficult to say *which* set of twins the second "they" refers to: Are we watching Siegmund and Sieglinde Aarenhold *react* to the goings-on onstage, or are we being told what is happening onstage? In such moments of blissful union, of spectator and spectacle, of brother and sister, it doesn't even seem to matter very much. But this moment of wordless unison is punctured when the onstage "Sieglind surreptitiously looked at the conductor," "got her cue, pursed her lips and related in all detail how matters lay."[56] When we are told that "Sieglind surreptitiously looked at the conductor," we realize immediately that the wordless bond has been broken. But which bond, and by which Sieglinde? Has Sieglinde Aarenhold looked away from the stage action, distracted rather than immersed? Or is it the actress onstage, giving away the fact she is an actress, no more related or attracted to the man across from her than to the man who will portray her Tamino the next day? The rest of the sentence makes it clear it is indeed the *actress* who has flinched, but the pervasive confusion of roles, the rapturous indistinction that envelops the scene, also makes it unclear who dares disturb the rapture—the spectacle, or the spectators. The way the scene is presented subtly indicts the Aarenhold twins' way of spectating the scene: they would like to think that they understand this story and the music better than the other "trivial ones" who attend the opera that night, but in fact it turns out they can't quite manage opera's Pascalian wager. Projecting their own "narrowing eyes" into the singers onstage, noticing the actors' "fleshy, rosy" arms, and their furtive glances to the *Kappellmeister*, the twins reveal that they are somehow not measuring up to the work they are witnessing, though the story leaves us wondering if anyone can.

SEX AFTER THE GESAMTKUNSTWERK

All the composers discussed in the following chapters address the entwinement of sexual relationship and operatic form, but they understand this entwinement as a problem (an "hereditary" one, as Bekker puts it) rather than an asset. The conjunction of sex and form they inherit from Wagner allows them to interrogate form through sex. As a result, we can observe their erotics shift in tandem with their relationship to the Gesamtkunstwerk.

For instance, when Zemlinsky, Schreker, and d'Albert turn to the incongruous and unassimilable detail that won't submit to the totality, they interrogate it by coding it as an erotically repellent object. But characteristically, the composers of these operas seem to identify (and seem to identify their operas) with the ugly characters rather than with the beautiful and well-integrated spectacle that surrounds them. When Wagner's Mime is out of step with the opera he is in, Wagner takes this as an occasion for moral denunciation; for Zemlinsky and his contemporaries, however, it is an opportunity for self-reflection and for sympathy. The composers who fear that their art may represent a "degeneration" from the Wagnerian apex (and those include Wagner's own son Siegfried) had an inherent sympathy for "degenerates" of all stripes, for outcasts and sore thumbs. It is this sympathy that marks them as modernists—modernists of an altogether different kind from the paladins of the Second Viennese School, but modernists nonetheless. Juliet Koss has recently argued that "modernism itself must be understood in reference to the theoretical elaboration and historical development of the Gesamtkunstwerk."[57] Operatic eroticism allows us to expand the scope of modernism and to refine our understanding of its origins.

In each of the following chapters we will show how opera composers of the post-Wagnerian generation reframed the sexual relationship, and how *this* reframing both reflected and shaped their evolving relationship to the Gesamtkunstwerk. Chapter 1 ("Mother Mime: Wagner and the Metaphysics of Sexual Difference") focuses on the *Meister* himself, showing how Wagner imbricated sexuality and the total artwork. We will see that *Siegfried*, and in particular its first act, represents a pronounced anomaly within the wider *Ring*

Cycle. Where the rest of Wagner's *Ring* narrative presents a sprawling, multi-generational arc, *Siegfried* starts out almost claustrophobically self-contained, focusing on two characters only dimly aware of their connection to the cycle as a whole. But this unawareness, though owed to the act's generic identity (it is drawn from the world of fairy tale rather than Germanic myth), is not value-neutral: Mime the dwarf keeps his ward, Siegfried, deliberately and maliciously in the dark about the wider world of mythos. The act's formal self-containment is thus an effect of guile, and of bad faith.

As the opera opens, Mime's schemes are running up against a powerful agent that serves to threaten his self-contained enclosure and to draw Siegfried to the wider truths (and the epic totality) of the Nibelungen myth—that agent is sexuality. Siegfried's awareness of sexual difference and paternity makes Mime's illusion untenable, founded as it is on the idea that Mime, the ugly, pathetic dwarf, gave birth to strapping young Siegfried. As Siegfried grows increasingly incredulous of Mime's story, Wagner cannily intertwines Siegfried's doubts about Mime's sexual potency with formal concerns: Mime starts trying to engage Siegfried in traditional operatic duets, to calm him with simple, four-square musical numbers, but only succeeds in enraging the youth further. Siegfried's erotic longing ultimately is a longing for the mythos and the operatic form that alone is appropriate to it; his rage against Mime's sexual impotence and his hatred for his songs, his voice, his ditty-texts are of one piece. The opera's first act tells of the erotic provenance of the total work of art, and of the erotic insufficiency of the operatic practices it seeks to replace.

This was the general equation Wagner's heirs turned to in order to articulate their fraught relationship to the *Meister* of Bayreuth. As chapter 2 ("Mime's Revenge: The Total Work of Art and the Ugly Detail") demonstrates, when Alexander von Zemlinsky (1871–1942), Eugen d'Albert (1864–1932), and Franz Schreker (1878–1934) turn to asymmetrical and one-sided erotic configurations—where one party is ugly, for instance—they are attempting to vindicate the particular against the whole. At least some of them still hew fairly closely to the integrated model Wagner had imposed, but in their deformed, deluded, and otherwise isolated characters, these composers allegorize the violence the operatic totality exerts on each of its constituent media. Where Wagner enlists the audience in Siegfried's enraged demand for the wider whole, Zemlinsky, d'Albert, and Schreker solicit our recognition of and sympathy for the partial, self-contained, and disjunctive aspect of operatic production.

Chapter 3 ("*Taceat Mulier in Theatro*: Richard Strauss's *Guntram*, Arthur Schopenhauer, and the Exorcism of the Voice") focuses on Richard Strauss (1864–1949) and his evolving relationship with Wagner. Strauss's first opera,

Guntram (1894), found Strauss at the terminal point of his infatuation with Wagner—"this one time Strauss, like a true epigone of Wagner, was ensorcelled and paralyzed by the master's pathos."[58] The opera's final scene, which restages the ending of *Tristan* in a highly peculiar fashion, replaces the fading subjectivity of Isolde's voice with the assertive subjectivity of his main character, while his love interest stands mute and increasingly invisible onstage. The final scene seems to have been inspired by Schopenhauer, whom Strauss read, inspired by Wagner. But Strauss realized how much of a misreading of Schopenhauer Wagner's "metaphysics of sexual love" was, and in presenting a genuinely Schopenhauerian finale for his opera, Strauss ultimately suggests that the Gesamtkunstwerk is unable to contain any genuine relationship to another at all, and is in the end antierotic.

On the face of it, Franz Schreker's *Der ferne Klang* (1912) seems like a radicalization of the Gesamtkunstwerk, both in terms of its musical-dramatic idiom and in terms of its erotic plot, which presents itself as a love-death in overdrive. But the opera's protagonist is drawn to his death not by his love for another human being, but by his desire for the titular "distant sound," which beckons always offstage, at times from the orchestra pit, at others from behind the scenes. Chapter 4 ("Erotic Acoustics: The Natural History of the Theater and *Der ferne Klang*") argues that by luring the drive offstage, Schreker ultimately interrogates rather than confirms the conception of the work of art he inherited from Wagner. The chapter puts Schreker's works into dialogue with the acoustic revolution of the opera house, drawing attention to the fact that the Gesamtkunstwerk was not just a matter of composition, writing, or dramaturgy, but that it also depended on a sophistication of technological means of production as well.

After *Guntram*, which he had both written and composed, Strauss did not present another opera for seven years. When he did, his mode of composing opera had shifted decisively: where *Guntram* had found the composer attempting to ape the *Meister* in writing both music and poem, after *Guntram* Strauss emerged as an inveterate collaborator. Chapter 5 ("Congenital Blindness: Visions of Marriage in the Operas of Eugen d'Albert") presents another composer with a similar trajectory: Eugen d'Albert's first forays into the form were heavily indebted to Wagner (both in content and form), but like Strauss he eventually came to work exclusively with libretti written by others. At the same time he abandoned the love plots of his first three operas in favor of plots dealing with marriages, and complicated ones at that: *ménages-à-trois*, domestic battlefields, a blind wife, and a hideous husband—almost all of the seventeen collaborative operas d'Albert went on to write dealt with marriages that were somehow off-balance. Even where he dealt with happy and seemingly straightforward marriages, d'Albert used both text and music to emphasize the dialogic and necessarily relational nature of marriage, and their dialogue and relationship is in each case mirrored in those of opera's constituent media.

Wagner's own son Siegfried (1869–1930) struggled throughout his life with his father's overwhelming legacy. Chapter 6 ("Occult Legacies: Eroticism and the Dynasty in Siegfried Wagner's Operas") investigates how questions of heredity and breeding impinge upon, and in many ways structure, the erotics of Siegfried's own operas. Siegfried's erotic plots are unusual for the period, and differ greatly from both his father's and those of his teacher Engelbert Humperdinck (1854–1921): where most composers turned to ever more simmered-down erotic plots, Siegfried's are expansive and almost baroque. This is because almost all of Siegfried's operas rely on a tension between an individual couple (or a love triangle) on the one hand and an expansive dynastic frame on the other. Richard Wagner had his lovers (paradigmatically the Valsung twins Siegmund and Sieglinde) resist that dynastic frame, and enlisted the audience's sympathy for their resistance; but his son again and again has the frame effectively delegitimate the central love relationship.

Chapter 7 ("The Power of the 'Verfluchte Lohe': (Post-)Wagnerian Redheads in *Das Rheingold*, *Fredegundis*, and *Irrelohe*") traces the entwinement of erotic attraction and operatic form after Wagner by focusing on a particular detail and tracing it through its Wagnerian and post-Wagnerian configurations; it uses this detail to show when the Wagnerian imbrication of sex and opera gave way to entirely new configurations of the two. In tracing the function of red hair as operatic fetish from Wagner's *Rheingold*, via Franz Schmidt's (1874–1939) *Fredegundis*, to Franz Schreker's 1924 work *Irrelohe*, the chapter shows that by the 1920s the protagonists of this study had begun rethinking the way operatic form and eroticism interacted and could be made to represent each other. As they take to increasingly exploding the overintegration of arts, they abandon Wagnerian eroticism in favor of a much more matter-of-fact treatment of love that points to the new objectivity of the Weimar Republic rather than to the decadent imaginations of Schopenhauer, Freud, and Wagner.

CHAPTER 1

Mother Mime: Wagner and the Metaphysics of Sexual Difference

In a letter to Theodor Uhlig in 1851, Richard Wagner writes that his *Young Siegfried* "has the enormous advantage that it presents the important mythos to the audience in a playful manner, the way one presents a fairy tale to a child."[1] Even when *Young Siegfried*, the prelude to a projected *Siegfried's Death*, transformed into the "second day" of the *Ring Cycle*, the opera remained something of a hybrid: *Siegfried* is mythos condensed into a fairy-tale setting, or conversely a fairy tale that hides a mythos. The doubleness that Wagner seems to find so advantageous, however, also constitutes *Siegfried*'s central contradiction. Act 1 of *Siegfried*, in particular, sees the story of the Nibelungs and the gods of Valhalla grind to a halt, as the cast pauses to stage a production of the Grimms' story of the "youth who went forth to learn what fear was."[2] The hybridity at the heart of the opera plays out both in the erotics and the music of *Siegfried*. The fairy-tale setting and the mythos that frames it come to speak about the music drama as form (as Gesamtkunstwerk), but they do so through the medium of sexuality.

As Carl Dahlhaus suggested with respect to *Siegfried*, a classic fairy tale is characterized by both timelessness and immanence.[3] In setting up its protagonist, in outlining that protagonist's travails and their eventual resolution, a fairy tale does not draw on any external resources, be they social, historical, or even logical. It answers exactly the questions that it poses, without leaving anything unresolved. Both mythos and fairy tale of course are centrally concerned with family and parentage, but they deploy it altogether differently. Where mythos concerns itself with origins, lineage, and causation, often with a connection to the present, the fairy tale tends to present its families as a static constellation of types. Insofar as they have mothers and fathers at all, they act only as ciphers, be they the absent parents of "Hansel and Gretel" or the classic evil stepmother. When Wagner distinguishes between *Mythos* and *Märchen*, he seems to be drawing on the same distinction between the historical axis and dynastic concerns of the epic/mythos, and the compressed and self-contained temporality of the fairy tale.

In Wagner's *Ring des Nibelungen*, this contradiction between genetic temporality and pure, ostensibly static form becomes a contradiction of genres. The cycle's "second day," *Siegfried*, as Dahlhaus argued, constitutes not only a fairy tale, but one upon which something foreign, namely the mythos, is always already encroaching: Instead of a "happily ever after," this fairy tale inaugurates a lengthy narrative, but that narrative "takes place outside of the world of the fairy tale and destroys it. The fairy tale of young Siegfried is like one of the Fortunate Islands, which is swallowed up by the myth[os]."[4]

A stark dualism seems to characterize Wagner's understanding of mythos and fairy tale, but at the same time the opera's undertakes to overcome that dualism. *Siegfried* stages an opposition between an epic plot, namely the story of the Nibelungs and the end of the gods of Valhalla, and a fairy-tale plot, the story of Siegfried leaving his forest and reaching (sexual) maturity. And since the intersection between the epic plot that needs to be advanced and the fairy-tale antiplot that attempts to suspend its development occurs precisely in the realm of sexuality, sexuality becomes a central thematic node of *Siegfried*. What is more, the dualism of self-enclosure and epic development plays itself out in *Siegfried*'s music as well, in ways that raise important issues for the immanence not just of the fairy tale, but operatic form itself. They were issues the generation of composers immediately after Wagner had to confront in thinking through the twinned legacy of Wagnerian erotics and Wagnerian operatic form.

The hero of both mythos and fairy tale persists in, or rather exists as, the intersection of fairy-tale timelessness and mythic provenance. He emerges from somewhere outside concrete historical sequence (like Romulus and Remus suckling on the teat of the she-wolf), yet comes to influence and even inaugurate historical sequence (the foundation of Rome). The spot where timelessness and development intersect is inherently contradictory, and the hero's position at that point in the story overdetermined—he or she belongs to two worlds at once. In *Siegfried*, more importantly, the hero is not alone at the intersection of myth and fairy tale: his foster parent and cunning exploiter, Mime, occupies that same vexed spot. In Mime's case, the opera obsessively asserts the impossibility of his position, turning him into the tortured citizen of two worlds. In the case of Siegfried, however, it just as strenuously denies that he is in an impossible position. Mime becomes in many respects the sacrificial lamb of *Siegfried*'s hybrid plot, or perhaps what Julia Kristeva has termed "the abject"—a loathed quasi-object, whose obsessive and repeated exclusion allows the opera to repress its own generic contradictions.[5] Mime's object is to preserve the immanence of the self-enclosed, imaginary space of the enchanted forest. What undoes him are the rumbles of the *Mythos* that, to return to Dahlhaus's image, threatens to engulf Mime's little island. And the rumbles become audible in *Siegfried*'s music.

Through the medium of sexuality, Wagner allows his Siegfried to transcend the limitations of the fairy tale toward the greener pastures of the mythos. Conversely, he forces Mime to act out the contradictions between the two through a sexual charade, by associating the epic with familial, dynastic sexuality and the fairy tale with a kind of asexual reproduction. In the course of act 1, Siegfried is launched on a quest to discover his provenance. And an increasingly panicked Mime, desperate to maintain the illusion that he is the boy's (sole) point of origin, begins to take on all roles, culminating in his desperate claim that "I am your father / and mother as well." Siegfried wants to know where he comes from, and suspects that it might not be Mime: "Now Mime, where have you got / your loving wife, / so that I may call her Mother?"[6] While Siegfried associates the woman he wants "to call mother" with sexual love, Mime refuses to acknowledge that link between sexuality and motherhood. Instead, he lays claim to being a nonsexual mother, an example of "cunning" manipulation based on the causal chains of instrumental reason. But it is *sexual* causation, of which Mime appears incapable, that proves to be his downfall.

Mime's dizzying carousel of sexual personae is at once strangely desexualized (in many ways it is the simple fact of sexual difference that proves Mime's undoing) and a kind of drag, and it is clearly played for a laugh in the opera. Mime's voice and use of figurative language already subvert the claims his charade forces him into, in the eyes of both Siegfried and the audience, for whose benefit Wagner supposedly turned mythos into fairy tale in the first place. As Mime's claims become increasingly outlandish, his voice, his mien, and the music that he is given to sing disclose with spectacular eloquence that for Mime sexuality is but a cunning machination. He tells Siegfried that he is his "father and mother," but his musical means betray that he is incapable of sexual reproduction and parental love.

Of course, being incapable of sexual love is not an incidental affliction in Wagner's system of thought, in which sexual love (*Geschlechtsliebe*) occupies a central position. Wagner's unsent letter to Arthur Schopenhauer speaks of "the predisposition toward sexual love" as "a path to salvation, to self-knowledge and self-negation of the will."[7] Being capable of love is the same as being capable of transcending the narrow bounds of the self—love "drives the subject beyond itself and forces that subject to connect with another:" But not everything that goes by the name "love" can claim to accomplish this much: "Not that 'revealed' love, imparted, taught and forced upon us from above— which for that reason has also never become real—like the Christian [love], but that love which springs from unalienated, real human nature; which is in its origin nothing other than the most active living assertion of this nature, which expresses itself in pure joy over sensuous existence, and which, starting with sexual love, progresses via the love of children, brothers, and friends to the love of all mankind."[8] Only sexual love is real in a concrete and effective way, as opposed to abstract kinds of love that are "taught and ordered." Thus when Mime tells Siegfried that he has taught him to love "his Mime," when he tells him that "you have to love him" (*so mußt du ihn lieben*), he is clearly imposing this false kind of love rather than the love on which the metaphysician Wagner pinned his hopes.[9]

The figure of Mime is central to any consideration of Wagnerian metaphysics and Wagnerian aesthetics, but above all to any discussion of Wagnerian anti-Semitism. Mime's cunning corresponds to a common topos of nineteenth-century anti-Semitism, and Wagner's score and stage instructions strengthen this parallel. Nevertheless, I do not contend that Wagner thinks of Mime as Jewish and of Jews therefore as somehow external to the metaphysics of sexual difference. Not because that argument cannot be made, but rather because, as Slavoj Žižek has pointed out, one cannot "characterize" a Jewish stereotype.[10] Indeed, although Mime appears undersexed and emasculated, Alberich has been read in precisely opposing terms.[11] Wagner's image of the Jew is not self-consistent, since a racist phantasm derives its force not from an inner stringency but rather from its functionality. In *Siegfried*, a particular set of organizing oppositions stages the coherence of Wagner's spectacle, as well as that of his intended audience;[12] in doing so, these oppositions overlap, but are by no means coterminous, with Wagner's anti-Semitism.

TWO HOUSEHOLDS UNALIKE IN DIGNITY

In German, the word *Geschlecht* can refer to both gender and to a dynasty or family. *Siegfried* could be described as a tale of two *Geschlechter* in that double sense. It concerns the existence of two sexes and the fact that they reproduce, and thus the question of motherhood. But behind this question looms the standoff between not just two families, but rather two kinds of families, which differ precisely with respect to reproduction.

In his 1908 article "Family Romances," Sigmund Freud points to a common fantasy that replaces the subject's own family with another.[13] This "family romance" (*Familienroman*) unfolds in two stages. Children as yet unaware of sexual procreation believe themselves to be switched or adopted, or their older siblings to be bastards; once children become aware of sexual procreation, they understand that *pater semper incertus est*, the mother *certissima*. Children then turn to the fantasy that a mysterious, unknown father from a higher station has sired them.

In many respects, the first act of *Siegfried* presents us with this kind of constellation: Siegfried, the orphaned spawn of the illicit love between siblings Siegmund and Sieglinde, is raised in complete isolation by the Nibelung blacksmith Mime. Mime is perfectly aware of his charge's illustrious provenance but tries to keep the youth in the dark about it, hoping to use him to reclaim the treasure of the Nibelungs. Scene 1 of act 1 traces Siegfried's discovery of his true origins; in scene 2, those origins themselves arrive in the guise of his grandfather Wotan.

And yet, the two scenes diverge in significant ways from the scenario Freud describes. For one thing, throughout Siegfried's attempt to decipher his true parentage, it is Mime who is *certissimus*; the mysterious object of the young man's fantasies is his mother. For another, Siegfried's interpretations are not firmly rooted in either awareness or unawareness of sexual difference, for he knows sexual difference but only by having observed it in the animal kingdom. At issue in his interrogation of Mime is sexual difference as such—whether it pertains to humans and what it means. Mime's sole concern in laying claim to androgynous parenthood is to keep Siegfried from realizing that there is such a thing as love between mothers and fathers.

In trying to convince Siegfried that they are a family, Mime recreates something along the lines of what psychoanalysts have described as the imaginary configuration between infant and mother, a dyadic construction in which the self is caught in a complex web of identifications and misidentifications with the mother. Mime himself suggests as much when he pleads with Siegfried to appreciate the fact that he "cared for you / as if you were my own skin."[14] This puzzling line sets up a strange parallelism in which narcissism is adduced as the metaphoric support for love: I love you as exclusively as I love myself. The way in which Mime sets up this imaginary circuit that knows no outside eventually undermines his attempts, hinting that the fairy tale is a defective form of myth, just as Mime's and Siegfried's dyad is a defective or pseudofamily. There is, in other words, something necessary in the unraveling of their dyadic pseudofamily and the fairy-tale world Mime sets up around it.

Wotan's appearance on the scene might seem to complete this defective family. But this itinerant father figure does not stabilize Mime's mother role. To the contrary, Mime notes with chagrin that "weak before [him] grows / my mother wit."[15] When Mime speaks of his *Mutterwitz*, his choice of words betrays the complex interplay between his subterfuge and questions of family and heredity. Prima facie Mime is simply complaining that Wotan is outsmarting him in their guessing game. Mime, as Theodor Adorno noted, represents for Wagner the failings and moral shortcomings of instrumental reason—the ability to manipulate the causes of the outside world without any insight into their quiddity or their raisons d'être, a preoccupation with mechanical causes and effects.[16] It is central to his attempts to manipulate the forces of nature (above all Siegfried) before which he is by himself powerless.[17] The word *Mutterwitz* links the idea of instrumental reason with maternity and thus heredity. In nineteenth-century German, the word designated nothing more than what modern German knows as *Gewitztheit*, "cunning." It refers to a quick ability to grasp and manipulate givens—a purely reactive, unoriginal facility, with a clear pejorative edge.

Although in its nineteenth-century usage, the "motherhood" of this *Witz* seems extraneous, the word's etymology points to the hereditary character of this kind of cunning, a matter of instinct rather than of acquired skill.[18] This etymology appears to have formed the basis for the Wagner family's use of the word. In *Deutsche Kunst und Deutsche Politik*, Richard equates *Mutterwitz* with "the natural understanding of a people";[19] Cosima's diary calls it "the wit that one has *inside*."[20] Wagner's personal understanding of "Mutterwitz" thus tends to valorize the word, as referring to wit that springs naturally from the autonomous individual or from the wisdom of a people. As such, it appears to be distinct from, and superior to, the rootless, roving cleverness of Mime. More important is the fact that the opera forces Mime into a revealing turn of phrase when he refers to his lack of *Mutterwitz*. Mime's language has a strange way of slipping out of his control; his wit and his language constantly bespeak what they lack, namely a natural, instinctual, inherited basis.

Mime's faltering "mother wit" constitutes his most damning disqualification in an opera in which the question of motherhood is a central preoccupation. In act 1, the recognition that Mime cannot be his mother launches Siegfried out of his fairy-tale enclosure. In act 2, the *Waldvogel*, who allows Siegfried to see through (and slay) his false mother Mime, seems to act as a medium of sorts, speaking for the dead mother: "It would surely tell me something, perhaps about my dear mother?"²¹ It is the bird, speaking for the "dear mother," who first redirects Siegfried's "yearning" (*Sehnen*): "Ho! Siegfried has killed / the evil dwarf! Now I know for him / the most marvelous woman."²² The moment he has slain his false father, Siegfried can accede to his true mother/lover. And in act 3, Wotan the wanderer who has lost his place in the world descends to Erda, the mother of Brünnhilde, who alone has remained stationary since we last saw her in *Das Rheingold*. The final scene of the opera then transposes mother into lover, as Siegfried finally learns to be afraid when he lays eyes on the female form: "O mother! Mother! / Your brave child! / A woman's lying asleep: / and she's taught him to be afraid."²³ The mother's image dominates the entirety of the opera's climactic scene. As Lawrence Kramer has observed, Siegfried "responds to the miraculous awakening with a maternal invocation that Brünnhilde at once echoes, the musical phrases of the couple overlapping and intertwining: 'O Heil der Mutter, die mich gebar,' 'O Heil der Mutter, die dich gebar' (Hail to the mother that bore me/you)."²⁴ When Brünnhilde informs Siegfried that his mother will not return, he is able to substitute her for his mother, the original object of desire.

In the opera, the image of the maternal object is always bound up with questions of epistemology: Mime's defective motherhood is tied to what Adorno calls his "Dummschläue,"²⁵ the cunning that turns him into a fool. Siegfried, in turn, is propelled by both his ignorance of his own origins (evident in particular when he fails to recognize the wanderer) and by the instinctive knowledge that Mime cannot possibly be that origin. As Adorno pointed out, Siegfried's ignorance is of an entirely different register from Mime's. In his cunning, Mime represents what the German Idealists called *Verstand*.²⁶ His actions are instrumental and always directed at the same, essentially conservative (or at least quietist) goal: "How can I help myself now? / How can I hold him here?"²⁷ Wotan, who goads him into posing questions to which he not only knows the answer, but rather to which he *is* the answer, represents the deeper, less mechanistic *Vernunft* characterized by insight into the conditions of possibility of the chain reactions that *Verstand* is content to manipulate.²⁸ Here, then, an anti-Semitic epistemology (the canard of the "cunning Jew") and an antibourgeois critique of specialized reason are explicitly linked in and through the medium of sexuality.

Since the knowledge that Siegfried seeks is always that of origins, the opera associates *Verstand* and *Vernunft* with variant approaches to sexual provenance. That is, *Vernunft* characterizes knowledge through genealogical descent, whereas *Verstand* corresponds to asexual transformation. Of course, the obtuse and shallow youngster Siegfried is neither *vernünftig* nor *verständig*, but the questions he poses (always in contradistinction to Mime) represent the first stirrings of *Vernunft* and a rejection of *Witz* or *Verstand*. In turn those two means of understanding origin vie to explain Siegfried's provenance in the first act of the opera. Mime claims to Siegfried that he "made him without a mother," and he plots against Fafner who has transformed himself from a giant into a dragon: dwarf and giant alike multiply laterally rather than procreating dynastically.[29] The distinction between the gods' procreative powers and the "horizontal dynasties" of iteration of the giants and dwarves (somewhat along the lines of what Carolyn Abbate has called the "cabinet of Wagnerian shape-shifters")[30] dovetails with the dichotomy of natural/unnatural. Even when Alberich begets Hagen, he does so as an unnatural "affront" (*Hohn*) against the gods since he has forsworn love.[31]

Wagner describes something similar to this biological narcissism in an 1849 fragment on "Jesus von Nazareth."[32] Here Wagner characterizes *Geschlechtsliebe* as the first self-alienation or self-externalization (*Wiederentäußerung seiner selbst*). In love human beings give away their life force (*Lebenskraft*) and multiply themselves into families. This voluntary surrender of life force necessitates the subject's eventual death. Wagner now sketches the opposite possibility "that man would not die, were he not to multiply by begetting offspring but rather using his generative power to continually reproduce his own body."[33] In this fragment Wagner explicitly declares self-reproduction a form of egoism, and associates it with "the acquisition of power and wealth." It is hard not to think of one particular "Wagnerian shape-shifter" in this regard—the giant/dragon Fafner: "Here I lie and I am master / let me sleep!"[34]—as Brechtian a line as Wagner ever wrote.

The juxtaposition of generative vs. "lateral" sexuality (or sexuality and antisexuality) has obvious racial implications. Indeed, neither Mime's attempt at keeping Siegfried in the dark about sexuality nor Siegfried's rage at the possibility of Mime's paternity make sense apart from a racial matrix of biological signification. One somewhat anachronistic testament comes from a rabid anti-Wagnerian, Max Nordau. "The disease of degeneracy," he would write in 1892, "consists precisely in the fact that the degenerate organism has not the power to mount to the height of evolution already attained by the species, but stops on the way at an earlier point." The degenerate may sink "somatically to the level of fishes, nay to that of arthropoda, or, even further, to that of rhizopods not yet sexually differentiated"[35]

The image of an organism too degenerate to be sexually differentiated resonates with Wagner's characterizations of the Nibelungs from his first prose sketches to the *Ring*. In his 1848 *Entwurf zu einem Drama*, Wagner describes the Nibelungs as follows: "With restless agility they burrow through the innards of the earth, like worms in a dead body."[36] The common denominator between Nordau's "degeneration" and the asexual nature of the Nibelungs and their ilk is the inability, or the immoral unwillingness, to self-alienate: Alberich's renunciation of love, of any "re-externalization of the self." The "retentiveness" of the *Ring*'s subhumans, their tendency to cling possessively to their essence and inability to beget newness finds its opposite in Wotan's (at least nominal) willingness to relinquish control to/via his offspring out of love. "Those I love, I let do as they please; / let him stand or fall, he is his own master."[37] It is of course significant that the egotism inherent in "lateral" reproductions of the self is also a common trope of Wagnerian anti-Semitism. For Wagner (who was influenced by Feuerbach in this regard), the Jews cling stubbornly to a particular identity, rejecting the universalization that can only come with the negation of the self.[38]

The moral ramifications of Mime's hesitancy before the realm of sexuality are illuminated by the opera that precedes *Siegfried* in the cycle: Love, in *Die Walküre*, has its own biological and deeply authentic basis (it is a love of likeness, of common origin), but because of this basis it is also incestuous. Natural, authentic attraction requires the relationship between Siegmund and Sieglinde; it is something that "happens by itself [*was von selbst sich fügt*]," as Wotan explains to Fricka. Nature, which seems determined to nourish in Siegfried an awareness of love and sexual difference, smiles of the Valsung's incestuous union—most famously when "winter storms leave behind a joyful moon [*Winterstürme wichen dem Wonnemond*]."[39] And of course their union is urgently necessary: Biologically begetting newness is entirely the province of transgressive relationships in the opera—the only two legitimate unions (Hunding-Sieglinde, Wotan-Fricka) are, for the purposes of *Die Walküre*, barren. Incest and adultery are where "kühn Kräfte sich regen"; it is where newness enters the world, where the self relinquishes control and allows something to happen "even if it has never happened before [*sei es auch zuvor auch noch nie geschehn*]."[40] The demands of biology, essential to bringing something new into the world, automatically conflict with the letter of the law—sexedness is in itself tragic. However, to cowardly shirk its tragic nature is to risk inauthenticity and immorality.

LOVE UNION AND ANDROGYNY

As Michael P. Steinberg has recently pointed out, *Der Ring des Nibelungen* tells an exceedingly bourgeois story, the "decline of a family" exemplified in

the German canon by Thomas Mann's *Buddenbrooks*.[41] The *Ring* is at its core
a story of the degeneration and decadence of a household. Paradoxically, of
course, in keeping with Wagner's revolutionary program the opera is dominated by an antibourgeois affect regarding both operatic genre (Gesamtkunstwerk) and organizing dichotomy (instrumental reason vs. love). At the same
time, this dichotomy relies on a parallel *Geschlecht* that persists side-by-side
with the Valsungs and at times interlocks with Wotan's household: the titular
Nibelungs, who shadow the Valsungs as their other, relying in each iteration
not on filiation but rather on changes in form. Alberich uses the ring to transform into a number of monsters and the giant Fafner turns himself into "a giant worm." Mime undergoes a similar transformation, appearing "in drag" by
claiming to be Siegfried's mother.

The precise nature of this "drag" is bound up with *Siegfried*'s organizing
generic aporia. Within the logic of the fairy tale, Mime is not in drag; rather he
attempts "to pass himself as an androgyne."[42] He stands outside sexual difference in that he banishes maleness and femaleness from the sphere of the
human, consigning them to the realm of "rabbit and fox." Siegfried, on the
other hand, instinctively yokes the question of origins to that of sexual difference and gender roles: which is it, Mime, father or mother?[43] To instill this
instinctual rage in Siegfried, the opera has to combine two tropes: the biological contiguity of "rabbit and fox" with Mime and Siegfried—a variation on the
naturalization of heterosexuality in Longus' *Daphnis and Chloe*—and the logic
of the fairy tale's generic other, the epic. Daphnis and Chloe learn from the
sheep they are herding, but they already have each other, whereas Siegfried's
naturalization of sexual difference can proceed only by positing the phantasm
of a never-glimpsed feminine outside Mime's magic circle.

Only vis-à-vis the epic context can the opera abject Mime's androgyny as
a stridently theatrical performance, obviously and spectacularly unnatural.
Only once we know of the epic-dynastic context beyond Mime's fairy tale
enclosure does his claim to fatherhood and motherhood become integrated
into a sexed context and thus clearly legible as cunning and instrumental deception. The question that *Siegfried* does not allow to come to the surface is
the following, famously posed by Judith Butler in *Gender Trouble*: "Is drag
the imitation of gender, or does it dramatize the signifying gestures through
which gender itself is established?"[44] Mime's drag is clearly imitative. In
fact, Mime is not "in drag" insofar as he is a man who presents himself as a
mother; instead, he is in drag whether he presents himself as man or woman,
offers himself as father or mother. In this figure whose very sexedness is a
ruse, *Siegfried* represses the second possibility Butler suggests, namely that

Mime's performance dramatizes the contingency of Siegfried's own dynastic, Germanic, heroic heterosexuality.

Mime's "drag" is thus the narrative obverse of the telos of *Siegfried* (the character as well as the opera), the "quest for sexual difference."[45] But that difference, in keeping with Wagner's metaphysical program, is necessary only so that it can be superseded in love. Siegfried has to leave behind the strange androgyne Mime, become aware of sexual difference, and then aspire to the (impossible) sexual union in love as another kind of androgyny.[46] The union Siegfried and Brünnhilde almost achieve at the climax of the opera is the opposite of the bizarre union of mother and father in the cunning blacksmith. For Mime's androgyny has not passed through the alembic of sexual difference, a stopping short before sexual determinacy that indicates his defectiveness. The *biologically* degenerate/egoistic relapses into a state prior to sexual difference (ontogeny recapitulating phylogeny); analogously, the morally egoistic is incapable of the self-alienation of love and thus remains outside the sexual relationship. Nevertheless, as the abject image of the "worms" in the earth's carcass makes clear, there is still an unsettling *productivity* to these loveless egoists: in spite of their barrenness, they counternaturally reproduce.

It is central to Mime's subterfuge that his performance of androgyny is, in a perverse way, reproductive (both in the sense of being mimetic and in the sense of reproducing the self). Mime's attempt to transform himself into a mother is thus not just one more instance of the Nibelungs' lineage of shapes and disguises. When Siegfried bluntly asks Mime whether he is his "father / and mother as well," he has hit upon Mime's secret motive: the Nibelung's ambitions to build a "lateral dynasty." Returning to the strange locution that Mime "cared for you / as if you were my own skin," we now see that "skin" not only points to an insufficient cleavage of self and other but also contrasts with "my own blood." Mime's relationship with Siegfried is skin-deep, just as Alberich's, Fafner's, and Mime's own transformations are mere changes of external form, since they seem to be barred from passing on their blood through procreation. It is indeed an index of Siegfried's lapse in *Götterdämmerung* that he himself begins to think/procreate laterally: his use of the *Tarnhelm* to abduct Brünnhilde disguised as Gunther, which sets off the opera's calamitous chain of events, is a lateral transformation in the mold of Mime and Alberich.

It is possible to read the first act as a struggle to integrate Siegfried into each of these lines. Wotan wants to restore the power of his dynastic line (and his own dynastic prowess), whereas Mime hopes to secure the transformative power of the ring, thus the power of lateral reproduction. At the beginning of *Götterdämmerung*, Siegfried entrusts the ring to Brünnhilde as a token of his love. It is, as Linda and Michael Hutcheon have noted, the first time in the cycle that the ring serves a ring's "proper" dynastic function, as a token of a love union. Before that, as well as later on in *Götterdämmerung*, it is a means of perverted dynastic ambition.[47] While he does not confront Siegfried directly in the first act, Wotan does remind Mime of the filial aspects of the struggle, turning him into the unwitting tool of his own dynastic ambitions.

Of course, Wotan's efforts in *Siegfried* have the strange tendency to assimilate him to the deceptive dynasties that the epic context pits him against. Wotan appears three times in *Siegfried*, each time in a different relation to the dynastic principle. In act 1, he simply serves as a reminder, and as a foil for Mime's cunning. The question with which Mime's life is ultimately forfeit is the question his *Witz* is unable to solve, that of how to mend the sword Nothung. In act 2, Wotan is himself engaged in a battle of *Witz* with Mime, aiding a scheme that act 1 made seem natural and inevitable. In act 3, finally, Wotan's designs paradoxically both are foiled and come to fruition, in a replay of the tetralogy's first oedipal scene: not recognizing "the Wanderer," Siegfried shatters the spear that represents Wotan's law; the spawn bests his elder.

The outline of this progression is illustrated by the role played by the sword Nothung. In Mime's forest, the shattered sword that his mother/father cannot mend comes to represent Siegfried's suspicions against him. In the second act, slaying both the dragon and the heinous dwarf, a repaired Nothung becomes the emblem of Siegfried's emancipation from the fairy tale world, his foray into the mythic struggle of the *Ring*, and his integration into the dynastic designs of Wotan. In the third act, Nothung begins to display its own efficacy, since Siegfried does not recognize his role in the epic design and uses the sword to smash Wotan's spear. Whereas in Mime's forest the shards of the sword functioned as a vexing reminder of the dynastic horizon looming beyond the fairy-tale enclosure, Siegfried's disinterest in where those same shards came from signal the unraveling of Wotan's dynastic plan: "What do I know of that? / I only know / that the fragments would have been useless / had I not forged the sword afresh."[48]

There is of course a dangerous suggestion in the eventual undoing of Wotan's plan: The possibility that the grandfather's designs are in fact not that different from fake father Mime's. Wotan spends as much of *Siegfried* skulking around caves and forests as Mime does. And his emphasis on love ("Those I love, I let do as they please; / let him stand or fall, he is his own master")[49] is no less a ruse than Mime's "so too you must love [me]." In fact, when he finally confronts Siegfried in act 3, Wotan seems to Siegfried nothing but a successor to Mime: "All my life an old man / has always stood in my way: now I've swept him aside."⁵⁰ Nevertheless, what still centrally distinguishes the two, at least for the audience, is the fact that the smashing of the spear constitutes a further step in the *Ring*'s tragedy, whereas Mime's comeuppance is at best comic.

Although *Götterdämmerung* will see both the lateral and dynastic projects come to naught, *Siegfried* at least concludes with the decisive victory of the dynastic principle. Leaving Mime's fairy-tale forest for a moment, it is clear that the biological and erotic solipsism of the opera's first act finds its glorious renunciation in the love union of the third act. It is here that Siegfried's budding awareness of sexual difference is finally realized, that his inchoate erotic longing attains to the status of true Schopenhauerian love, and that the union that Mime can only feign of "father and mother in one" is finally (albeit only momentarily) realized. And lest we forget: it is here that the youth who went forth to learn what fear was learns just that. When Siegfried first ascends to Brünnhilde's fiery resting place, he is looking for his mother but still sees a man: "Look! A man in armor: / how strangely enticed I am by his image!"⁵¹ The homoerotic tinge of the scene should not eclipse the fact that Siegfried is at this point unaware that his mother might well look different from a man. Nevertheless, his instincts once again stand him in good stead. Just as he rejected the false father Mime for not being masculine enough, for not being able to mend Nothung for him, so he feminizes the unknown "man" through his phallus sword: "Come, my sword, / cut the iron! / That is not a man!"⁵² The recognition that "that is not a man" brings to a conclusion the fairy tale of the "youth who went forth to learn what fear was" (even though in the fairy tale, the youth never does learn to be afraid).

Žižek characteristically reads the fact that Siegfried's "quest for woman" and thus "for sexual difference" is "at the same time the quest of fear"⁵³ understood as castration anxiety. This is certainly plausible, given Nothung's role in the discovery and "feminization" of Brünnhilde. Still, it fails to take into account the specific link Wagner himself proposes between sexual difference and fear. Woman strikes fear into Siegfried's heart by confronting him with difference, with something that exceeds the narcissistic configuration in which he has persisted with Mime. The "man" Siegfried describes before he opens Brünnhilde's harness may, at least in Wagner's vision, be simply Siegfried: "Oh, how beautiful! / Shining clouds hover on the waves / of the bright sea in the sky; / the gleaming sun's laughing gaze / beams through waves of cloud / his breast heaves."⁵⁴ What shock, then, when his mirror image sports a pair of breasts! Sexual difference and sexual relationship finally becomes a sensuous reality for Siegfried when he disarms Brünnhilde. For not only does he invoke the matrilineal dynasty of which he is a part ("Mother! Mother! Think of me!"), but he also understands that overcoming this fear requires a dialogue with the sexual other: "If I myself am to wake up, / I must awake the maiden!"[55]

In every respect, then, the love relationship to which the opera's final scene offers its encomia constitutes the opposite of the relationship Mime has tried to foist upon Siegfried. Whereas Mime mainly postulated love ("so you *must* love him") and claimed it as something unknowable ("What mother? What father? / Idle question!"),[56] in this final scene knowledge and love are nearly identical: "You yourself I am, / If you in my bliss love me. / What you don't know, / I know for you; / Yet I have knowledge / Only because I love you!"[57] Mime's claim to Siegfried's love was a matter of "caring for you as for my own skin." But Siegfried was entrusted to Brünnhilde's care "before you were even conceived," and her love for him is a matter of blood: "As streams of my blood rush towards you"; "as our blood streams set one another alight."[58] Her care, love, and knowledge of Siegfried are not "taught and ordered" but rather are matters of instinct and dynastic heredity: "My inheritance, my own, one and all,"[59] as Siegfried and Brünnhilde proclaim in their climactic dialogue.

THE INTERRUPTED DYAD AND THE FAIRY TALE

Dahlhaus observed that "what separates *Siegfried* irredeemably from *Götterdämmerung* is the timelessness of the fairy tale, as opposed to the temporality of the mythos."[60] This timelessness of *Siegfried* is intimately bound up with the question of filiality. The fairy tale's protagonist never belongs to a family tree (a *Geschlecht*, to speak with Wagner)—all he or she has are "father" and "mother" (or, more often, stepmother), who constitute family prototypes rather than a dynastic line. The arrangement of these prototypes can be broken, skewed, incomplete, or even phony, but that status itself has neither etiology nor consequences beyond the causality of the fairy tale. No fairy-tale orphan has ever lost his or her parents to an historic event, to a family history of disease, or to a boating accident. No fairy-tale protagonist has ever avenged his or her family, or set off a feud with, for example, the evil stepmother's own offspring.

Indeed, then, in insisting on being "your father / and mother as well," Mime is acting in the interest of generic purity as well as his own interest, attempting to banish the threatening echoes of the epic. Wagner's "poem" for *Siegfried* makes quite explicit that what disrupts the fairy-tale act is not so much Wotan, the father figure, as sexuality itself. The cracks that start to appear in Mime's and Siegfried's dysfunctional dyad are occasioned by Mime's double insufficiency. Siegfried's father would have to be able to craft a sword that his son could not break—a rather strange supposition. He is not man enough for young Siegfried, unable to create a sword that the youth wouldn't break in two like "trashy toy[s]" (*Tand*);[61] moreover, he is unable to sustain the illusion that he is man enough to have given birth to Siegfried, a bizarre position into which scene 1 of act 1 increasingly forces him.

The impossibility of Mime's paternity stems from questions of descent rather than of family in a narrower sense. Plenty of children are able to best their parents; in fact oedipal impulses require that they do so eventually. That Mime's failure before his "son" is not oedipal, but rather means that [the fact that] Mime cannot be Siegfried's father, is a matter of heredity. Siegfried's suspicions are aroused by his observations of nature: "And so I learnt what love is: / from their mother I never took her whelps away. / Now Mime, where have you got / your loving wife, / so that I may call her Mother?"[62] More heavily than this introduction to "what love is" (namely coupledom) weighs Siegfried's self-observation. In watching reproduction among the animals in the forest, he notices how "the young look like their elders." Eventually he comes across his own image: "There I also saw my own shape; completely different from you I seemed to be." The difference between Mime and Siegfried is thus framed in terms of the descent of species. Siegfried does not simply doubt that Mime is his father because he does not look like him but rather suggests that they are of different species. He and Mime are "as like as a toad to a glistening fish; but never a fish was born to a toad!" What first looks like a family romance turns out to be something different: in realizing that he cannot be of the same species as Mime, Siegfried realizes that he cannot be Mime's offspring.

Mime in turn deflects Siegfried's inquiries by chalking up sexual difference to a difference in species: "Are you either a bird or a fox?" he asks, suggesting that sexual difference obtains only in the animal kingdom.[63] The very question after his descent, which for Siegfried is coextensive with the quest for his mother, is relegated to the animal kingdom. In a puzzling fragment written in 1883 and intended as a concluding chapter to "Religion und Kunst," on the theme "das Weibliche im Menschlichen," Wagner introduces the opposite line of argumentation, emphatically linking the sexuality of animals and humans. Although Wagner tries in the fragment to capture the "Reinmenschliche" in the "relation [*Verhalten*] between . . . the male and the female," he ranks animal coupledom very high. Animal species are able to maintain themselves "in great purity" (*in großer Reinheit*) because they do not get together based on the acquisition of wealth (*auf Eigenthum und Besitz*).[64] On the other hand, they also do not marry. Monogamy is the way in which human beings raise themselves, or have historically raised themselves "above the animal kingdom" (*über die Thierwelt*). Clearly the basest of these three different forms of *Verhalten* between male and female is the marriage that is entirely drained of its biological content. If the institution is abused for external purposes (Wagner speaks of a "Mißbrauch der Ehe"), namely gaining wealth, power, and influence, it occasions mankind's degeneration "bis unter die Tierwelt."[65] Mime's claim that descent is something that characterizes only the animal kingdom thus paradoxically represents his utter debasement of the love relation between humans.

Significantly, introducing a cleavage between animal and human love represents a full reversal in Mime's line of argumentation. Mime has previously argued that "Young things long for their old ones' nests; that longing is love: and so you pine for me also."[66] Siegfried is to love Mime like his offspring, but he is not the result of reproduction; other species may constitute a model for the love relationship that is to obtain between the Siegfried and Mime, but they cannot provide a model for their filiation. As already noted, Mime here takes recourse to an abstract love "from above," which lacks natural grounding and requires language to assert what *Geschlechtsliebe* simply knows. Mime offers this as the human form of love, as opposed to the brute *Geschlechtsliebe* characteristic of *Vogel und Fuchs*.

The disjunction Mime insists on between filiation and *Geschlechtsliebe* means that love becomes an ideological construction, a conceit of language as self-sufficient as the fairy tale loop the dwarf is trying to maintain around Siegfried: "Won't you ever remember /what I taught you about gratitude? / You should be glad to obey / the man who did so much for you."[67] The second part of Mime's question is strangely circular: Siegfried is to remember what Mime taught him about being grateful for what Mime taught him. Mime's efforts are focused on calling on the Siegfried that he himself has constructed—with the additional proviso, however, that the opera posits a real Siegfried behind the linguistic one Mime attempts to fashion.

We might well wonder if Mime's claim of fatherhood and motherhood is not perhaps a metaphorical one. Is Mime really laying claim to preterhuman sexual prowess, or is he simply claiming that he is *like* mother and father to Siegfried? If Mime's statement is metaphorical, it is obviously evasive: His claim that he is "dir Vater und Mutter zugleich" is an answer to Siegfried's question "Du machtest wohl gar ohne Mutter mich?" only if he means it literally. The assertion that he cares for Siegfried just as much as the combination of a father and a mother would is certainly interesting, but it offers nothing by way of explaining how Siegfried was "made." Only if the claim is on some level literal does it answer Siegfried's question. While Mime's exact meaning (and thus its relation to Siegfried's query) is thus not decidable, it is clear that in this instance only Mime has a choice in registers (literal or metaphoric). Siegfried can pose exclusively existential questions; whereas, Mime in answering them can treat them as questions of existence or of language.

If language is Mime's province, he is not therefore the lord of his domain. Just as it is not clear whether his claim "ich bin dir Vater und Mutter zugleich" is a machination of his *Witz* or follows from his desperation, the fact that he must speak literally to answer Siegfried's question of paternity indicates that Mime is at the mercy of his language. For at all times Mime is either being metaphorical or outright lying. Language is thus the last resort of those that can't lay convincing claim to paternity. And indeed, Mime's strange locutions betray him again and again. Take for example a line we have examined twice already: Mime claims that he "cared for you / as if you were my own skin." In German, as in English, when one saves or protects "one's own skin," this is usually a selfish, cowardly act at the expense of others. To protect someone else like one protects one's own skin thus means that one will think of the other first the same way one thinks of oneself first. The metaphor contradicts its supposed intended meaning.

VOICE, SONG, SATIRE

Freud's article on *Family Romances*, at least in its English translation, involves a strange confusion of genres—for Freud's text in the original is titled "Familien*roman* der Neurotiker," thus invoking the *novel* rather than the *romance* as the generic patron saint of the phantasmatic construction under consideration in the text. Similarly, as we saw, the narrative of *Siegfried* is precariously perched between two genres—the atemporality of the fairy tale and the historicality of the mythos. It should not come as a surprise, then, that musically as well, *Siegfried* performs a kind of travesty, almost an act of transvestitism. Nor should it come as a surprise that it is Mime who is forced to enact this travesty. There is a different operatic form lurking in the background for much of *Siegfried*, and it is a form to which the opera hearkens back only to travesty it—a kind of derisive citation that employs its idiom, thoroughly Wagnerized but nevertheless legible, as a code for not just aesthetic, but dramatic, and, I would argue, sexual *mauvaise foi*.

To begin with, the self-enclosed loop characteristic of many of Mime's claims asserts itself in the music as well. The backstory that grounds Mime's claim to motherhood returns at least three times in the opera's first scene, resurfacing as something closer to a song number than a leitmotif. Twice Mime repeats it in order to remind Siegfried of his debt of gratitude, whereas the third time Siegfried turns the song against Mime, demanding to know where he "als zullendes Kind" came from.

In fact, whenever Mime repeats the song, the opera's poem reproduces the text in quotation marks: the song does not recur; rather, it is quoted. The circulation of distinct song numbers is of a piece with Mime's deceptiveness and his defectiveness as a parent. As Abbate claims, "He sings it even though it has been sung countless times over the years (Siegfried's irritation makes this clear) and though his audience has had more than enough: he is harping."[68] But it is above all Mime's choice of genre that is meant to condemn him in the eyes of this "audience," meaning both Siegfried and us, which again has implications for the opera's stance toward sexual difference.

The first act of *Siegfried* is notable, among other things, for its comedy, even its downright satiric character. The opera's original draft, *Der junge Siegfried*, was explicitly conceived as the comedic companion piece to the tragedy *Siegfrieds Tod* (later to be rechristened *Götterdämmerung*).[69] The opening conceit (explored in Mime's "Zwangvolle Plage") of a master blacksmith too specialized, too "witzig," to craft a lasting blade, already takes rather obvious satirical shots at what Hegel called the "animal kingdom of the spirit" (*das geistige Tierreich*) of extreme specialization and the social division of labor.[70] Mime's repartee with Siegfried—the only time in the entire *Ring* that the word "repartee" might be justified—with its tempestuous mood changes, Mime's constant attempts at ingratiating himself, and Siegfried's constant rejection of these, constitutes one of the cycle's most overtly comedic scenes.

Not least among the libretto's comic flights ranks Mime's increasingly desperate attempt to harmonize Siegfried's growing awareness of sexuality with the elaborate web of lies with which he seeks to keep the boy in the dark about his ancestry. At least part of the comedy of their exchanges, then, issues precisely from the fact that, in trying to maintain his deceptions, Mime is pushed by Siegfried into claiming ever more outlandish sexual powers. The more fervently he asserts these powers, however, the more Siegfried realizes that Mime cannot really possess them: in its very plaintiveness, Mime's voice bespeaks with ever-greater eloquence the extent of his impotence. This dissonance, to which Siegfried responds with instinctive rage, furnishes much of Mime's comedy.

This points to a strange ambivalence in Mime's villainy as well as his comedy: his comedy is villainy thwarted by bodily insufficiency. Of course, as Adorno knew already, Wagner's operas are able to "do" comedy only in a very strange, refracted fashion. In order to laugh at Mime, we have to be able to despise him a little, and it is difficult to despise him without a bit of a chuckle. Wagner's villains, Adorno has noted, "become humoristic figures and victims of denunciation," insofar as Wagner presents them as objects both of ridicule and pity.[71] Mime's ridiculousness and pitifulness are both staged in a spectacular fashion that links him to earlier operatic and singing types.[72] If *Siegfried*'s first act is structured much more like a traditional opera than the rest of the *Ring*, this rests mostly on Mime's shoulders. Recitative, aria, and dialogue, all but banished from Wagner's operas, reappear in Mime's forest, while leitmotivic development plays only a secondary role.[73]

Adorno already argued for the anti-Semitic aspects of Siegfried's instinctual rejection of Mime's paternity.[74] "I can't abide you," he reminds Mime, providing a litany of Mime's bodily expressions that rouse him to violence.[75] As Marc Weiner has added more recently, it is difficult to hear Mime's whining, plaintive song and not be reminded of Wagner's infamous indictment in "Das Judentum und die Musik" of 1850.[76] In Wagner's words "A shrill sibilant buzzing of [the] voice" characterizes Jewish speech and song, so that in listening, "we are involuntarily struck by its offensive manner and so diverted from understanding its matter."[77] Others have contested the identification of Mime's voice with that which Wagner attributes to the Jew. Hermann Danuser for example has pointed to the fact that Mime too uses that (to Wagner) ur-German poetic form, the *Stabreim*.[78] However, it seems that it is not so much the intricacies of Mime's sound (which is indeed *zischend* and *schrillend*) that lend credence to the identification, but rather the preponderance of the *how* over the "*what* contained in*" Mime's speech. Mime's use of *Stabreim* would thus be itself a kind of masquerade, but a masquerade that is flamboyantly obvious to both Siegfried and the audience.[79]

Whether or not we read Mime as anti-Semitic, then, at least one parallel to the Judaism essay emerges as obvious: Mime's voice, like that of "the Jew," has a problem with "how" it says "what" it says. "The Jew," Wagner claims, is characterized by a range of vocal effects that draw attention to themselves to the point that they eclipse the actual "content" conveyed in speech. These vocal effects seem to run the gamut from pronunciation ("zischend") to timbre ("summsend").[80] Similarly, Mime throws himself at Siegfried as a friend, yet his voice and his mien betray him as a repulsive "Nicker." Mime attempts to fool Siegfried, yet his voice tells the dragon-blood-addled Siegfried everything that he means to conceal (with the help of his "real" mother speaking through the *Waldvogel*).[81] Although Mime offers himself as a cunning artificer, we hear him to be a fool.[82] And, centrally for our line of inquiry, Mime offers himself as

"Vater und Mutter zugleich," yet both Siegfried and the audience can hear that this is not true: his voice signals that he is lying and betrays that he could not possibly be Siegfried's father or mother. For Mime, whether he is put forward as an explicitly "Jewish" character or not, is clearly offered for "ridicule and pity" as a castrato of sorts.

The musical form that Mime turns to (the "how") heightens the obviousness of his insufficiency, for Wagner provides Mime's pleas with a generic subtext that subverts both his intentions and his literal meanings. We have already noted that the self-enclosed loop in which Wagner places Siegfried and Mime asserts itself in the circulating "song numbers," forgoing developmental or motivic considerations. And it is clear that this melodic insularity is related to the insular form of the fairy tale. Dahlhaus thus points to the "song- and rondo forms" that predominate in particular in the exposition "between Mime and Siegfried, in which the fairy tale atmosphere is most obvious."[83]

Like Mime's voice, however, these forms are not just subversive but also comical. We are meant to laugh at Mime's songs as much as we are to laugh at his outrageous attempts to cover up his lies. "Als zullendes Kind" is not just a song number, fully detachable, as Dahlhaus pointed out, "from the dramatic-symphonic context;"[84] it is also a song parody. Keeping in mind David Levin's point that "Jews in Wagner's works are dogged by aesthetic qualities that the composer loathed,"[85] it becomes clear that Mime, whether he is an anti-Semitic caricature or not, is ridiculous because he represents a remnant of an "inferior" operatic practice. He declaims his arias, draws an unwilling Siegfried into duets, and comes close to speaking, returning almost to a recitative-aria schema.

Mime's music is not simply a throwback to outdated aesthetic practices and genres; its generic insufficiency is coterminous with his generative insufficiency. His voice and song offer eloquent testimony of his lateral lineage and its allegorical dimension. As Abbate puts it: "It is no secret that such empty formalism, though the librettos present it more harmlessly as the outmoded or antique, was what Wagner had in mind, when he decried Jewish music, its 'false mimesis' and artistic incapacity."[86] Mime, who as "parent" cannot beget newness, is also an aesthetic reproducer. As Martin Puchner has noted, "Mime is the scapegoat for everything that is suspect about theatrical mimesis"[87]—including, it seems, its supposed barrenness, its artificiality, and its overdependence on language and rule. Seen in light of his own erotics of creativity, then, Wagner's notorious assertion that "the Jew" can only imitate (*nachsprechen, nachkünsteln*)[88] has the equally ominous corollary that the Jew Mime cannot but always recreate himself—that his "Mime-sis" is also a form of (biological, musical, generic) egoism.

Wagner himself proposes a similar link between song-dominated musical practice and the lack of sexual relationship in a startling discussion of what we might term "tonal exogamy": In the third part of 1851's *Opera and Drama*, "Dichtkunst und Tonkunst im Drama der Zukunft," Wagner turns to the metaphor of exogamy for a discussion of melody and modulation: Each tone, he writes, is a member of a "family clan" (*Geschlecht*), namely a scale. But each member of this scale is itself tied by a kind of yearning to the notes of another scale; harmonic modulation thus resembles healthy exogamy, the unification of the members of two separate families, while the tonal endogamy practiced by, for example, folk melody that remains wedded to a single key, can know nothing of the love between two tones. Here, then, family and sexuality (because, once again, Wagner is not interested in platonic love, but rather in sexual attraction, *Geschlechterliebe*) are thought as opposites: An involved kinship system secures transcendence of the "patriarchal limitation" (*patriarchalische Beschränktheit*) of the "family melody" (*Familienmelodie*).

While Mime's song numbers, most prominently "Als zullendes Kind," do modulate and are thus (to use Wagner's schema) "exogamous," it is clear that Wagner thinks of song-based operatic practice as tending toward a kind of familial solipsism that is coterminous with the absence of love. Insofar, then, Mime's reliance on song resonates with this earlier Wagnerian text as well: Mime's voice banishes sexuality, in particular the incestuous genesis of Siegfried, but the generic form of that voice ends up reenacting the incest, as it were. Mime's musical means of self-assertion are song-based and thus tend toward tonal endogamy. Nevertheless, the net result of this endogamy is the same as that of a wholesale banishment of sexual difference: the impossibility of love. As Lawrence Kramer has pointed out, there is an obvious racial dimension to the charge of endogamy, "Jews, runs the anti-Semitic bromide, care only for other Jews; they incarnate endogamy."[89] In Hegelian philosophies of religion this charge of clannishness was transformed into a more metaphysical quality: beholden to the particularity of their group and its relationship to its God, Jews are incapable of sublating the particular into the "universal." The immoral hesitation before the necessary relinquishing of the self into a larger whole through love once again marks Mime's self-containment as a strange mix of moral, sexual, and racial failure.

The harmonic self-referentiality that parallels Mime's biological solipsism as well as the closed-loop structure of the fairy tale he constructs around Siegfried, is thus once again explicitly marked as barren and as "egotistical"—incapable of love, which is "the motif . . . that drives the subject beyond itself and forces that subject to connect with another."[90] This tonal love of course obtains in particular in the case of a scale's tonic keynotes (*Haupttöne*): They are, Wagner writes, the adolescents of the tonal family, which yearn to separate from their family and unite with the scion of another family, a tonal maiden.[91] Like Siegfried, they have to recognize themselves as also members of another family, another tonal dynasty. Analogously, Mime's melodic self-enclosure is of one piece with his incapacity for, and utter disregard for, the alienation of the self in sexual love.

It may appear at first, then, that Mime's "endogamy" is nothing other than the Valsung's incest, which has produced Siegfried—the value judgment implied in Wagner's family metaphor would thus be offset, or at least to some extent relativized. It is worth noting, however, that Wagner does not say that single-scale harmonics are incestuous, and only modulation produces desirable exogamy. In his image, he seems to regard family and *Geschlechtsliebe* as fundamentally opposed: It is not that harmony within the scale family is incestuous and bad, it is simply *not love*. This is why I claimed that Wagner may regard Mime's songs as insufficiently exogamous: They are not incestuous, since they are not characterized by any love relation whatsoever, and it is the latter fact rather than the former that marks their moral turpitude.

In the wider context of the *Ring* cycle, this moral turpitude is of a distinctly different character as that with which Mime is associated in *Rheingold*, mostly because he represents or speaks for a different class there than he does in *Siegfried*. *Das Rheingold* presents Mime as the spokesperson for a proletarian underclass, which it positions as the object of both pity and disgust. That Mime is very different from the songster, trickster, and conniver of *Siegfried*—not least of all since he appears to be married and part of a *Geschlecht*.[92] *Siegfried* similarly presents Mime as an object of pity and ridicule, but the reason for that pity and ridicule have changed. The victim who laments the labors his treacherous brother has laid upon his kind has become an instigator—in some way the fairy-tale atmosphere of *Siegfried* is entirely of his making.

The introduction of Mime's bizarre sexuality, of asexuality as deception, coincides precisely with Mime's change in class type—and that type and his sexual *mauvaise foi* are, as we have seen, of one piece. If, for example, Adorno is correct in recognizing in the wanderer's accoutrements the trappings of the frustrated nineteenth-century revolutionary,[93] might we not see in Mime another type, that of the bachelor? Domestic and fussy, obsessively doting on his idyllic *Heim* with Siegfried, Mime clearly resembles the *Spiessbürger* in his Biedermeyer domesticity; but since that hypostatized domesticity is precisely lacking a "minniges Weibchen," he may in fact be closer to the later Victorian type of the bachelor.[94] It might thus be nothing other than this Victorianism that explains Mime's resistance to the sexuality Siegfried's persistent questions introduce into his domestic existence. Just as Wagner's critique joins certain antibourgeois topoi (the vituperation of *Verstand*, atomization and overspecialization) and an attitude to sexuality and the sexes, Wagner here links Biedermeyer or Victorian domesticity to a repression of sexual difference itself.

Once read in the context of Wagner's own speculations on the ground and meaning of sexual difference, the generic hybridity of *Siegfried* takes on distinctly moral undertones. Its fairy-tale self-sufficiency and its first two scenes' comedic trappings, holdovers from earlier developmental stages of the opera and the *Ring Cycle*, are transformed into sexual signifiers that open up an almost Darwinian morality of origins, sexual relationship, and community. Thus the characterizations of Mime and Siegfried's dysfunctional dyad are shot through with a much more black-and-white morality that is at base biological. As Patrice Chéreau has famously noted, it is almost impossible to watch Siegfried's treatment of his foster parent and think Mime at least somewhat justified in plotting his revenge.[95] It is also impossible not to recognize in Siegfried's supposed superiority a good deal of shallowness, obtuseness, and downright idiocy (in particular when compared to the cycle's two other heroes, Siegmund and Wotan).[96] Nevertheless, on my reading, there is a level of signification that transcends or grounds Mime's and Siegfried's particular characters, and this biological-genetic, as well as musical-generic, level marks even the victimized Mime as somehow unnatural and contemptible, while marking Siegfried even at his most brutish as naturally superior. Wagner's biological "supremacism"[97] distinguishes between a domain of the properly human (coterminous with the domain of the sexual) and one of the not-quite-human (coterminous with parasexual reproduction). Wagner's musical drama then strains to give this defective or "lower" phylogeny a voice by which its defect can betray itself.

But Wagner's "cabinet of . . . shape-shifters"[98] raises yet another problem: While the "burrowing worms," the Nibelungs, the giants, the lateral procreators constitute a *Geschlecht* too degenerate, too weak, and too cowardly to take a chance on (sexual) difference, they and other exponents of what Abbate identifies as Wagnerian metempsychosis have another function, one concerned less with philosophy and more with the artwork itself. Metempsychosis, the fact that Wagnerian characters have a tendency to "bundle" multiple personas (for instance, in *Parsifal* Klingsor claims of Kundry that "you were Herodias, and what else? / Gundryggia there, Kundry here."[99]), aims ultimately for a transcendence of drama with individual, discrete characters, a drama of the *principium individuationis.*

Shape-shifting is thus implicated in the project of a Schopenhauer-inflected Gesamtkunstwerk, to ensure the metaphysical enclosure and compactness, rather than the sprawling casts and plots of "outmoded" operatic styles. This raises the possibility that if what Mime is trying to arrange in his bachelor pad in the forest is much the same thing as what Wagner is reaching for on the opera stage. And if that were true, the question becomes whether the mythic masquerade ultimately hides nothing but another fairy-tale enclosure, self-sufficient, solipsistic, where the composer can be *Vater und Mutter zugleich.* Is the flop-sweat drenched actor and deceiver Mime not perhaps an abjured mirror image of the composer whom Friedrich Nietzsche called the "most enraptured mimomaniac"[100]?

It is this conjunction of problems that confronted the generation of composers immediately after Wagner: Was the fairy tale justifiable? What was its relationship to the Gesamtkunstwerk? This was a question Wagner's son Siegfried ran up against his operas, it was one that informed Zemlinsky's own highly fractured turns to the fairy-tale genre. But the first to engage with these questions explicitly in the terms of the concepts of myth and fairy tale suggested by the *Ring* were the composers of the fin-de-siècle "fairy-tale operas" (*Märchenopern*) whose reflections on sex and form continued many of the concerns raised in the first act of *Siegfried.*

MIME'S LEGACY AND FAIRY TALE OPERA

That Mime's inferiority is emphatically linked to the defectiveness of the fairy-tale genre casts an interesting shadow over those post-Wagnerians, who "built a small hut in the shadow of the Wagnerian art work, a modest 'happiness in the arbor,' which shuns the peaks and . . . affords the advantage of security."[101] The "happiness in the arbor," inspired in part by Mime's own "small hut," that the composers of fairy-tale operas (in particular, the followers of Engelbert Humperdinck) carved out for themselves, is, according to the master's own standards, intrinsically defective. The Romantics still associated the fairy tale with the love relationship, Novalis the poet, for example, noting in his *Allgemeine Brouillon* that "all novels in which true love appears, are *fairy tales—magic events.*"[102] But after Mime's hut, this equation appears to have been to some extent reversed; Mime's forest uncovers an unspoken enmity between the fairy tale and sexual relations. And it was to Mime's dyadic enclosure much more than to the sprawling dynastic canvas of what Novalis understood as his "fairy tales" that Humperdink and his followers hearkened back.

In many cases they explicitly followed Wagner's equation of the fairy tale with claustrophobia and limitation, even as they themselves wrote emphatically diminutive operas themselves. One such composer was Richard Wagner's own son Siegfried. When staging the *Ring Cycle* during his tenure as artistic director in Bayreuth (1908–1930), Siegfried always took particular interest in the first scene of *Siegfried*. As Kurt Söhnlein recalls in his memoirs, Siegfried progressively changed the design to make Mime's cave "smaller and more oppressive." In 1911, when he had first decided to jettison the older, more spacious sets, Siegfried included "a neutral frame in grey-black canvas," but in 1928 he suggested a "plastic rock-frame." A final design draft from 1930 made these "heavy hanging rocks" even more prominent. Söhnlein finished the design only after Siegfried's death, and in July of 1931 Mime moved into his new cave in Bayreuth.[103]

Siegfried thus accepted the idea that Mime's fairy tale was intended to be "oppressive," though that acceptance did not dissuade him from turning to the fairy tale form himself time and again. His teacher, the composer Engelbert Humperdinck (1854–1921), proceeded similarly: accept that the fairy tale was a defective, limited genre, but forego attempts to transcend it in favor of an outside corrective. Humperdinck's *Königskinder* (libretto by Ernst Rosmer, a pseudonym for Elsa Bernstein-Porges), which premiered in a melodramatic version in 1897 and as an opera in 1910, opens on a situation very much reminiscent of *Siegfried*'s first act. A young goose girl lives in a forest with a woman she is told is her grandmother, but who is in fact an evil witch, who keeps the girl entirely isolated. Just like Mime, the witch wants the goose-girl to be her child, but is finding this extremely difficult: "All my toil and exertion / can't make you into a witch-child."[104] While she tries to raise her fake granddaughter to be a witch, but finds the girl unreceptive to her teachings, the first stirrings of the girl's awareness of the outside world ultimately condemn her plans to failure.

Musically, the witch's songs constitute one of the main remainders of the opera's early melodramatic version. When those were widely judged to be unsuccessful, Humperdinck reconceived the melodrama as opera—originally, the witch's attempts to keep the goose girl isolated were musical; the disruptions of that isolation were dramatic. Here too, then, old forms, forms that fall short of "true" opera, live in fairy-tale settings. First among the outside intrusions is the arrival of the king's son, the first man the goose girl has ever laid eyes upon. The two young people promptly fall in love. Secondly, a group of citizens from the nearby town of Hellabrunn arrives to consult with the witch, who they believe to be a benevolent wise woman. They are accompanied by a fiddler, who notices the goose-girl. He realizes right away that the witch cannot possibly be the child's grandmother, telling her, "You are free and she keeps you locked up."[105] The witch then claims that the goose girl is the child of a convicted murderer and the hangman's daughter—"the sinner's dress [*Sünderhemd*] is your father's garb, the harlot's wreath [*Dirnenkranz*] is your inheritance from your mother."[106] The fiddler consoles the girl: "Two royal human beings full of power and force, gave you your breath and your earthly form." Through a Siegfried-like invocation of "Mother! Father!," the girl finally manages to escape the witch's spell.

The realization of her provenance does not do the girl much good in the world outside. Neither she nor the prince are ever recognized as *Königskinder* outside of the forest, and they find each other only in a sort of *Liebestod*, where, destitute and near starvation they fall unconscious and are slowly buried by snow. But what enables the two to find and recognize each other? Not the external force that has propelled the goose girl from the witch's forest, not the dynastic intimations, nor even the erotic force of the prince's presence. In the first act, the witch tells the goose girl to bake a cursed loaf of bread intended to kill those who eat it; in defiance the goose girl instead blesses the bread, saying that those who eat it will see what they want most. It is this loaf of bread, that is to say, a resource that comes from the same place as the witch's deceptions, that brings the two youngsters together.

Restricted, inauthentic, and unloving the witch's hearth may be—but it alone can furnish the resources that overcome that limitation. No mythos swoops in here and helps offset the limitations of the fairy tale. Humperdinck's opera rehearses the Wagnerian characterization of the fairy-tale form as severely compromised, but his plot suggests that the resources for overcoming its limits come from the fairy tale itself, not from some external corrective. As the next chapter will show, at least in this respect Humperdinck's *Königskinder* is symptomatic for the erotics of post-Wagnerian opera more generally: The erotic no longer represents and enforces the cosmic tug toward totality, and thus toward the Gesamtkunstwerk. Rather, eroticism resides in the unfinished, ununified, and at times ugly particulars that resist, or are incapable of, their sublation in the total work of art. As the next chapter will show, ugliness in particular becomes a figure for those elements of opera which cannot be sublated in this way—in the ugly characters who abound in Wagnerian opera, and who composers and librettists treat with much more sympathy and care than Wagner did, Mime finally got his revenge on Siegfried.

CHAPTER 2

Mime's Revenge: The Total Work
of Art and the Ugly Detail

In what was generally a laudatory review of *Die Gezeichneten*, published in a special issue of *Anbruch* dedicated to Franz Schreker and his music in 1922, the music critic Joachim Beck opens with a puzzling remark: "In looking at a phenomenon like Franz Schreker, it seems to me necessary to keep in mind that there are two kinds of creative genius: the genius which starts something, and that which is in decline. However, the exhaustion of this second type can have something intoxicating to it as well."[1] The notion that Schreker is a "genius in/of decline [*deszendentes Genie*]" may strike us as a strange compliment to begin with, but it is made even stranger by the fate that would befall *Die Gezeichneten* sixteen years later.[2]

The Nazi government put on the *Reichsmusiktage* in Düsseldorf on May 22, 1938, Richard Wagner's one hundred twenty-fifth birthday. The event was organized at the behest of Joseph Goebbels, who sought, as his speech on the occasion put it, to elaborate "the principles of German musical creativity." Two days after the festival kicked off (with Richard Strauss conducting his *Festliches Präludium* in a new arrangement for orchestra), the musicologist and director of the Weimar *Nationaltheater*, Hans Severus Ziegler, presented an exhibition entitled *Entartete Musik*, in deliberate reference to the exhibition *Entartete Kunst*, which had toured Germany the year prior to great success. The exhibition was intended to hold up for ridicule and rejection much of the music of the early twentieth century, music that was either atonal, influenced by non-European traditions, or written or promoted by Jews. "We descendants of Richard Wagner should possess the acuity to unmask the charlatans of the most recent past, who lorded over our opera and concert life for decades,"[3]

Ziegler wrote in an essay accompanying the show. Schreker, who had passed away four years prior, was one of the most prominent of those supposed "charlatans." The exhibition catalogue described him as "the Magnus Hirschfeld of the opera world. There was no sexual-pathological aberration that he didn't set to music."[4]

Both the *Reichsmusiktage* in general and Ziegler's exhibition fell short of the organizers' expectations, perhaps not surprisingly. After all, *Entartete Kunst* had physically presented modernist visual art of the kind the Nazis deemed "degenerate" and had brought the German public directly face-to-face with the art the organizers wanted them to reject. The *Reichsmusiktage* by contrast did not present any actual "degenerate" music, and indeed could not readily do so. Commandeering a few paintings by Max Pechstein and Otto Dix, slapping them into a lazy display, and counting on the average Fritz's kneejerk aversion to all things abstract or formalist was one thing. Getting orchestras to study, rehearse, and perform the music by Schreker, Schoenberg, Weill, Hindemith, or Krenek, and risking people applauding at the end of the performance was quite another. Ziegler's exhibition almost by necessity relied on paraphernalia—posters, photos of composers, and the like. Ziegler's essay on *Entartete Kunst*, printed as a kind of exhibition guide, features seventeen images: The vast majority are unflattering photographs or cruel caricatures of (preferably Jewish) composers, conductors, and critics, a few others show stage design or actual performances. There is only one picture of a score, from Weill's autograph of the *Dreigroschenoper*—with a note that we are meant to judge his handwriting, rather than the music.[5] In his May 28 speech at the *Reichsmusiktage*, Goebbels conjured up "a past we have at last overcome," of which "we can barely imagine any more that it was once reality." And of course, it was not going to be the job of the assembled musicians and Nazi-aligned composers and musicologists to bring back into reality this spectral past. The composers (to say nothing of the performers and conductors) the exhibition insulted were silenced more thoroughly than Pechstein and Dix.

But there was another problem that made *Entartete Musik* a perplexing concept and undertaking. Goebbels's remarks present a racialized aesthetic, unwittingly highlighting the fact that there were no purely aesthetic properties in "degenerate" music the Nazis objected to, analogous to, say, their allergy to all things abstract or subjectivist in the visual arts. In his speech Goebbels charged "Jewish elements" with "trivializing" the "German folksong"; he charges "Jewish cliques of publishers and conductors" with "falsifying the German masters," rails against "kitsch and jazz," and praises a "new" German music that has supposedly replaced "the constructions of a barren, atonal expressionism" with true "artistic intuition." As the phrase "barren, atonal expressionism" shows, it is unclear throughout Goebbels's speech what kind of music he has in mind here (only the kind of person who made or championed it): "expressionism" was even then a label only rarely applied to music, and the music it might plausibly be attached to was anything but "atonal," to say nothing of "barren." Conversely, the atonal musicians attacked in the *Entartete Musik* exhibition were often concerned with the exact opposite of subjective expression.

Ziegler's own screeds, as close as *Entartete Musik* comes to theoretical underpinnings, are similarly opaque. Kurt Weill, Arnold Schoenberg, Franz Schreker, the operetta composer Oskar Strauss, Darius Milhaud, Otto Klemperer, and jazz musicians are all and sundry attacked as "cultural Bolsheviks." What features of their music mark them as such, Ziegler won't say. He mentions "foreign" tonalities and rhythms, but his essay cites not one musical example. Again and again, he appeals to "our German feeling," "our healthy understanding of art."[6] This contrasts with the case of the Degenerate Art exhibition, which clearly set itself the task of distinguishing a "good" (i.e., Aryan) modernism and a "bad" modernism.

Another problem confronted by Ziegler and Goebbels in putting on their show is perhaps less immediately obvious, but becomes clear in view of Joachim Beck's review of Schreker, and the many like it in the teens and twenties. Beck was not a Nazi, and his review was overall extremely positive. And yet his invocations of "decline" and "exhaustion" uncomfortably anticipate the terms of Joseph Goebbels's exorcisms of "degenerate music": the attributes that Beck admiringly attaches to Schreker's work are generally those that would lead the Nazis to suppress the opera as "degenerate" music.

By dint of a peculiarity of music history, music castigated as "degenerate" found itself in a very different position than, say, the paintings expurgated from museum collections, or the books burned at Berlin's Opernplatz after 1933. There was a long tradition of querying opera for possible "degeneracy" by the time the Nazis got around to it, so long in fact, that the medium itself had begun to grapple quite self-consciously with the label. What counted as "degeneracy," and what ought to be done about it, was no clearer than in the tirades of Goebbels and Ziegler, but the term hovered as a threat over the operas produced in the forty years after Wagner's death. They were, as the critic Leopold Schmidt said about *Die Gezeichneten*, not just "works," but "questions" requiring positioning.[7] This stems at least partially from the fact that much of the music the Nazis labeled as "degenerate" was modernist in only a highly ambivalent sense, and often enough hewed quite self-consciously to neo-Romantic, nineteenth-century idioms—this was still very much the music of decadence.

By comparison, the kind of visual art that understood itself as somehow decadent or degenerate was several decades old by the time the Nazis staged their
"degenerate art" exhibition in Munich in 1937.

This peculiarity has also affected the reception history of the operas silenced by Goebbels, Ziegler, and their ilk. Not every work the Ziegler branded
as "degenerate" had self-consciously grappled with the label. But those that
refused to do so, the ones we label today as "avant-garde"—the music of Berg,
Schoenberg, and Hindemith, for instance—entered or reentered the musical
canon with much greater ease after the war (in both Germany and the US),
while works like *Die Gezeichneten*, works understood as "genius in/of decline,"
had a much harder time doing so, and in some cases still remain in the wilder-
ness into which Ziegler and his cohorts cast them. *Die Gezeichneten*, for one,
had its American premiere in 2010. While it may do—in the case of the visual
arts—to simply reject the suggestion of "degeneracy" out of hand, this is not
possible when it comes to opera, whose works had obsessed over their relationship to decline, degeneracy, and decadence for nearly forty years by the
time the Nazi arbiters of musical "health" actually set about to decide which
works were to be deemed degenerate, and which weren't.

But if the terms *degeneracy* and *degeneration* were everywhere in discourses
about opera after Wagner, there wasn't a clear narrative one could attach to
them. Just who was degenerate, and what *genus* they were degenerating from,
was subject to changes and slippages depending on the cultural politics of the
day and the political orientation of the writer employing the concept. When
the term *Entartung* had first attained currency in the wake of Max Nordau's
book of the same title, it had attached itself above all to the work of Richard
Wagner—that is, someone the Nazis were not very likely to attach it to. The
fact that Ziegler and Goebbels opened their *Reichsmusiktage* on the *Meister*'s
birthday points to the fact that the "degeneration" they had in mind required
a return to Wagner. In the decades since the composer's death, the general
discourse around opera had frequently suggested (even if not in the biologistic
terms of Nordau, Ziegler, and Goebbels) that opera had undergone something of a degeneration *since* Wagner, rather than *with* Wagner. As Richard
Batka put it in 1899: "What if Wagner's work of art . . . was the peak of this
development, and perfect in itself, such that every attempt at making him more
perfect would be useless, and that every attempt to change it would necessarily
lead to a degradation [*Verschlechterung*] of this wondrous artistic organism?"[8]
The anxiety-provoking possibility that they constituted a "degradation" was
inscribed into post-Wagnerian music dramas in ways entirely different from
other musical genres or other arts.

And here Mime makes a reappearance of sorts in the story of German opera after Wagner. The first act of *Siegfried* musically staged two modes of being in the world: Siegfried who navigates his world by instinct, and Mime who has to use cunning to simulate what comes naturally to his young charge. The feelings that spring spontaneously from Siegfried's heart, Mime is forced to learn and endlessly rehearse; Siegfried's cocksure decisions contrast with the flop sweat-drenched anxiety with which Mime ties himself into knots trying to explain the seemingly most natural questions. And Siegfried notices. He recognizes that this anxious, prevaricating imp is not, cannot be related to him, cannot even be a member of the same species. Mime's spectacular insufficiency, which he himself is all too conscious of, is the condition of the possibility of Siegfried and the opera that bears his name.

The composers who self-consciously followed Wagner, the "geniuses in/of decline" of Beck's review, told Mime's side of the story, and turned the formal implications of his abjection on their head. Perhaps they recognized themselves, their own anxieties, their own worries about insufficiency and degeneration, in the character, or in characters like him. They seem to have grasped the fact that Mime, and the terrible way in which Siegfried the character and *Siegfried* the opera treat him, had ramifications for the very structure of the Gesamtkunstwerk. Post-Wagnerian opera abounds in outsider figures, and they are treated with extreme tenderness and understanding. In many cases, these outsider figures can be seen as allegories of the operatic form itself—and their ugliness or perceived degeneracy should be understood as an interrogation of the questionable heredity and viability of operatic form. If *Tristan* bequeathed on opera a scenario in which a symmetry of attraction could become a figure for the harmonization of opera's constituent media, Mime's abjection stands for the opposite scenario. The ugly outsider elicits asymmetrical desire (these outsiders are almost always in love with women who do not return their affections); and he structures the work of art through the repulsion he inspires in others.

In what follows, I will first chart the reception of one such ugly outsider figure, and then outline the question of ugliness in early twentieth-century opera more generally. I will draw both on works that were eventually suppressed as "degenerate," and on works that were never in any danger of such suppression. I believe that this way of proceeding is justified by the highly haphazard way in which the Nazi allergy to modernism manifested itself—as Strauss himself is reputed to have asked Ziegler, if *Erwartung* was out, then why not *Electra*?[9]

We begin, however, with a work that, while not itself suppressed by the Nazis, spawned a number of adaptations in early twentieth-century German music that all were suppressed. Oscar Wilde's "The Birthday of the Infanta," which first appeared in a collection of fairy tales titled *A House of Pomegranates* in 1892, describes the festivities attending the twelfth birthday of the Infanta of Spain. Unconcerned with the cruelty, grief, and destitution impinging on the world of the *Escorial* from all sides (the exploitation of the colonies, the Spanish Inquisition, and the wars of religion all creep in between the masques), the princess enjoys a lovingly described cavalcade of spectaculars, from a mock bullfight to a puppet show. Eventually, a surprise gift is brought in: a deformed dwarf, found in the woods by some courtiers the day before. The children are beside themselves at the strange creature, its dance, its attire, but the good-natured dwarf realizes none of their malice. Instead, he falls in love with the infanta almost as soon as he lays eyes on her, and she, in a bout of whimsy, gives him a white rose as a token of her mock affection. Elated, the unsuspecting creature wanders the halls of the palace, only to encounter a giant mirror—its first. Only now the dwarf realizes his deformity, the extent of his humiliation by the courtiers, and dies of a broken heart.

THE BIRTHDAYS OF THE INFANTA OF WILDE, SCHREKER, AND ZEMLINSKY

"The Birthday of the Infanta" proved to be one of Wilde's more popular works, especially among composers. Franz Schreker, Alexander von Zemlinsky, and Bernhard Sekles (Adorno's composition teacher in Frankfurt) all adapted it—Schreker and Sekles into ballets (in 1908 and 1913 respectively), and Zemlinsky into the opera *Der Zwerg* (1922). There is something in this outsider story and its satire of decadent sophistication that seems to invite reading in terms of the creator's biography, a trend inaugurated by none other than Edith Ellis (i.e., Mrs. Havelock Ellis), who opined in 1918 that "Wilde, till the blow fell which led to his arrest, had been frolicking, as it were, in a forest of fancies like the dwarf with the gypsies."[10] When Georg Klaren adapted "Infanta" into the libretto of *Der Zwerg*, he similarly modified the character to rather obviously echo the details of Zemlinsky's own biography.[11] Zemlinksy himself was a fairly unattractive man, well-known for relationships with women far more beautiful, and self-debasement seems to have been an important part of these relationships.

Given its emphasis on the brutal derision and abjection of the different-looking outsider, the story also invites a reading in terms of Jewish identity. Its oriental inflections, as the foreign dwarf is brought before the court, makes for an easy depiction of culture clash, as the music critic Walter Niemann observed in 1913 apropos Bernhard Sekles's version of the *Infantin*.[12] While the (auto)biographical charge of this material is undeniable, it does not exhaust the sources of the fascination with Wilde's story. As I will argue, the dwarf (and in particular his ugliness) allegorizes a particular kind of operatic form, or at least a set of problems of operatic form. The dwarf's ugliness stands in for a kind of "degeneration"—but a kind that has nothing to do with the compos-ers who gravitated toward "Infanta," and instead everything to do with their work's relationship to the history of opera. The dwarf's ugliness is the part that sticks out of the harmonious whole, but the fact that everyone else gath-ers around him actually helps constitute that harmonious whole. The dwarf is both a victim of illusion and strangely colludes with illusion—an ambivalence that turns out to characterize the attitude toward operatic coherence among the composers who turned to Wilde's dwarf and his ugly brethren in the wake of Wagner.

Schreker's, Zemlinsky's, and Sekles's adaptations hew to Wilde's story with varying degrees of closeness, but generally they tend to emphasize the dwarf. While in Wilde's story he is just "the funniest part of the whole morn-ing's entertainment,"[13] he becomes the main attraction in its German musical adaptations. Zemlinsky's opera originated with his desire to write an op-era that would tell "the tragedy of the ugly man"—he asked Schreker for a libretto, but Schreker decided to explore the theme of the ugly man on his own. The result was *Die Gezeichneten*. Both operas and ballets are dwarf-focused, and focused moreover on the dwarf's ugliness, rather than, say, his in-nocence. Even the ballets, which naturally dwell on the birthday party's many other entertainments—the "procession of noble boys, fantastically dressed as *toreadors*," the "marvelous bull-fight," the "Italian puppets"—retain the focus on the dwarf and tend to organize the spectacle around him (an exception is Schreker's reworking of the *Infantin* in the 1923 concert suite "Spanisches Fest," which removes the climactic mirror scene and thus pretty much aban-dons Wilde's plot).

These adaptations share their focus on a spectacularly ugly character with a whole slew of operas, but easily their most famous ancestor is *Rigoletto*. Verdi's opera premiered in 1851, but was popular in Germany throughout the post-Wagnerian era, even though Verdi's position in Germany was an ambiguous and at times precarious one.[14] The ways in which Rigoletto's post-Wagnerian heirs differ from their forebear point to what is specific to operatic ugliness af-ter Wagner. While not a dwarf, the misshapen court jester Rigoletto is another shunned artist figure in the mold of *Der Zwerg*. Unlike Oscar Wilde's dwarf he is all too aware of his condition. But though he knows about his ugliness, he is offered some surcease from this knowledge, because the opera carves out a space that allows him respite from the spectacle his ugliness creates around him, even if that space is brutally invaded in the course of the opera. *Rigoletto* opens on a series of pageant-like court scenes, but before long the jester retires to his own home, where his vivacious daughter Gilda greets him.

Within the confines of his home, Rigoletto's ugliness is not occasion for ridicule, but instead for compassion. In his professional, that is to say, his artistic life Rigoletto is "made evil and corrupt," "but here," he says, in the confines of his own home, "I become another person." And he is right: at home he does not just *appear* different to his daughter; rather her gaze seems to effect a real transformation. Among the nattering courtiers, Rigoletto gives as good as he gets, a fact he reflects on right before entering his house in the aria *Pari siamo*; but under Gilda's adoring eyes he becomes a doting, even sentimental father. Similarly, he tells us of Gilda's mother: "She felt, that angel, pity for my sorrows. I was alone, deformed, poor, and she loved me out of compassion." The world of *Rigoletto* is profoundly compartmentalized. In one part of it, the title character's ugliness keeps him in a universally abject position, hated and ridiculed by all, capable only of hatred and ridicule in turn; in another, he arouses and exudes equally unwavering sympathy instead.

Rigoletto's ugliness plays out in two arenas, and plays out differently in each. In fact, this "tragedy of the ugly man" unfolds only when the two worlds he inhabits collapse into one, when the Duke invades his domestic preserve. The German musical versions of the *Birthday of the Infanta* have that tragedy unfold in one unitary world instead: the ugly character is afforded no space of retreat; his abjection is total. Any surcease from the horror of his condition is brought on by deception rather than sympathy. Moreover, in each of Verdi's two arenas, Rigoletto's deformity structures a different kind of musical drama—the exaggerated choral dynamism of the Ducal court on the one side, and the muted domestic scene (*"Figlia!" "Mio padre!"*) on the other.

Both of these differentiations disappear in the musical iterations of Wilde's *Infanta*, in which the dwarf alone is ignorant of his own ugliness, and in which the dwarf is always surrounded by the moveable feast of the royal court. In fact, the only moment he is left alone he promptly seeks out a mirror and discovers his deformity. In so doing, they dichotomize more heavily the unfortunate dwarf on the one hand and the decadent spectacle that eventually chews him up on the other. In Wilde's story, there are some members of the court unamused by the dwarf, and even sympathetic to him; there is another character entirely opposed to the gay proceedings, namely the Infanta's father, the King himself. In Schreker and Zemlinsky, matters are more starkly divided. Though Zemlinsky's plot adds a benevolent lady-in-waiting, who "wants to make those happy who are joyless and ugly," and eventually gets the dwarf to recognize his delusion, her motherly affections too serve to keep the dwarf at arm's length. She pities him rather than ridiculing him—but she is far from being on his side.

Musically, too, there is no intervening mediator in the vein of Rigoletto's domestic idyll between the self-deceived individual and the world that mocks him. Of course, it is difficult to compare a ballet pantomime and an opera. But in one central respect, both Zemlinsky's and Schreker's versions of *Infanta* live off the juxtaposition of diminution (dwarf) and overweening spectacle (court). Both works open with a grand fanfare, which is put almost directly into contrast with smaller instrumental groups: flutes, oboes and solo violin at different points in Schreker's opening fanfare, which Schreker's directions tell us are to be played "soft and indistinct [*zart und verschwommen*]." As such, these isolated instruments also anticipate the dwarf's own dances, in particular his initial hesitation, where the dancer skips to the sound of a "hesitant [*zurückhaltend*]" theme carried by a single bassoon. As the dwarf becomes increasingly comfortable and unselfconscious in his movements, the solo instruments in p, pp, and mp are quickly joined by a crescendo of other instruments until a tutti statement of the dance's main theme. From the very get-go, then, the diminutiveness of the dwarf is contrasted with, and literally dwarfed by, the outsize character of the spectacle around him. As he becomes deluded about his relationship to this spectacle, the music to which he moves becomes itself more spectacular. And as he learns the true nature of his relationship to the spectacle, the initial fanfare becomes increasingly disfigured, as the spectacle that has thus far aided his delusion now rends it asunder. Part and whole are in stark opposition in Schreker's ballet: the asymmetry of the spectacle, with all its erotic and cultural baggage becomes the central, organizing opposition of the piece.

This spectacle is much reduced in Zemlinsky's version of the same story. Klaren's libretto reduced Wilde's story to an allegory of man's relation to woman in general, dropping much of the pomp and pageantry Schreker's "dance pantomime" still traffics in. But *Der Zwerg*, despite its brevity, is not exactly compact: dances, parades, and play acting, while reduced vis-à-vis the cavalcade that saunters through Wilde's story, still interrupt the opera's main action at every turn. However, as Sherry Lee has recently shown, the opera goes out of its way to ally this pageantry with the princess and to oppose it to the dwarf. *Der Zwerg* is not the story of two individuals whose dramatic arc then furnishes the occasion for much pomp and circumstance; the dwarf may think it is, but the music puts the lie to this delusion. In terms of meter, "the music of the Infanta and her companions skips and lilts in triple time," while the dwarf with his duple meter is "figuratively and literally out of step."[15] We are witnessing instead a magnificent spectacle of which the Infanta is simply one aspect, with the dwarf entirely alone in being "out of step." Even though Zemlinsky, when compared to Schreker, reduces the extrinsic pageantry, he maintains and even heightens the opposition between individual and spectacle.

The starkness of this opposition is owed to an element of Wilde's narrative that disappears in both Schreker's and Zemlinsky's version of the story: Wilde's fairy tale has not one but two characters spectacularly out of joint with the spectacle around them—one is the dwarf, the other is the king of Spain himself, still grief-stricken over the death of his wife twelve years earlier. Not that one could really fault either Schreker or Klaren for leaving the episode out: The king's grief is something of an odd addition to Wilde's story—the old man's desolation as he watches his daughter and her attendants from a balcony, irrupts into the flow of the fairy tale without seeming to impact either its plot or its psychology. Removing the king enhances the schematism and stark dichotomization of the opera's setup; it uncouples the goings-on from individual psychology and instead places it in the metaphysical realm—as Sherry Lee demonstrated in her ingenious reading of *Der Zwerg*—along the lines of Hegel's concept of recognition.

While the king hovers spectrally over Wilde's story without ever interceding into its plot, he does provide a complement and counterweight to the dwarf. The king, much like the dwarf at the end of the story, becomes a broken-hearted and uncomprehending observer of the courtly ritual, a joyless participant in his own narcissistic isolation. And, again like the dwarf, he is entirely misunderstood by the revelers themselves—the shallow girl only thinks him unconcerned with her enjoyment and preoccupied with "stupid State-affairs,"[16] and seems to know nothing of his grief. However, the effect of the irruption is of course that the dwarf is not alone in bucking the spectacle around him.

In Zemlinsky's opera, the courtiers spend the first part of the opera admiring each other's beauty, but mostly that of the Infanta—only with the dwarf does ugliness enter into the picture, only then does anything seem amiss in the beautiful ambiance. Moreover, while in Wilde's story, the dwarf simply has not met enough people to be told the truth about his condition, in Zemlinsky's, the whole world seems to be in on the joke—a Sultan sends the dwarf to the Escorial as a joke, he is carried in by slaves like a king, and the Chamberlain announces him as "a knight, as beautiful as Narcissus." Contained in this joke is the strange morality of this version of the Narcissus story: Narcissism is usually the fault of the narcissist, who is hubristically obsessed with himself and neglectful of the outside; the dwarf's narcissism on the other hand reflects badly on his surroundings rather than on the narcissist himself. There is something deeply touching, human, and vulnerable about his self-deception, and something conversely monstrous in the people who maintain the illusion for him.

UGLINESS AND OPERATIC TOTALITY

Beyond any biographical or existential reading of this configuration, in which the individual's narcissism is goaded on by something of a world-spanning conspiracy, the way in which these German adaptations overemphasize the distinction between dwarf and surrounding spectacle seems to have formal implications as well. The dwarf and his ugliness—an ugliness that requires the consent of all and that unites all in sadistic delight—allegorize a set of problems of operatic form. The way the dwarf becomes the only detail amiss in the lavish spectacle, and the way in which that ugly detail in turn structures the spectacle around him, suggests that deformity, degeneration, and disharmony are not merely problems of content in these works, but rather represent problems of form. Just as Wagner turned to fulfilled sexual relationships as ciphers and enactments of the Gesamtkunstwerk, so do the asymmetrical, skewed and sadistic erotics that dominate the operas of Wagner's successors articulate a somewhat less totalized form of operatic spectacle.

Ugly characters abound in German operas of the turn of the century. However, while they are many, they are also solitary, usually surrounded by an eager audience of normal, or even explicitly beautiful, characters. Wherever ugliness appears in these operas, it appears in tandem with an audience that ridicules or exploits, but in any case feels compelled to interact with the central character's deformity. Normally ugliness comes to matter, in particular, in relation to spectacle: it gathers an audience around the ugly character, united in their derision or incomprehension. From naturalism and decadence to expressionism, German literature of the time not only trafficked in ugly characters, but it also frequently depicted communities enscorceled and united by their fascination with single ugly characters. In Lion Feuchtwanger's novel *Die Häßliche Herzogin* (1923), the political skill and ambitious achievements of Margarete, the "ugly duchess" of Tyrolia and heroine of Feuchtwanger's historic novel, remain invisible to her subjects who instead lavish their attention on her beautiful rival, the fair Agnes von Flavon.[17] Thomas Mann's early stories, such as "Tobias Mindernickel" (1898), "Der kleine Herr Friedemann," and "Luischen" (1900) abound in outsider characters whose ugliness gathers around them a veritable community of gawkers.

In *Der Zwerg* and other operas of its era, ugliness unifies that audience into a community of spectators, but it usually doesn't turn them into a community of listeners. That is because music doesn't make, or help make, the distinctions these operas and their staging of ugliness depend on. Music's beauty unifies the audience, and it doesn't make distinctions either onstage or among the audience; the visual, however, is inherently asymmetrical. The ugly characters of the period sing just as beautifully as everyone else, but no one seems able to pay any attention to their discourse, as one is distracted by their visual repellence. Even where characters are content with the ugly individual's voice, the operas of the fin-de-siècle will eventually force them to confront his (and it is usually his) visual ugliness. In Eugen d'Albert's *Die toten Augen* (a work Zemlinsky himself conducted at the Neues Deutsche Theater while writing his *Zwerg*), the ugly Arcesius is married to the blind Myrtocle who believes him to be beautiful, due to the wonders of his voice and the softness of his touch. When she miraculously regains her sight, she cannot tolerate the truth and stares into the setting sun, once again consigning herself "to the realm of dreams."

These lonely grotesques are particularly prevalent in those operas that still operate in a late Romantic, decadent, or post-Wagnerian idiom. In d'Albert's *Stier von Olivera* (1918), the central union is instead doomed to lopsidedness by the fact that one partner's deformity is dreadfully, spectacularly visible, a fact which his vengeful wife brutally exploits. In *Die Gezeichneten*, too, it is only Carlotta's fascination with the hunchbacked Alviano that sparks his love, which she then spurns even in death. To be sure, ugliness also constitutes a preoccupation of works that break with the post-Wagnerian idiom—for instance, the operas of the Second Viennese school; and ugliness was important in operas composed outside of Germany. But neither of these groups relies so centrally on the ugliness of one lone character to organize every other player onstage.

This is because the ugly dwarf and the birthday party he crashes hearken back to two central problems encountered by operatic composition after Wagner: there is for one the question of how his diminutiveness relates to the scope and size of Wagnerian "music-drama," and there is for another the question of how opera's different media ought to be integrated. In this respect, it is significant that *Der Zwerg* is a short piece, partakes of a miniaturized genre that Wagner's heirs were quite ambivalent about (the fairy-tale opera) and combines leitmotivic techniques with distinct numbers, such as the *Reigen* that opens the stage action proper. Schreker in turn embarked on his *Infanta* while wrestling with writing what was to become *Der ferne Klang*, his first opera to be performed. His first effort, *Die Flammen*, had been widely judged a failure precisely because it never successfully integrated poem, drama, and music—something that Schreker's operas from *Der ferne Klang* onward would pursue with almost obsessive (and Adorno would say, "phantasmagoric") intensity. When Schreker set out to formulate "my musical-dramatic idea" over a decade later, he identified it as "musical drama in total purity [*Reinkultur*]" (i.e., in a unity that "broaches the vexing discrepancy that constitutes the problematic of operatic form").[18]

This unity rather than "vexing discrepancy" has ramifications for the relationship to the audience—in 1933 Paul Bekker, Schreker's friend and tireless promoter, identifies the "magic theater [*Zaubertheater*]"[19] as Wagner's central legacy. By this he means that Wagner's stage action is not pure spectacle to be consumed by an audience, but instead postulates that this spectacle be *believed* by the audience. Most of the composers of his day, Bekker asserts, are still very much beholden to this postulate—only the precious few are beginning to develop the necessary "will to abandon the magical theater." Schreker, Bekker suggests in article after article, was the first after Wagner to take seriously the problem that opera's reality, as the more or less successful collaboration of different arts, in an overdetermined, underfunded, and often incongruous whole. And unlike other post-Wagnerians he did not seek to simply repress the awkwardness of that whole by either intellectualizing opera, or by turning it into an ersatz religion.

> The artistic element of this art form derives from the ability to fuse the seemingly inferior [*Minderwertige*] of means and ends in the suggestive power of the instant, . . . to create a transitory moment in which the stage life stands as the only truly existing, built of cardboard, painted in colors one shouldn't look at in the bright light of day, carried by sounds set down in the score really only as a stopgap measure, mimed and sung by people whose real existence is only a vegetating between two scenes. Everything is false, inauthentic, means to the end of deception—in the unity [*Einheitlichkeit*] of the real inauthenticity of all the factors lies the true, compelling truthfulness of the Whole.[20]

But Bekker is not alone in recognizing opera's authentic inauthenticity. Zemlinsky's dwarf, Schreker's Alviano, d'Albert's Arcesius, and even Schreker's mute but dancing dwarf all do two things: they reenact the quasi-moral demand opera places on its audience (not to notice the cardboard, the overweight singers, the lack of integration of orchestra and singers), and they trace out post-Wagnerian composers' discomfort with that demand. These two features of the music drama—the way it combines different media, and the way it requires the audience to buy into their combination in an aesthetic leap of faith—come to inform the way Wagner's heirs deploy ugliness. Ugliness, in short, stages the discontent with, the friction within, the total work of art.

As I showed in chapter 1, the notion that whatever falls short of the totalized music drama may have ugly, and perhaps even dwarvish features, goes back to Wagner's *Siegfried*. There the ugly dwarf Mime tries to blind young Siegfried to the dynastic tetralogy that looms in the background and tries to convince him, one could say, that he is actually starring in a fairy-tale opera. His arsenal in this ultimately foolhardy effort consists of a series of plaintive songs and ditties stridently out of synch with the work in which they appear, and often enough stand-ins for older operatic practices Wagner himself loathed.[21] Mime's only audience is the strapping lad Siegfried, who can see through Mime's lies, precisely because Mime is so ugly: There is no way, he reasons, that such a beautiful creature as him could be related to "a toad" like Mime.

Among those composers who, as Schreker put it, engaged in "at times rather forced attempts to free themselves of Wagner,"[22] Mime finally got his revenge—or, at the very least, has his story told, on his aesthetic terms. As in the different incarnations of the *Birthday of the Infanta*, these operas are dominated by an asymmetry of desire, compounded by an equally uncompromising asymmetry of spectatorship, which, as we shall see, undermines the phantasms of the perfect union onstage and that between stage and audience. After all, in Klaren's version of Wilde's story, the dwarf matches the discordant ugliness of his exterior with an almost implausible level of delusion. Wilde's dwarf has never seen himself because he is a child of nature; Klaren's has lived in civilization all his life, has steadfastly avoided looking at mirrors and, when encountering his own visage, he believes it is an evil twin haunting him. Just like Arcesius' marriage to Myrtocle in *Die toten Augen* depends on the prestabilized harmony of ugliness and blindness, so the ugly dwarf's—imagined, ironic, and fantastical—integration into the spectacle surrounding him depends on a leap of faith so great it beggars belief.

This leap of faith dominates the drama of the ugly man in fin-de-siècle opera, but it is also usually for naught. There is, in all these operas, a pronounced will to deception, often enough as a moral imperative. *Der Zwerg*'s chamberlain facetiously announces the deformed dwarf as "beautiful as Narcissus," but his joke hides a demand for a peculiar kind of narcissism: in order for his spectacular delusion to continue, he must not look in the mirror, but rather rely on his recognition by others exclusively. D'Albert's Myrtocle recommits herself to her marriage by recommitting herself to the blindness that sustains it.[23] The lady-in-waiting Ghita in *Der Zwerg* struggles with herself, mirror in hand, over whether or not to shatter the dwarf's delusion. Disillusionment is here an ethical lapse, illusion a moral demand placed on the characters—but it is a demand they cannot readily fulfill. There is a demand for narcissism in these operas, a demand that the protagonists only fulfill to their own detriment and at their own peril—and a demand that the operas themselves seem less than sure is justified.

The marriage at the center of D'Albert's *Die toten Augen* is at once profoundly lopsided and perfectly harmonized; Arcesius' ugliness finds its harmonious complement, its better half, in his wife's blindness. As we shall see in chapter 6, the imbalance implicit in their marriage in many respects models the awkward synesthesia of opera, its attempt to merge and unify separate media into a seamless whole. That experience, the opera suggests, is predicated on blindness—a willingness not to see what is perfectly obvious. What threatens that relationship is the fact that one partner's deformity is dreadfully, spectacularly visible. It is the central scandal of the opera, the element that gins up its works, that upends its prestabilized harmony. Not just on the level of plot, where Arcesius's ugliness makes Myrtocle's blindness a problem: but also on the formal level, where it is our own blind faith that is challenged by Arcesius's deformity. What if our love, the audience's love for the character is weaker than Myrtocle's and instead of staring into the blinding rays of the rising sun we cannot but stare at the ugly physiognomy onstage?

At the end of *Die toten Augen*, we are left with the same question the Infanta asks of the dwarf once he has realized the truth: Can you unsee what you have seen? "If I were to tell you [that you're not ugly] / would you believe me? / Didn't you see yourself in the mirror?" The relationship between the on-stage audience and the ugly man thus mirrors that of the audience of Bekker's "magic theater": an ethical demand is placed on us to see something in the goings-on onstage, to focus on some and disregard others. And it implies that to fall away from willing submission to those goings-on, to look where we're not supposed to look, constitutes an irreversible lapse: we cannot regain our faith in the stage action once we have lost it. There is a will-to-narcissism in these operas, a willingness to live in a world of illusion, that is directly homologous to the demands the ritualistically heightened post-Wagnerian opera places on its audience—be ensorcelled or be cast out.

But like Ghita and the dwarf, we may, as Bekker suggests elsewhere, be unable to "unquestion" a questionable form; in fact, Bekker seems to suggest that we are increasingly unable due to historical changes and transformations wrought on operatic form itself. When Bekker asks, "What to do with opera?"[24] during the 1920s *Opernkrise*, he is to some extent recasting Ghita's question as one of music history. Operatic form had always been more ostentatious in its representational character than other musical, literary, and dramatic forms that traced themselves, with whatever justification, to the rituals of the spiritual or everyday life of antiquity. In its awkward mixture of the musical, the dramatic and the balletic, "is it a paradox which we cannot really take seriously?" Have we passed that moment of recognition, where representation ceases to ensorcel like it ought to, a point of no return after which we can *no longer* take this strange mongrelized form seriously in the cold, clean space delimited by modernity? "Is opera a representative social pursuit of a past age, which we kept alive by sheer force of thoughtless habit?"[25]

That the audience's relationship to the stage may no longer constitute a lived, ritualistic unity, but rather a fashionable and arbitrary "social pursuit," was a worry that animated Wagner's own conception of the music drama, as well as the music dramas he produced. After all, the title character's task in the first act of *Parsifal* is exactly the one asked of the modern operagoer, and Parsifal has a difficult time with it initially: He is forced to make sense of a timeless ritual and he comes away not understanding what he needs to about it. His seductress, Kundry, has similarly witnessed a most holy ritual, the crucifixion of Christ, but has been unable to react with anything but laughter. But what in the form is it that the audience might no longer be able to believe in? There stands behind the question of ugliness a serious philosophical problem as well, one that links what Bekker called opera's "hereditary problem"[26] to the hereditary material, the Wagnerian Gesamtkunstwerk itself.

Nietzsche, in *Twilight of the Idols*, proclaims Socrates' ugliness "almost a refutation [*beinahe eine Widerlegung*]"[27] of his thought. It put Socrates at odds with Greek harmony, betrayed his non-Greek character and marked him as a "decadent." Ugliness was marked by excess, by disharmony of the parts that hinted at degeneration and decadence[28]—all matters of high anxiety for Wagner's uneasy heirs. Was their art a debasement of Wagner's hereditary material? Was their reliance on older forms a kind of relapse, a slide back down the musical (evolutionary) ladder? Or were they, in the sense of Max Nordau, perpetuating Wagner's "degeneration"?[29] When a stranger came to Athens, he diagnosed Socrates (on the basis of his physiognomy) as a "monster," to which Socrates replied, according to Nietzsche: "You know me, sir."[30] Ugliness is diagnosable and thus spectacular; it is eminently meaningful to the community of those in the know.

In his highly influential *Aesthetics of the Ugly* (*Aesthetik des Hässlichen*, 1853) the Hegelian philosopher Karl Rosenkranz suggested a similar reading of ugliness as disharmony, the undue prominence of part over whole. For "the truly ugly is the free which contradicts itself through unfreedom," in which whatever is characteristic is rendered absolute, "insofar as the individual . . . puffs itself up as the species."[31] Rosenkranz points out that the off-putting ugliness of caricature, for instance, resides not merely in the exaggeration of certain characteristic features, but rather in the fact that those features begin to encroach upon the rest of the creature and threaten to usurp the whole person. "A mean [*gemeine*] physiognomy as such is not yet caricature; when however a face seems to dissolve entirely into one of its parts, if it seems to consist entirely of lower jaw, nose, forehead etc.,"[32] caricature results. The part that renders invisible the rest of the whole is ugly.

Of course, the worry that one aspect may overwhelm the whole is a persistent one in opera, usually asserting itself in the charge that a particular opera needn't have been an opera at all, but would have made a perfectly fine novel, play, cantata, or (later) film. It is also a persistent concern of both Schreker and Zemlinsky. Their worry about this kind of usurpatory one-sidedness was among the central motivators of their musical aesthetics: For instance, Bekker's rejection of the operas of Pfitzner stemmed from the fear that word or thought might overwhelm the music, might become "a drama, which almost accidentally happens to avail itself of singing and music"[33] to express itself; Schreker's self-professed dislike of hyperindividualized instrumental or vocal sound goes in a similar direction: "Nothing is more off-putting than a celesta that obtrusively announces itself as such. . . . I deny the overly clear, differentiable sound and want to recognize only one instrument in its service of the opera: the orchestra itself."[34]

Bekker similarly worries that in modern opera (especially in Wagner and his followers), the "sound world" of the human voice that had been opera's distinguishing feature was increasingly pushed aside by "the ideas of drama and all the illustrative elements," such as "action, staging and presentation."[35] In "musical drama," then, drama threatens to eclipse the music. And composers and critics frequently charged that "literary" operas (such as Franz Schmidt's ill-fated *Notre Dame*), fairy-tale operas (the aforementioned Siegfried Wagner), or historical operas might be grafting music, text, and drama incongruously onto one another—"a symphony with some obligatory singing," as Schreker scathingly lampooned this trend.[36]

Common to all of these diagnoses is the worry that an opera may be all libretto, all idea, all any particular detail—in short, that opera might become misshapen, one-sided caricature. D'Albert's later librettist Richard Batka charges apropos *Tiefland*: "Modern music is conceived from the direction of the *stage*, d'Albert's however is conceived from the parquet. The former is an organic part, an inextricable means of expression of the drama; the latter is a sonic carpet, upon which the theater piece transpires."[37] Music is but the carpeting on which opera transpires—it is neither "organic" nor "inextricable," an autonomous, threateningly mobile detail. This is why critics often derided d'Albert's works as "cinematic" drama: the relative autonomy of the "sonic carpet" and the proximity to popular genres meant that d'Albert's operatic practice risked having one part overwhelm the whole, to turn it into a caricature of an opera.

As the previous chapter has made clear, the very genre of Wilde's *Infanta* was frequently charged with a similar one-sidedness around the turn of the century. To be sure, *Der Zwerg* belongs in the vicinity of the fairy-tale opera, though not all contemporaries would have placed it squarely in that category. In the very first German-language study of the genre, Leopold Schmidt insisted that all that smacked of historicity (such as myth) and specific locality (such as orientalism) disqualified a work as a fairy tale opera.[38] Nevertheless, its identification with this rather amorphous genre seems to have been widespread, not least because it draws on a famous literary fairy tale, and actually heightens its fairy-tale character vis-à-vis its source material: Wilde's story is much more specific about history and culture, character and place than Klaren's libretto. Even the change in title is significant: A work with an *Infanta* in the title can take place only in a circumscribed set of cultural contexts, but a dwarf is a timeless occurrence.

Its creators thus actively ushered in *Der Zwerg* into this peculiar genre, and their treatment of the dwarf's deformity stands in dialogue with the genre's own perceived diminutiveness. The fairy-tale opera was widely regarded at the time as a diminutive genre, perhaps a bit unambitious and without hope of ever attaining the lofty heights of the music drama. Wagner's dwarf Mime essentially tries to arrest the *Ring* epos and stage a fairy-tale opera as a kind of cover-up, deceiving Siegfried, and he is brutally punished for it.

Zemlinsky himself seems to understand his dwarf's self-deception in much the same terms: "My Dwarf seeks his fortune in *fairy-tale-like* ignorance of his deformity,"[39] he wrote in an article about the opera.

The popularity of the fairy-tale opera among Germany's composers was, as Walter Niemann observed in 1913, widely understood as a "bankruptcy of the post-Wagnerian composers."[40] Rudolf Louis, for instance, charged that fairy-tale composers had cowardly sought to "build a small hut in the shadow of the Wagnerian art work," which "at the price of an absolute renunciation of aspirations of individual power and grandeur, affords the advantage of security."[41] Bekker speaks of a "miniaturization" of Wagnerian form.[42] And Niemann himself claims its popularity is owed to the composer's unwillingness to bring plausible psychology and effective dramaturgy to bear on the material, and constitutes a retreat into "mere" composing: "And lo and behold, gray theory, the complications of music drama no longer hinder [the composer], who can just make music to his heart's content."[43] If the fairy-tale opera, for all its virtues, constitutes an evasion of the demands placed on music by the legacy of the music drama, it is not an entirely successful one: Bekker's study on Schreker suggests that the fairy-tale opera is fatally torn between "the naïveté of the genre" and its "artfully overburdened musical style"; this constitutive contradiction, well hidden initially by Humperdinck's technical skill, eventually doomed the form and "found its final expression in the stammering in word and tone of Siegfried Wagner's simple-minded and sorry efforts."[44] Fairy-tale opera as such was a failure of nerves, an attempt to sidestep the demands placed on opera by Wagner's aesthetic. Its diminutiveness was a form of prevarication, of not putting the cards on the table.

However much the dwarf, his deformity, and the cruel reaction he elicits from those he delusionally thinks of as his peers invite or even demand a reading in terms of biography, the story provides a clear allegory for opera as an integrated work of art. The harmony of parts on which its success rests requires a constitutive and willful blindness on the part of the audience, and a willingness to live in a "world of dreams" guided by voices. It is a willingness that, like Myrtocle's blindness, has to be willingly chosen once the illusion is destroyed. Ugly characters help post-Wagnerian operas to both enact this willing and allegorize the consequences of not being able to unsee what one has glimpsed behind the illusion.

At the same time, such ugly characters themselves render the world they inhabit more coherent: The spectacle necessary to sustain the web of illusion and delusion around Arcesius, around the dwarf, around Alviano allows the different components of the opera to move closer together, to conspire. As the one detail amiss in the sumptuous spectacle, these ugly characters guarantee the beautiful coherence of their surroundings. Rosenkranz programmatically claims that ugliness is not a quality that attaches to objects "in itself," but describes it instead as the "positive negation"[45] of the idea of beauty. Accordingly, what makes ugliness at once repellent and comical is the fact that "it reminds [us] of its ideal opposite," namely harmonious organic integration of whole and part.[46] The offensive autonomy of the hyperindividualized particular thus necessarily refers back to an ideal of complete and harmonious integration, which it violates.

And indeed, ugliness in post-Wagnerian opera turns out to be a uniquely one-sided affair. Wagner's Mime's dwarvish deficiency is not left up to the actor portraying him, the director or the makeup artist—even if Mime were dressed in a hyper-Germanic loincloth, we can hear his insufficiency in his voice. Not so in d'Albert, not so in Zemlisky, and, in terms of movement rather than voice, not so in Schreker. With regard to those aspects that matter to the performance itself, the dwarves of both Schreker's and Zemlinsky's *Birthdays* do not stand out from the spectacle that surrounds them. Schreker's dwarf is ugly and misshapen, a feral woodland creature, but he dances just as well, if not better, than those that mock and hector him; in *Die Gezeichneten*, Alviano is obsessed with beauty both visual and sonorous until his illusion is shattered. And Zemlinsky, by changing the dwarf from a child of nature to an accomplished bard, makes sure that the dwarf's ugliness is present only visually—the dwarf sounds, if anything, much more ravishing than the derisive and disharmonious titter with which the Infanta and her ladies-in-waiting interrupt his songs. Zemlinsky's dwarf even "moves with complete *grandezza*, which is rendered grotesque only by his physique," as the stage directions make sure to note. Similarly, when the dwarf initially emerges from his carriage, it is the *orchestra* that marks his deformity, of which his voice betrays nothing.

Operatic ugliness, by virtue of sounding beautiful, and balletic ugliness, by moving perfectly, thus makes visible the nonconcomitancy of different media of operatic production. In Wagner's dwarf, they coincide; in Schreker, Zemlinsky, and d'Albert they cleave apart—they almost have to. On the one hand, this falls short of Wagner's prescriptions for music drama—something that was of great concern to these composers even forty years after the master's death. The dwarves are symptoms of a falling short of the integrated work of art. But on the other hand, these dwarves with their ugly exterior who yet move and sing so beautifully, register the cruelty inherent in the integration of media in the Gesamtkunstwerk. It is really only the libretto or scenario that tells us that these dwarves are in fact ugly; in *Siegfried*, all media conspire to brutalize

Mime, just as the Infanta's courtiers gang up on their dwarf. The songs Mime turns to, the words he uses, the voice in which he pleads his case, the movements prescribed by Wagner's stage direction—they all combine and conspire to make him other, abject, ugly.

The abiding fascination for the *Birthday of the Infanta* among those writing music drama after Wagner, is at least partially motivated by the fact that it grants Mime some measure of justice, and along with him, the abject detail for which Wagner's operas displayed such marked "impatience."[47] The deformed dwarf's delusion and its brutal disillusionment allows us to question on the one hand Wagner's "magic" theater, in which the audience is asked for an aesthetic leap of faith, and on the other hand the integration of media, which, the dwarf figure suggests has something terribly repressive and potentially violent about it. What makes these operas so interesting, then, is that they liberated the voices of those characters on the losing side of the Gesamtkunstwerk—that they destabilized the overweening spectacle, the overweening integration and the overweening Germanness of the Gesamtkunstwerk.

The Nazis had characteristically little patience for the losing side of the Gesamtkunstwerk, as Goebbels's *Musiktage* made clear. But Richard Strauss, who conducted his own works there and who was a guest of honor, seems to have disagreed. When he asked Hans Severus Ziegler why his own *Elektra* was not "degenerate music," while Schoenberg's *Erwartung* supposedly was, Strauss pointed to the fact that the grappling with the Gesamtkunstwerk that animated so much of the music the Nazis branded "degenerate" had crucially informed his own work as well. The complicated and fractious relationship between the man on whose birthday the *Musiktage* started, and the man whose composition opened it, will be the topic of the next chapter. Just as in the story of Mime's revenge, eroticism will turn out to be at the center of that story as well.

CHAPTER 3

Taceat Mulier in Theatro: Richard Strauss's *Guntram*, Arthur Schopenhauer, and the Exorcism of the Voice

Arthur Schopenhauer, in what is perhaps the most stridently misogynist text of the nineteenth century, describes how women ruin a man's concertgoing experience by "continuing their chatter" even "during the most beautiful passages of the greatest masterworks." This terrifying vision of man's masterworks, disrupted and destroyed through feminine chatter, moves Schopenhauer to make a modest proposal:

> If it is true that the Greeks did not admit women into their theaters, they were right; at least it would have been possible to hear something in their theatres. For our own times it would be proper to add to the *taceat mulier in ecclesia* a *taceat mulier in theatro*, or to substitute it and put it in large letters on the curtain of the theatre.[1]

It was not Schopenhauer's self-proclaimed disciple, Richard Wagner, who made good on the philosopher's proposal—there was no such command emblazoned on the curtain at Bayreuth. Rather, it was the young Richard Strauss who purged the theater of irritating feminine chatter, if only onstage. Where Schopenhauer envisions a theater that allots a voice only to men, Strauss's first opera, *Guntram*, populates the stage almost exclusively with men, only to then winnow down the remaining number of women to one, who spends the opera's climactic scene standing on the stage in perfect silence.

It is of course not accidental that *Guntram* (for which Strauss served as both composer and librettist) is also deeply indebted to the philosophy of Schopenhauer, to the point that it can be (and has been) read as a downright illustration of Schopenhauer's doctrine of the "self-negation of the will." While Strauss, like Wagner, turned to Schopenhauer as the anchor of an operatic-aesthetic program, his opera is nevertheless quite anti-Wagnerian. As Charles Dowell Youmans has argued, *Guntram*'s debt to Schopenhauer emerges from a situation in which a young Wagnerian realized that Wagner and his crowd had consistently distorted and misread the philosopher and had perverted his philosophy for their own aesthetic ends.[2] In writing and revising *Guntram*, Strauss clearly juxtaposed Wagner and Schopenhauer (rather than taking the composer's alleged fealty seriously), attempting to write a Gesamtkunstwerk animated by a more accurate reflection of *The World as Will and Representation*. The way Strauss confronts Wagner and Schopenhauer, interrogating and rethinking both gives rise to the theory of vocality that seems to animate the composer's mature operas from *Salome* on, a theory which will be the focus of the following chapter.

This chapter reads *Guntram*'s exorcism of the female voice in terms of the opera's debt to Schopenhauer. Of course, the Schopenhauer Strauss was responding to was not the curmudgeon of "Ueber die Weiber," but the master thinker of *The World as Will and Representation*. Nevertheless, there is enough of Schopenhauer's "taceat mulier in theatro" in *Guntram*: sexuality and voice, theatricality and silence come to define the sexual politics in the opera's climactic scene. This scene indeed features the silent woman Schopenhauer fantasizes about—but in the process, silence becomes a multifarious and rather mysterious quality. How subjective is a silent subject on the opera stage? How objective is it even?

Guntram tells the story of a minstrel, a member of a secret sect called the Champions of Love (*Streiter der Liebe*) that seeks to transform humanity through love. In the opera's first scene, Guntram becomes acquainted with the effects of the villainous rule of the evil Duke Robert. Guntram saves an unknown woman from committing suicide, only to discover that the mystery woman is in fact Robert's wife, Freihild. The two fall in love. At her urging, and in keeping with his mission, Guntram sings a song to convince Robert to mend his ways, but the duke accuses Guntram of sedition. Robert attacks Guntram, who kills him by accident. While imprisoned for what is universally presumed to be a regicide, Guntram is visited by his mentor, who enjoins him to submit to the jurisdiction of the Champions of Love. Guntram rejects this counsel and proclaims that "No group may punish me, for the group punishes the deed! Only my will may punish the sins of my heart!" However, he also renounces his love for Freihild, which he now recognizes as selfish rather than ideal—as the curtain falls, she stands "in transfixed remembrance," while he walks off into exile.

Even this cursory summary should make clear that *Guntram* bears more than a passing resemblance to Wagner's operas. The characters, their names, and their language seem inspired, to put it mildly, by the master of Bayreuth. The singer hero seems to have been self-consciously adapted from *Tannhäuser*, and the topos of authentic versus inauthentic music (the former embodied by the Champions, the latter by a host of minnesingers and monastic choirs beholden to secular and church authorities) wears its kinship with *Die Meistersinger* on its sleeve. Moreover, the concept of a mystic brotherhood and the doomed love relationship seem inspired by *Parsifal* and *Tristan*, respectively. Romain Rolland, in his discussion of *Guntram*, remarks that "la tyrannie de Wagner s'y fait sentir, ce qui est rare dans les autres oeuvres de Strauss."[3] But while the Tristan echoes in particular are audible throughout *Guntram*, they peter out into spectacular silence in the opera's final scene. Rather than stage a Liebestod duet, Strauss has his protagonist forswear love, while his Isolde remains entirely mute. Strauss's most Wagnerian opera replaces the love-death *dialogue* (in which Tristan delivers a final monologue, echoed by Isolde's own over his dead body) with a love-renunciation *monologue*.[4]

It is clear from Strauss's own writings that this shift was explicitly conceived as a move beyond Wagner: Strauss's original ending did not feature either the rejection of the Champions' authority nor the renunciation of Freihild's love; instead, Guntram submitted to the (divine) judgment of his brethren.[5] The revision in which Strauss introduced this new ending greatly displeased his friend and mentor Alexander Ritter (a rabid Wagnerian and an ardent Catholic), who regarded it as a rejection of Wagner and of Christian ethics.[6] Instead of a Wagnerian fulfillment of the love union, even if that fulfillment were to come at the cost of the lovers' lives (as in *Tristan*), the opera's final scene stages man alone, facing and renouncing a woman reduced to utter silence. And since she is not the target of some action (such as the object of salvation, as a similarly silent Kundry in *Parsifal*), but rather only of a withdrawing of action, her silence is coterminous with an uncertainty about her very objecthood.

What is more, Strauss's stage directions suggest that the illumination of the stage should be reduced as the scene goes on, until the curtain closes on almost perfect darkness. In this context, of course, although it is Freihild, not

Guntram, who is left standing as the curtain closes, Freihild's muteness renders her almost imperceptible—Guntram is left singing essentially to himself and to us. A contingent fact of *Guntram*'s reception makes this imperceptibility nearly total: Strauss's opera saw only a few performances at Weimar in 1894 and, after one ignominious further performance at Munich, was not performed again for decades. Even today, performances are extremely rare; most of those follow not the score written in the 1890s but rather a redacted version Strauss completed in the 1940s. In other words, we the audience, as a matter of pure happenstance, approach this opera almost always as listeners or readers, not as spectators—and some parts of the opera are inaccessible to us other than as readers of scores. While she is inaudible but somehow present to the opera's rare viewers, Freihild's remaining onstage must have seemed mysterious and opaque to most of those who encountered *Guntram* outside the opera house.

At least part of the reason why Strauss, dissatisfied with the opera's reception yet convinced of its quality, nevertheless chose to revisit the score toward the end of his life has to do with matters of voice. Strauss streamlined some of the more tedious philosophical passages—the repetitive songs that cycle through the scenes at court in act 2—but mostly he aimed to make Guntram's part more singable. By Strauss's own admission, this part suffered in the original from something of a surfeit of voice, both in terms of the actual amount of singing required ("so-and-so many more bars than Tristan") and in terms of the technical demands on the singer ("insane," in Strauss's own words).[7] And while the Freihild role is itself anything but easy, it is the part of Guntram that draws (in the original version apparently undue) attention to itself. When this overweening vocality is confronted with a mute heroine, a strange drama of voice, causality, and identity ensues.

PHANTOMS OF THE OPERA

The third act of *Guntram*, as Youmans has pointed out, is "a kind of exegesis" of Schopenhauer's *The World as Will and Representation*.[8] Indeed, the trajectory it traces from a doctrine of universal love (the project of the *Minnesinger* brotherhood) to a renunciation of love as fundamentally contaminated by egotism, dovetails exactly with Schopenhauer's "transition from virtue to asceticism."[9] This transition is accomplished by what Schopenhauer terms the "denial of the will,"[10] which delivers the subject from a love still attached to the *principium individuationis* to objectless renunciation of the will.[11] At its highest stage of refinement, the human spirit retreats from "the deception of appearance" (*Täuschung der Erscheinung*), and "stops wanting anything, takes

care not to attach his will to any one thing, tries to instill in himself the greatest indifference towards all things."[12]

On one hand, then, we have a renouncing subject; on the other, an object
to be renounced—or, perhaps better, a very concept of objecthood (namely
Erscheinung) to be renounced. And Schopenhauer makes clear that one prime
aspect of the denial of the will, of the detachment from phenomenal objecthood, is sexual abstinence: the ascetic "wants no sexual gratification" (*er will
keine Geschlechtsbefriedigung*). The renouncing subject, even though its geni-
tals are left undetermined, is clearly a man (*er . . . er . . . er . . .*), and the thing to
which he wants to become indifferent is a woman.[13] Guntram similarly considers his sexual bond with Freihild the "last, most precious rope by which the
world ensnared me." Questions of objecthood and renunciation thus feature
prominently in both Schopenhauer's philosophy and Strauss's musical exegesis. In *Guntram*, this question is literally sounded out, its depths plumbed
by voices present and absent.

Freihild is, somewhat paradoxically, Guntram's object only in renunciation—she attains a status as an object only insofar as she is pushed away. She
thus bears a family resemblance to what Julia Kristeva has called the "abject,"
with the essential difference that the "abject" is obtrusively physical, whereas
Freihild's semiobjectivity is bound up with a lack of physical presence.[14]

All structural homologies with the ending of *Tristan* notwithstanding, poor
Freihild cannot be a mourned object in a *Tristan* with reversed genders: she is
too alive to be a proper object for mourning. Unlike Tristan, whose dead body
remains onstage, cradled by Isolde, Freihild is barely physically present at all.
But precisely what kind of object is she? Is this strange apparition an object
in any sense, even one to be renounced? If she did not open her mouth, sing,
and touch Guntram in the very beginning of the opera's final scene, we might
be confused as to whether dramaturgically she is the real Freihild at all and not
perhaps her specter, an imaginary object of Guntram's to which we as audience are also privy. Are we hallucinating along with Guntram? The kiss she
plants on Guntram's hand is the only physical contact the two share; for the
rest of the time, she is reduced to gestures and glances.

Freihild's silence is what marks her as Guntram's object. She has no way
of asserting her desire (much less renouncing it); her silence allows desire and
renunciation to remain an exclusively male preserve, a one-way street emanating from the male subject and visited upon or retreating from the female object.
There is nothing sadistic or possessive to Freihild's status, Guntram wants to
do nothing with his control over her beyond relinquishing it. Nevertheless,
her reactive objectivity entails a lack of what Johann Gottlieb Fichte called

"dignity"—she is deprived of agency, prevented from actively renouncing and thereby controlling her surroundings and her destiny.[15] The fact that she is present at all, that she is even onstage, seems dictated by the need to certify that there is indeed an object to be renounced within reach of the desiring (and thus renouncing) power of that same male subject. But what kind of an object is it that presents itself only so that it may be renounced? Is this woman that Guntram (and, by extension, the audience) can only *see* on the dimming stage real, or is she a figment of the very desire that masochistically renounces her?

The question of how real the silent apparition Freihild is in this last scene dovetails with a perennial epistemological question of the early nineteenth century: what distinguishes our constitution of an object of perception from seeing something that appears in space and time, but is not in fact an object, for instance a ghost? The seeing of ghosts [*Geistersehen*] was thematized by Kant, Fichte, and Schopenhauer.[16] And indeed, Freihild's strange para-objectivity may owe something to Schopenhauer's essay "Versuch über das Geistersehen und was damit zusammenhängt." As we noted above, the opera's libretto is quite thorough in sketching a physics of *Geistersehen*—there is but one touch, an elaborate pantomime, and not a sound. Seeing ghosts, as both Kant and Schopenhauer knew, is in principle no different than the spontaneous use of our categories to structure raw sense data. In his essay, Schopenhauer writes:

> It is commonly supposed that we have falsified the reality of a ghostly apparition when we can show that it was subjectively constituted; but what weight can we give such an argument, when we know from Kant's teachings how great a part subjective conditions have to play in the constitution of the physical world, namely the following: that the space in which it appears, and time in which it moves, and causality in which consists the nature of matter, that is to say in its very forms, is but the product of brain functions.[17]

In other words: just because something is "subjectively constituted" doesn't make it less than real. Freihild's presence may well be just a mute reminder of exactly whose love Guntram is renouncing, a figment in Guntram's and a mnemonic in the viewer's head—her objectivity may be only an effect of the constituting work of someone else's subjectivity. Yet, as Kant tells us, any object that is physically ready at hand, real in the common sense, is also "subjectively constituted." Wherein, then, lies the difference? The concept of a (phenomenal) object of experience, Schopenhauer claims, depends on three factors: locatability in space, in time, and in a causal chain. It is an object we must be able to place and whose substance we must be able to trace through transformations; and we must be able to assume that we (or the other objects around it) can in some way interact with it, impinge upon it or have it impinge upon us.

Clearly, Freihild occupies space on the stage and performs her pantomime in a temporal sequence—but the question of causality becomes an increasingly vexed one as the scene progresses. After all, she does not interact with any other body (e.g., Guntram), she does not respond to him physically (the one kiss notwithstanding), and, most important, she never replies. When Freihild gestures, glances, but does not touch or sing, she is admitting precisely to being "not quite an object." In *The World as Will and Representation*, Schopenhauer turns to the voice as an instance of causation: if I hear a voice, I look for the body that has produced it.[18] Freihild's "not quite objecthood" is thus of one piece with her voicelessness. She cannot cause sound, cannot interact; and even if she is located in space and time, she can at best be semiobjective. The misogynistic trope that man and woman could be thought of as transcendental subject and the object constituted by that subject's categories respectively is an exceedingly old one, running from at least Fichte to Weininger—she has "no I," as Weininger puts it, receives her reality and content only as a reflection from the (male) transcendental subject.[19] This trope, however, does not exhaust the relationship between Guntram and Freihild, for Freihild precisely fails as a constituted object. This is both to her detriment and her great advantage; on the one hand it makes her not just his projection, but also an unsuccessful one; on the other hand it also gives her an uncanny independence that a perfect Romantic "speculum,"[20] as Julia Kristeva has called it, would not have.

Just how much causation a human voice is capable of in *Guntram* becomes evident in the fact that Guntram is the scion of a brotherhood of singers. Of course, Wagner's Lohengrin and Parsifal both come from a (suspiciously) similar group, but unlike *Guntram*'s Champions of Love, singing is not the grail knights' primary occupation. The Champions of Love, in other words, champion love through their voices—political efficacy in the opera seems intimately bound up with vocal performance (even evil Duke Robert has minnesingers celebrating his awesome power). Guntram's attempted conversion of Duke Robert makes the vocality of (political) action particularly clear: his song, a rather opaque allegory of war and peace, is aimed at convincing Robert, the Old Duke (Freihild's father), and the attending vassals—but it does not seem to be the semantic content of Guntram's song that each of them reacts to.

Robert proves immune ("What's with this singing?"), the vassals are entranced ("Hear the singer! Never have I heard anything like it!"), the Old Duke seems on the verge of giving in to Guntram's entreaties (praising his "art"), and

Freihild is won over ("Like tidings from heaven the notes strike my heart!"). What the courtiers collectively respond to, then, whether positively or negatively, is the song insofar as it is sung, not in terms of what it says. They are not convinced by any sentiment or argument laid out in the song; they are ensorcelled by Guntram's voice alone, much like Siegfried is repelled by Mime's (see chapter 1).

Losing her voice thus means far more for Freihild than it does for, say, Kundry in *Parsifal*—all efficacy, in *Guntram*'s universe, is channeled through vocality. Parsifal is just as mute as Kundry in the first scene of *Parsifal*'s third act, to the point that Gurnemanz assumes that his visitor has taken an oath of silence, wondering whether "an oath binds you / to be silent towards me [*dein Gelübde / dich bindet, mir zu schweigen*]"; when Guntram is "silent witness" to events at the court, on the other hand, he reflects on what he sees in song—he is not yet "politically" active (as when he sings his song to the Duke), but he forms a plan of action by vocally relaying it to the audience. According to Guntram's refusal of the Champions' judgment over him, it is this efficacy alone that falls under their purview. The fact that his subsequent renunciation of Freihild constitutes precisely the kind of vocal action he has just renounced along with the Champions' project is a perplexity we will have to return to.

Freihild's voicelessness thus commits her to a lack of activity; it also more broadly commits her to a lack of efficacy. In fact, Guntram himself initially doubts Freihild's objectivity when she first appears in his dungeon—and with good reason, since he has just been visited by another vengeful phantasm. However, it is precisely touch and voice, the two means of contact of which the Freihild of the final scene seems to be deprived, that convince him that she is the real thing. In the original version, Guntram's dungeon is visited by Duke Robert's angry ghost, who accuses him of murder—a claim that Guntram rejects. In the revised opera, only this rejection survives, but Robert makes no personal appearance either in the score or the stage directions. (In fact, Robert's presence is so tenuous that it is easy to misread Guntram's exorcism as a warding off of the guilt brought on by the monks' requiem for Robert, the sounds of which waft into the dungeon at the beginning of act 3, scene 1.) By insisting on the justness of his action, Guntram banishes Robert's specter, but just as his shape disappears, Freihild appears in the doorway of the cell. In both versions, Guntram now thinks that Freihild too is another ghost ("trickery of the senses" [*Trug der Sinne*]) or a fantastic manifestation of his guilt ("beautiful shape of terrifying thoughts" [*furchtbaren Gedankens schönste Gestalt*])—in any case his projection, of his making. Only when she calls his name and touches him is Guntram at last convinced of her reality ("Freihild? Truly, Freihild?" [*Freihild? Wirklich, Freihild?*]).[21]

By the time the act is over, however, we are once again left asking: "Wirklich, Freihild?" The opera skirts her troubling "not quite objecthood," the possibility that Freihild is not quite real, by granting the mute object ersatz, and that means visual, expressiveness: even though Freihild is silent during Guntram's final monologue, she still communicates. We may not hear her voice (and the vast majority of the opera's listeners hearing a recording may wonder whether she has perhaps exited the stage), but the opera's score provides a veritable pantomimic routine through which she is to communicate with Guntram. Of course, purely gestural performances to music have been part of operatic form since at least Restoration opera. But usually (as in ballet) the stage is neatly divided between those who produce sound and those who do not produce but rather move to it. Even pantomimic interludes usually concern characters (such as jesters) who are external to the plot that is advanced by the music. While *Guntram* thus clearly partakes of a silent tradition, the opera nevertheless stages something rather more scandalous: a passing into pantomime of a previously vocal character. What's more, the transition occurs with shocking suddenness; upon her rejection by Parsifal, Kundry similarly "loses her speech, changes into a mute shadow, and finally drops dead" in the third act of *Parsifal*, but years have intervened between her confrontation with Parsifal in Klingsor's garden and the events on Good Friday.[22] All that Guntram needs to silence Freihild is a word.

The fact that Freihild's loss of voice appears within the context of a scene in which love is renounced cannot be accidental. Man's sexual renunciation finds its correlate in the muteness of his object. On one level, this loss of voice is mostly a loss of the body behind that voice (what Roland Barthes has called "the grain of the voice").[23] For it is not agency or subjectivity that she forgoes: she does act (or at least act out), and the opera wants us to know how she feels. As Guntram forswears physical love, the object of that love becomes almost exclusively visual, which for the opera seems to mean a specter, without a desired or desiring body. Pantomime, as Martin Puchner has pointed out, is also frequently marked as inauthentic, as overly theatrical, as opposed to the essential authenticity of the (embodied) voice.[24] This is what makes her a (quasi-)object of renunciation: the ascetic renunciation of love strips not only the "saint" of his body, but his object of hers as well. In renouncing her, he renounces the very part in her that he could potentially desire.

In other words: Freihild's musical silence figures as a more metaphysical passivity. Guntram can actively (performatively) renounce her. She is asked to renounce him in turn ("Freihild, do you forswear me?"), but all the opera really allows her to do is watch him walk away—she never actively renounces, partially because such activity would require speech and voice. Freihild's passage from a body with a voice to a voiceless pantomime is also a passing from the production (or causation) of sound to a pure passivity of moving to the sound of others. While the voice is the place where bodily objectivity can actively assert itself, Freihild's silent pantomime is pure mirroring: "Freihild, who has been seized by excitement at Guntram's proclamation, expresses her impression in a grand gesture" and "remains standing across from the erect Guntram in this way."

The fact that Freihild can only react and the fact that she can only react silently are thus one and the same: a sonic reflection would upend the logic of the voice that pervades the scene. Of course, pantomime is etymologically always already reactive, mirroring some other thing—it is mimicry (from *panto* "all" and *mimos* "mimic"). Just as for Schopenhauer "all other arts represent" different "objectivations of the will," whereas only music "represents immediately the will itself," Freihild's exclusively visual performance lapses into a representation that Guntram's song is automatically raised above.[25] This of course only heightens the problematic of communication in this quasi monologue: the only way the opera can construe a "dialogue" between the renouncing subject and the object of its renunciation is through an anacoluthon of registers—by having visuality echo sound.

VOCALITY AND PANTOMIME

"Incapable of a word of reply," Freihild is reduced to pantomime—but since she is voiceless, we have only the score's word, as it were, for Freihild's incapability. Why this should be so is not immediately obvious; after all, operatic-dramatic convention may allow silence or taciturnity to become quite eloquent. Since not every sung expression needs to correspond to a diegetic act of speaking, characters that are being perfectly mute onstage as characters can still inform the audience about their feelings, desires, and schemes quite effectively. Guntram himself is described as "a mute witness of the glittering feast" in act 2; however, his "muteness" is actually quite loquacious, for Guntram has been singing to himself (and to us) continually, broadcasting his attraction to Freihild and his distaste for her husband, his wavering between leaving the empty world of the court and his desire to remain close to the duchess. In the operatic playbook, then, even if Freihild is "incapable of a word of reply," that does not mean that she cannot sing at least to herself and us. During Guntram's song monologue in act 2, Freihild does intercede, but only "to herself" [*für sich*]—something Guntram's final monologue no longer allows her to do.

By depriving Freihild of an inner monologue, the opera does not, however, render her entirely unfeeling, without subjectivity—it just has her channel her feelings differently. For most audiences, Freihild's position onstage is not particularly dynamic: she stands, increasingly statuesque, in the gradually dimming light and does not say a word. Any audience member who decided to consult the score would be shocked to find, however, that the composer librettist asks Freihild to run a veritable gauntlet of emotions, some of them easily conveyed for an audience a few dozen yards away, others almost impossible to convey to anything but a television camera.

The voice is of course securely located in an opera score: we know what words go with what note. Performance is an entirely different beast. Always parenthetical, stage directions can span an entire line while describing what happens "in one note," as it were ("Freihild starts crying bitterly"); or they can describe a process, and it is left up to the director to decide what action falls where in the music. The typographic (that is to say, linguistic) representation of a scream, for instance, can easily occupy a few measures, although no singer would hold a scream for the entirety of those measures. At other times, directions are entirely dislocated graphically, printed cursively at the beginning of a scene, leaving their mapping onto the musical score up to interpretation. Whatever dynamic spin director and performer may put on them, if it were solely up to the stage directions, most of opera's figures would just stand around between parenthetical bursts of activity.

This is not much of a problem if we as audience members have the figures' words to go by—usually, they inform us whether a character is horrified, angry, or defiant. But that is precisely what is missing from Freihild's performance. Freihild's stage directions in the opera's final scenes necessarily have to describe actions, since she can communicate only pantomimically. All of Guntram's directions are almost entirely adverbial ("sehr innig"), and thus modifications of the voice—while all of Freihild's directions are an ersatz for a voice: they communicate just enough of her state of mind to keep her in the picture as a renounceable object, but they entirely deauthorize her as a subject. Since many of Freihild's more outré gestures involve fainting and then rising again in sudden resolve, we may in fact be reminded of a puppet flopping mutely up and down the stage.

Whereas Guntram's directions are relatively succinct, Freihild's pantomime is exceedingly elaborate, to the point that it is unclear who is interpellated by these stage directions: is it the audience who encounters these words only as embodied and transmitted by the pantomime? Or is it the score's reader who is to be reassured that, in spite of her silence, Freihild still has a home on the page? After all, instructions such as "with pained meekness" would be difficult to convey in any performance context outside of a film close-up—unless, of course, the person feeling the "Demut" were singing! And when one reads that "Freihild rises and, in calm reconciliation, looks straight and clearly into Guntram's eye," one really wonders how any audience, however eagle-eyed, is supposed to espy these nuances on a (rapidly dimming) stage.

The addressee, in other words, is the reader of the score, not the viewer of the opera; and as previously discussed, for much of its history, *Guntram* has been available only to readers. The point of these elaborate instructions seems to be the graphic reassurance that Freihild still exists as a *possible*, though inactive, voice. In other words, rather than provide empty measures for her part (which the Universal Edition's revised score does for the first few pages of the scene), she is turned into text. Strauss's dejection at *Guntram*'s disappearance from the opera house strongly suggests that Freihild-as-text was an accident rather than her creator's design. And yet, Strauss, the reader of Schopenhauer, seems to have unconsciously written a role that was fully available only to those who read the score, not those who saw it performed.

Freihild's excessive textuality is symptomatic of a philosophical drama overdetermined to the point that its own status as drama becomes a problem— after all, Wagner had admitted the necessity of the drama in "musical drama," because it alone could provide guidance that was "lacking in a mere reading of the score."[26] But in *Guntram* the reverse seems to be the case; we have to read the score to understand what we are (or are not) looking at. Freihild's vocal inactivity does not necessarily translate into a more active stage performance (unless one considers "pained meekness" an activity); it rather finds its ersatz in writing. On the ever-darkening stage, Freihild is expressionless, present only as writing. The score, however, provides a plethora of emotions she *could* potentially express—if only she weren't lost for words.

FREIHILD'S SCREAM AND THE VICISSITUDES OF RENUNCIATION

And yet, it is not entirely accurate to describe Freihild's performance in the opera's final scene as "mute." She may not speak or sing a word, but she does use her voice, if only once: Strauss's stage directions indicate that "Freihild gives a loud scream and threatens to faint." This moment is indicated only in the stage directions, and the 1985 BBC production of *Guntram* left it out of the opera entirely. Much like Kundry's screams (she "emits a terrible scream"), laughter ("Kundry breaks into uncanny, ecstatic laughter that turns into convulsive wailing"), and groans ("Kundry [gives a] muffled groan"), and unlike Klingsor's laugh, it has no location in the score's musical notation.[27] And yet, here the written word reintroduces something of a voice into Freihild's performance. At this vital juncture, the only moment of something that could be termed "dialogue" between Freihild and Guntram, the scene thus stages an opposition between the renunciation of emotion, which is the province of spoken text and voiced meaning (*phone semantike*), and the inarticulate, meaningless scream that expresses unfiltered emotion.[28]

Ever since Aristotle, *logos* was founded on *phone semantike*, signifying sound—as opposed to nonsignifying noise (*agrammatoi psophoi*), which was essentially animalic, and whose expressivity was not tethered to subjective states, but rather, like a sneeze or hiccup, simply a biological necessity.[29] Kundry's muteness in act 3 of *Parsifal*, as Elisabeth Bronfen has observed, moves this Aristotelian topos into the purview of the emergent study of hysteria—Kundry's groans, screams, and above all laughter are no longer merely reflexes; they are hysterical symptoms.[30] When Schopenhauer claims that "animal voice is used entirely to express the will in its excitations and movements," he is integrating this Aristotelian topos into his own metaphysics.[31] The scream is thus the exact opposite of the renunciation of love: the basest assertion of the will, as opposed to its repudiation.

As Strauss's rather loquacious stage directions indicate, Freihild gestures because she is "incapable of a word of reply."[32] At least at this one point, then, Freihild's inability to vocalize is a matter of organized speech rather than a lack of (animal) voice—her scream finds her momentarily lost for words, but not for voice. And conversely, Guntram's words ("I renounce your love"), which are supposed to transcend the snares of the will, are fatally contaminated with the very animal musk they want to shed. The magic formula can only be uttered as voiced—and gloriously so, in the case of Guntram. The "so-and-so many more bars than Tristan"[33] give Guntram full control of the opera's final scene; however, they also bind him to the world of "representation [*Vorstellung*]," precisely at the moment when he is supposed to leave it behind.

The role of voiced meaning (*phone semantike*) in music is a vexed one in Schopenhauer's metaphysics. And given that *Guntram* is "a remarkably well-informed piece of philosophical drama," it is more than likely that Strauss was aware of this problem and its bearing on the opera.[34] Music, according to Schopenhauer's account, has a peculiar relationship to mimesis: it does not represent the world of appearances, as all other arts do, but rather represents the will, the thing in itself, without detour via the world of objects. Since it offers privileged access to the will itself—an access that the spoken word, as lyric poetry, for instance, does not—it is difficult to make sense of opera in Schopenhauer's scheme: what can be said about a genre that attains the representation of the will, only to then weigh itself down with words that recapitulate the false world of the *principium individuationis?* Schopenhauer, who seems to have personally enjoyed opera quite a bit, struggled considerably with the answer to this question, and indeed the first and the second volumes of *The World as Will and Representation* offer slightly divergent answers to it.[35]

This question ultimately concerns the legitimacy of opera as a form. It may be imaginable to have an opera without words, in which the voices would function literally like instruments. Indeed Schopenhauer suggests that the text of oratorios, which functions without regard to its entirely liturgical meaning and is in most cases incomprehensible to its audience, amounts to exactly that—its Latin text is in some sense purely formal and not meant to impart additional meaning. But this is something a music drama in the Wagnerian mould cannot do. Over and over the master of Bayreuth insisted on the need for a specific relationship between German music and the German language that was sung to it. *Gesang* was not canto, a *Gedicht* was not a libretto,[36] and those who attempted to combine German words with Italian forms destroyed both: "Since forever the German language has been mistreated by German [opera] composers according to a arbitrary norm, since they derived their treatment of language from the usage in the operatic practice of the nation from which opera has been transplanted [to Germany] as a foreign product."[37] An organically integrated "poem" (*Gedicht*) in a language (German) listeners could understand was thus central to Wagner's Gesamtkunstwerk.

Wagner's linguistic parochialism thus runs counter to his attachment to Schopenhauer's metaphysics of the will, according to which music precisely leaves behind language, and, in more general terms, anything that communicates with an audience through discrete semantic units (of plot, character, psychology, etc.). How could an opera, in particular after Wagner's reformulation of the operatic project as "music drama," do without, well, drama? For Schopenhauer, this once again poses the question of why the dramatization of actual, particular passions (the will in its subjective form) would be necessary or profitable at all in a musical setting, since music's "absoluteness" refers back to "the will" as a metaphysical entity.

It is quite possible that Strauss realized this problem while writing and composing *Guntram*, since the question is particularly pressing and intractable in Strauss's plot: how can a form that ostensibly represents "the will itself" tell the story of the renunciation of the will? In the second volume of *The World as Will and Representation*, Schopenhauer himself suggests an answer to this question: he proceeds from the assumption that "song with comprehensible words" is enjoyable, and offers as the reason the fact that "in it our most immediate and our most mediate forms of cognition are excited at once and in unison."[38] Our "most mediate" form of cognition is language ("comprehensible words"); the "most immediate" form is the hearing of music. In other words, then, as a libretto, *Guntram* can indeed tell about an individual renouncing its will—it can stage this renunciation as drama. And yet, as music, *Guntram* inescapably expresses or represents the (suprasubjective) will.

This is the fact that appears to have dawned on Strauss upon reading Schopenhauer: any Schopenhauerian story line would have to be dramatized without drama—a Schopenhauerian opera, at least at first blush, threatens to become a *contradictio in adiectum*.[39] Not only did Wagner's program of *Musikdrama* represent a misappropriation of Schopenhauer; any such program would run exactly counter to Schopenhauer's own aesthetics.[40] This is at least in part Nietzsche's point in the famous passage in *Nietzsche contra Wagner*, in which he derides the master of Bayreuth as the "most enraptured mimomaniac," and really "a theater-man and actor."[41] While it can be argued that Strauss's opera tries to have its cake and eat it too by outsourcing the drama to a silent woman character, the very renunciation the plot demands of Guntram depends on performative language, upending any aspirations to musical "absoluteness." And while *Tristan* can be read as essentially an allegory of the coming into being of absolute music (where drama—and voice—are slowly purged or sublated into pure instrumental music[42]), *Guntram* cannot effect any such sublation—because Guntram depends on speech to renounce, and Freihild depends on theatricality (pantomime) to be a possible object of this renunciation.

In some sense, the brief sonic break in the pantomime—Freihild's scream—functions as a reply of sorts to the project of renunciation. The scream occurs in response to Guntram's declaration that "renouncing you, who I love so passionately, removed from you forever, eaten up by the ardor [of love], will I make up for my sinful existence." To renounce—just as to declare love—requires language, and this utterance manages to renounce and declare at once. It is the question that, according to Georg Lukács, animated Søren Kierkegaard's purposely ill-fated romance with Regine Olsen: how do you renounce an object without saying so?[43]

By contrast, Freihild's scream, a sound of "animal voice" [*thierische Stimme*], without any words or semantic content, is an assertion of the voice as music, that is to say as a matter of will rather than (linguistic) representation. Wagner's Beethoven essay analogously calls the scream "the most direct expression of the will," and for this reason posits it as the paradigmatic musical moment.[44] It is thus a representation of the will in two different ways: it betrays the subject's will "in its excitations and movements," *and* it represents the suprasubjective will, since it is music unobstructed by words, drama, or semantics.[45] In other words, Freihild's scream represents not only a strange irruption of an otherwise exorcised voice; it also represents the opera's bad conscience, the repressed fact of its own problematic generic identity. And as Philip Friedheim has pointed out, at least in Wagner's own operas there is no passive-reactive screaming; screaming is active expression, a moment of paradigmatic subjectivity rather than objecthood— "Sieglinde cries out when she sees Siegmund stabbed; Siegmund himself does not cry as he is killed."[46] For this brief moment, Freihild trades her passivity for pure activity—only then to fall silent once more.

If Catherine Clément is correct and opera involves essentially an undoing of women (*défaite*), then *Guntram* is uniquely extreme in this undoing: after all, the *défaite* of Woman has taken place even before the final scene gets under way—Woman is undone already, as we saw, only semiobjective.[47] Yet if Clément is correct and the scintillating beauty of the voice obscures the brutal *défaite* of such operatic women as Cio-Cio-San, then the silence into which *Guntram* forces its heroine is profoundly ambivalent. On one hand, it robs her of singing back, of asserting her own subjectivity; on the other, however, the opera oddly enough recapitulates Clément's gesture, divorcing Woman from the voice that might cover up her subjugation, leaving her abjection dreadfully visible.

The opera tiptoes back from this brink, but it never manages to resolve this problematic. Instead, Freihild falls silent again, Guntram goes on renouncing, and in the end we are left with a perfectly silent woman standing alone on a dimming stage, as the music takes over:

> When Guntram has disappeared from Freihild's view, she threatens to collapse once again of the most overwhelming pain; however, remembering his pronouncement, she gathers all her strength and rises, in transfixed remembrance until the curtain closes.

Guntram, unlike Freihild, is allowed to make a clean escape: rather than linger visually on the stage, he disappears along with his voice. His voice, the stage directions assure us, lives on in Freihild's "Gedenken" and "Erinnerung." The voice of (his) memory is a stronger presence in this final moment than Freihild's actual presence onstage. Her visual presence is nothing but an echo, a remembering reflection, basking in the paladin who has just "escaped her gaze." Freihild ends the opera once more as Guntram's silent mirror. Guntram's last question to his mute lover is, "Freihild, do you forswear me?" Her only reply, according to the score, is silence.

But Guntram renounces not just Freihild in the opera's final act—he also rejects the Champions' juridical claim on him. It was this plot point that irked the Wagnerian Ritter: the individual rejects not only love, but also the community; not only Woman, but also (homo)sociality. Unlike in, say, *Parsifal*, there is no band of brothers to accompany the exorcism of the female voice: the (male) voice in monologue is not accompanied by (or, as Ryan Minor has suggested, amplified by) the "communal body" of a chorus.[48] This also means that the opera's final scene is musically ambivalent about its relationship to Schopenhauer. After all, it offers a wordy renunciation of words, a dramatic disavowal of drama; it is similarly unclear about its relationship to the *principium individuationis*. Granted, Schopenhauer was not a communitarian by any stretch of the imagination, but how does one square Guntram's extreme individualism in the final act with the asceticism that *The World as Will and Representation* seems to call for?

At least one possible answer would center around, and in turn account for, the fact that the opera's final sequence features a protagonist who renounces an object of dubious objectivity; renunciation of the kind that requires an object to renounce—a *Gegen-stand, ob-iectum*, something posited over and against the renouncing subject—is indeed primarily an action that returns the subject into itself and thus constitutes a reiteration, rather than a transcendence, of the *principium individuationis*. This is not what Schopenhauer's ascetic does; rather, he "stops wanting anything" and supercedes any subjecthood that would depend on an object (of the will).[49] It is this exact move that Freihild's actual physical presence would make impossible—just as Guntram has to renounce his love for her, so the opera has to renounce her bodily, vocal physicality.

It is of course quite striking that Strauss, of all people, should end an opera with the echoes of a monolithic male voice—after all, such later Strauss operas as *Der Rosenkavalier* or *Ariadne auf Naxos* are notable precisely for a preponderance, indeed dominance, of female voices. It is clear that, Strauss's unflagging enthusiasm for his debut opera in later years notwithstanding, this embrace of the feminine voice constitutes something of a repudiation of *Guntram*'s sexual politics. But not just the female voice is recuperated in what can be counted as Strauss's mature operatic oeuvre. The (temporarily) voiceless

female body, too, becomes anything but the bizarre puppet of the stage directions—as Linda and Michael Hutcheon have pointed out, Strauss's *Salome*
features "one of the most provocative dancers in opera."[50] Salome's Dance
of the Seven Veils is in fact the exact opposite of Freihild's mute pantomime:
wordless yet part of an intricate negotiation, mute and yet astonishingly physical. And, of course, in *Salome* it is the woman who ends up the ultimate cause,
and it is a man who ends up as a quasi object of her fancy. Where Guntram
renounces a woman who is barely there, Salome makes love to her own partial
object. Perhaps, then, the severed head of Jochanaan serves in some sense as
Freihild's revenge. Where *Guntram* treated a silent woman as almost bodiless,
Salome understands woman's silent movement as imbued with an uncanny
efficacity. As the next chapter will show, in *Salome*'s voice, far from being the
only way in which woman can be a cause, voice serves as a guardrail against
what a silent woman is capable of.

Guntram, Strauss's first opera, marked the only time the composer endeav-
ored to serve as his own librettist. After the failure of *Guntram*, Strauss, who
had been slow to venture into opera to begin with, waited another seven years
to write another opera. *Feuersnot* marks a break from the world of *Guntram*
in many respects: The opera leaves behind Wagner's musical language and,
perhaps not coincidentally, decisively breaks with Wagner's erotics. Where
Guntram confronted Wagner with Schopenhauer, creating a Gesamtkunstwerk animated by a more accurate musico-dramatic reflection of *The World as
Will and Representation*, *Feuersnot* is already much heavier on female voices,
and it adheres to a parodic Wagnerian schema, culminating in a salvation
through sex: Here, in order to rekindle a town's festival fires during a midsum-
mer celebration, the virgin Diemut has to sleep with the evil sorcerer who has
extinguished them. This "salvation through sex" is not accomplished through
a dialogue or a monologue—in a joking nod to *Tristan*, it is moved into the
orchestra.

Perhaps even more centrally for the further trajectory of Strauss's career
weighed another change: The Wagner-inspired composer librettist of *Guntram* had, almost immediately after *Guntram*'s failure, begun casting about for
collaborators. *Feuersnot* was written by Ernst von Wolzogen, who also wrote
numerous libretti for Eugen d'Albert. It seems that just as *Guntram* ended with
a man singing to and renouncing a woman who may be nothing his projection,
so the opera found its composer overly enveloped in the solipsistic world of
the total work of art. Instead, then, Strauss seems to have turned decisively to
the irreducible alterity and dialogue involved in setting someone else's words
to music. As chapter 5 will show, several composers around the turn of the

century turned to this kind of dialogism as a means to free themselves from the oppressive monologic weight of the Wagnerian legacy.

In the following decades, Strauss would collaborate with a number of German and Austrian writers on his operas, and initiated projects that never came to fruition with several more. One of them was the dramatist Frank Wedekind, whose plays *Erdgeist* and *Die Büchse der Pandora* eventually formed the basis for Alban Berg's *Lulu*. The two men came into contact in 1896 and began planning several opera and ballet projects together. All of them came to naught, but Wedekind's draft survives—and they, too, deal extensively with questions of voice and voicelessness, in particular voicelessness of female characters. Together with the libretto Hofmannsthal wrote for the opera Strauss did end up writing, these never-were projects serve to chart the fate of vocality in Strauss's oeuvre once he had freed himself from his overreliance on Wagnerian and Schopenhauerian erotics.

CHAPTER 4

Erotic Acoustics: The Natural History of the Theater and *Der ferne Klang*

In his 1964 *In Search of Wagner*, Theodor W. Adorno claims that "until its self-dissolution in Schreker, the New German School remained committed to the idea of the 'distant sound'; the sound in which music becomes static and spatialized and mystifies social models into nature itself."[1] This chapter traces the trope of the "distant sound" and asks what is specific about operatic distance after Wagner and before the New Music. This, however, requires thinking of the "distant sound" as more than just a compositional technique, but instead as a product of particular technologies as well. The "sound in which music becomes static and spatialized" depends not only on a certain mode of composing, but also on a certain kind of concert hall or opera house, a dependence that is explicitly thematized in Schreker's operas. Leaving behind the philosophical discourses that have framed the discussion in previous chapters, we will instead turn to the then-emergent field of acoustics, asking how fin-de-siècle notions of gender influenced theories of operatic architecture and acoustics, and how their conjunction informed opera, its staging, and its reception.

Adorno identifies Schreker as the endpoint of the idea of a "distant sound," because Schreker raises the idea of a "distant sound" to a centrality it did not have elsewhere, and he raises it to self-consciousness—especially in the opera to which Adorno is alluding in the passage cited above, *Der ferne Klang* (*The Distant Sound*) of 1912. For Adorno, *Der ferne Klang*, much like Wagner's operas, represses the mechanisms (musical, mechanical, social) that collude behind the stage to produce its spectacle—this is what Adorno famously called opera's "phantasmagoria." Yet Schreker's protagonist spends all of *Der ferne*

Klang searching for the titular "distant sound," a sound located offstage, behind the scenes. The opera presents the story of a quest for the space that, as
phantasmagoria, it has to pretend doesn't exist. Not only does *Der ferne Klang*
put its secret animating principle onto the stage, it thereby manages to interrogate the very category of distance on which it depends.

What is at stake, as the music critic Paul Bekker makes clear in his 1918
essay on Schreker, is nothing less than the "deep connection between textual
and musical creation." After Wagner, Bekker argues, only Schreker was able
to effectively connect his dramatic and musical instincts, because "his basic
dramatic ideas rest on sound symbols."[2] Schreker's operas abound in distant,
disembodied, dislocated sounds, but they tend to be explicitly acknowledged
by the operas' characters and tend to be integral to the opera's plot. Schreker's
use of distance thus is another attempt at making opera a coherent synesthetic
artwork, rather than a play set to music, or a symphony with words. Schreker's
distant sounds fuse the mélange of media that have to come together in opera.
But beyond that, they are also attempts to create a coherent operatic experience
in which, as Adorno puts it, the senses "unite to create a totality, a unified and
guaranteed world of essences." This unity and cohesion runs the gamut from
the metaphysical "world of essences" all the way to the much more pedestrian
world of sense stimuli: in Wagner's totality the senses coincide rather than running alienated side by side—in everyday experience, on the other hand, "the
senses, which all have a different history, end up poles apart from each other, as
a consequence of the growing reification of reality as well as of the division of
labor."[3] Wagner's revolution of musical technique is thus inseparable from his
revolution of the architecture and technology of the opera house.

Since both distance and the kind of Gesamtkunstwerk it is adduced to support are on the one hand matters of compositional technique and on the other
heavily dependent on technological means of production, our discussion will
draw on two kinds of thinking about operatic distance and operatic sound.
When Schreker thinks of the operatic, he means the score, the text and their
integration; but Schreker's operas seem to understand that opera and integration go further, that they include the building and social codes that make a
performance possible.

FRANZ SCHREKER AND OPERATIC DISTANCE

What is at stake above all in these operatic "phantasmagoria" is the cancella-
tion of difference and distance. When the cursed sailor in *The Flying Dutchman* beholds Senta's image for the first time, he remarks that "as though from

the distance of long-ago ages this girl's image speaks to me."[4] Of course, as Carl Dahlhaus has remarked, the Dutchman's recognition of Senta (and her later recognition of him) in a way contains the entire opera in the shape of a distant image. He sees the woman who can release him from his curse, she the man whom she wants to save. All outward trappings of plot (the love triangle with Erik, most notably) serve only to inflate this double recognition to opera length. The distant image of Senta is actually identical with the opera, all plot mechanics, all appearances of development and characterization are mere window dressing—what appears to unfold in time as plot is in fact only a timeless, instantaneous image; what presents itself as a narrative to be followed, untangled, and responded to turns out to be distant—by the time events are in motion they are already in the rearview mirror.

Such deceptive distance and timelessness dominate not only Wagner's plots, but, according to Adorno, Wagner's music as well, where melody gives way to static harmony, development gives way to repetition and leitmotivic structure subordinates musical logic to narrative logic. In an essay on Schreker, Adorno claims "Schreker read out of Wagner the moment of phantasmagoria and made it total."[5] In looking for distance in Schreker's operas, one does not have to go to his libretti, or to his harmonies, however. The "distant sounds" that Schreker "reads out" of Wagner are often quite literal—sounds that appear unmoored from the stage action, that comment on it from metaphysical remove, or beckon its characters with otherworldly calls. This is a kind of phantasmagoric distance that Wagner's operas frequently traffic in—in Schreker its deployment becomes a central organizing principle.

This aesthetic principle is made most explicit in Wagner's *Parsifal*: "You see, my son, time here becomes space," Gurnemanz explains to young Parsifal as the two enter the grail castle.[6] It is, according to Adorno, Wagner's spectacle at its most phantasmagoric. Wagner's stage directions call for an "imperceptible" shift in setting, as the scenery gradually transforms from a forest knoll into a domed structure. Their walk is accompanied by the faraway "sound of trombones" and "approaching bell chimes." When at last Gurnemanz and Parsifal arrive in the grail hall, where "the only light emanates" from a "high-vaulted dome," the bells instead come from "high above the dome." As the grail knights file in, their solemn is soon joined by "younger male voices" that are audible "from the middle height of the hall,"[7] and eventually by "boys' voices" "from the highest point of the dome."[8] As ailing King Amfortas is brought in on his bier (as well as later when the grail is finally unveiled), the ritual onstage proceeds almost wordlessly—until "from the farthest background, from a arched niche sounds . . . , as though out of a grave, the voice" of old Titurel.

At least in Bayreuth, the only place where the *Bühnenweihfestspiel* was allowed to be performed (or at least staged) until 1914, the solemn action onstage
is almost wordless, while most of the scene's participants are offstage, invisible
and present only as distant sounds: the orchestra from its pit, the bells from
"above the dome," the boys' choir from the top of the dome, the young men
from the middle down and Titurel from below the stage. However, it is also
striking that Wagner provides an astonishing range of distances from which
sound can impinge on the stage. The stage directions almost unfurl a topography of the opera house, with a space "above" the dome, a space below the
stage, behind and before it, all of which seem to represent different physical or
spiritual topographies. What is more, it is difficult to determine whether any
one element of this geography corresponds to a real physical place, or whether
it represents an ideal one instead. Is there a bell tower above the dome? Are
angels physically present in the dome? The entire elaborate geography Wagner
lays out hovers between a representation of actual physical spatial relations and
a cosmological topography.

Of course, Lawrence Kramer has recently made the case that a "wandering
voice," that is, a voice disengaged from and mobile vis-à-vis any body onstage is
characteristic of opera as a form.[9] However, while homeless, offstage voices may
thus constitute opera's paradigm rather than any sort of exception, the role and
the ideology of that "wandering voice" is anything but invariant. To be sure,
there are offstage voices in opera since its origins, and the nineteenth century
delighted in them in general. Mozart's *Idomeneo*, Verdi's *Aida* and *Don Carlo*,
Offenbach's *Les Contes d'Offman* are but the most prominent examples. At the
same time, Adorno seems to suggests that there is something unique about
the deployment of "distant sounds" in German opera after Wagner and until
Schreker. That may be overstating the case, but comparison with *Idomeneo*
makes clear that, when the distant sounds came to invade the post-Wagnerian
stage, they did so with highly particular functions, and in dialogue with a new
(often erotic) ideology of the opera. Older operas like *Idomeneo* often turned to
offstage sounds to integrate into the stage action events or persons whose size,
scope, or appearance rendered their physical representation onstage less than
practical. After all, when the voice of Neptune intervenes in the eighth scene of
Idomeneo's third act, the voice's distance (designated simply as "La Voce" in
the score) reflects not so much the god's metaphysical distance from the action
onstage, but rather introduces another character into the drama that might be
otherwise a bit difficult to set apart from the other actors onstage.

The offstage voices of the fin-de-siècle, on the other hand, come not just
from another place, but another world altogether. They could not, with

whatever technology and whatever compositional inventiveness, be brought onto the stage. This metaphysical charge of the offstage space complicates the eroticism the offstage object is supposed to elicit—very rarely is an offstage voice or instrument a simple, straightforward erotic object, for instance an absent person, or a faraway locale (such as the clamor of the Burgundian court that wafts tauntingly over to the outcast Telramund and Ortrud in *Lohengrin*). It is, often enough, not a person at all and interacting with it is exceedingly difficult. And yet, this distancing strengthens rather than weakens the erotic desire solicited by the distance of the offstage sound.

This conjunction of factors informs much of the obsession with "distant sounds" in opera after Wagner: The stage action is in dialogue with a highly differentiated and specifically located set of offstage sounds, but this differentiation and specificity combine to create an uneasy ambiguity about the physicality of operatic space. Is the distance of a muffled trombone, of a boys' choir representative of actual, physical distance—is it simply a simulation of sound from the distance or does it represent a kind of transcendence? This raises the question what we are to make of opera's variegated "distances" and their sounds. How is orchestra-pit transcendence related to backstage transcendence, how is physical distance represented by an orchestra behind the audience different from physical distance represented by instruments behind the stage?

Distant orchestras (*Fernorchester*), distant choirs (*Fernchöre*), and individual, displaced instruments abound in German music around the turn of the century; as do musical instruments that leave the orchestra pit and participate in the opera's main action onstage. While distance effects are common to opera and orchestral music, they tend to predominate in narrative musical forms—be this an opera, a symphonic piece with an actual plot (for instance, Mahler's *Das klagende Lied*[10]), or simply program music (for instance, the second brass section of Richard Strauss's *Alpensymphonie*, op. 64). Like Wagner, Mahler and Strauss were quite specific where "distant" orchestras were to be located, and often provided for more than one distant location in the same score[11]—for instance in Mahler's Symphony no. 8, in which different instruments are "positioned in isolation" in the distance.[12] Mahler's symphonies put the full orchestra in a complicated dialogue with instrumental groups actually placed beyond the stage, orchestral instruments that play "as though from a distance," and groups of soloists.

Even given this prevalence, however, Schreker's use of distance effects is unusually sustained. What is more, Schreker's *Fernorchester*, writes Bekker, was "more than an accumulation of instrumental means," but rather "symbolizes the fateful intrusion of supernatural [*übersinnliche*] forces."[13] All of

Schreker's operas feature music, in other words, that makes sensible not feelings or interactions, but rather stand in for that which cannot be made sensible; usually, this supersensible is a "symbol" on the level of plot only—for the supersensible usually impinges on the plot as sound.[14] These are instances of distant orchestras and instruments, or diegetic musical pieces that not only feature in the plot, but in fact drive it—from a sounding grotto in *Die Gezeichneten*, the titular *Spielwerk* of *Das Spielwerk und die Prinzessin*, and of course the distant sound in *Der ferne Klang*.

At the same time, Schreker almost inevitably moves some of his operas' orchestra onto the stage, by including them in the opera's diegetic action. This is music that the opera's characters actually hear, to which they respond, and with which they interact. Especially in his earlier operas, Schreker delights in placing small musical ensembles, troubadours, and single musicians onstage. Schreker deploys these in order to enhance the realism of a scene, or the accuracy of the description of a particular setting or milieu—Schreker himself acknowledged explicitly that this was owed to "a kind of verismo."[15] Here, then, operatic distance is not a matter of otherworldly symbolism, but rather analogous to Roland Barthes's *reality effect*—it aims at immersion in the scene itself, rather than at something that transcends it. Distant sound in Schreker is not something that dissolves sets, characters and stage action into an all-enveloping music; instead, it becomes prop, character, and action in itself.

At other moments, Schreker instead turns the stage itself into a musical instrument of sorts, a producer of sound. In his *Memnon*, an abortive project from the 1910s, the stage is dominated by a colossus, which, at the opera's climax, begins to hum as the first rays of the sun hit it; *Die Orgel* (*The Organ*), later retitled *Der Singende Teufel* (*The Singing Devil*, 1924, 1927–28), is dominated by the titular organ commissioned by the abbot of a monastery—in the opera's climactic scene, as the monastery burns all around it, there emerge from the wreckage the otherworldly sounds of the organ in its dying wheeze. The sets themselves, in other words, are supposed to intervene into the music. Schreker's operas thus obsessively toy with questions of distance and immanence, geographic sounds and transcendent ones, sounds that are meant to enhance the realism of a scene, and sounds that are meant to make sensible the ineffable. Taken together, the kinds of geography unfurled by Schreker's distant and roving sounds map out the totality of the composer's competing influences—Wagnerian music drama, verismo and *Künstleroper* engage and entangle in Schreker's competing and differently valenced distances.

This entanglement is perhaps most clearly felt in Schreker's first great success, *Der ferne Klang*, a *Künstleroper* rife with the echoes of verismo and yet in many respects indebted to Wagnerian music drama. The opera opens as the young artist Fritz leaves his provincial town to become "an artist by the grace of God," embarking on a quest for the "distant sound" which is drowned out by his mundane surroundings. He leaves his girlfriend, Grete, behind, promising her that he will return with fame and riches. A mysterious old woman observes the scene. Grete's father, who can be heard drinking and gambling with his friends in a nearby tavern from offstage, returns to announce that he has lost Grete to the tavern's proprietor in a game of bowling. Grete refuses to assent to the deal, revealing that she is "engaged to another," and flees the scene. In an enchanted forest, she contemplates suicide, but a strange vision of sexual passion ("love and happiness all day") stays her hand. She falls asleep by the side of the lake that was to be her grave and is found by the old woman.

The second act takes place in a brothel in Venice, where gondoliers' songs and gypsy bands accompany the raucous goings-on. Grete, who now calls herself Greta, lives the life of a courtesan, though she is dissatisfied with her life and still longs for Fritz. A stranger appears: Fritz, who has been unable to find his "distant sound," and has spent years searching for the love he left behind. Just now, he explains, he has heard his sound and it has led him to Grete's island. The lovers recognize each other, but once Fritz realizes Grete has become a prostitute, he insults her and leaves. Desperate, Grete acquiesces to a liaison with one of her wealthy customers. The third act opens in a café in an unnamed city. Two friends of Grete's father from the first act discuss Fritz's opera (based on the events of his own life) now being performed at the Hoftheater: *The Harp*. Apparently, the premiere is going well. Suddenly, Grete enters: now a common whore, she is recognized by her father's friends. Together, they are told that *The Harp*'s premiere has turned into a scandal: apparently the last act has turned out disastrous. Moreover, we are told that Fritz is terminally ill. The friends, racked with guilt for their role in young Grete's downfall, agree to bring her to Fritz. There, the lovers are united, but Fritz dies in Grete's arms as the "distant sound" can be heard once more.

Its deployment of distance, as well as what we are supposed to look (or listen) for in that distance, make *Der ferne Klang* both a paradigm of fin-de-siècle "roving voices," and an interesting limit case. As is the case in virtually all of Schreker's operas, what beckons offstage comes to dominate the action onstage. At the same time, however, *Der ferne Klang*'s protagonist, Fritz, sets out to capture the elusive distant sound, to ultimately bring it from offstage onto the stage, and to turn it quite literally into opera. On the one hand *Der ferne Klang* represses the mechanisms (musical or mechanical) that produce operatic spectacle, but its main character is in the search of the titular "distant sound," a sound located offstage, behind the scenes. The opera obsesses over a space that its form represses. The disappearance of that space, the fact that the opera house beyond the stage could communicate otherworldly forces beyond the realm of human commerce, and that it could unfold such diverse geographies as the Venetian lagoon or the main square of a modern German metropolis (complete with opera house), depend not only on changes in musical technique, but mostly on changes surrounding operatic performance and technology.

THE SILENCING OF THE OPERA HOUSE

Adorno's invocation of the "distant sound" refers at once to certain compositional tendencies and to a cognitive problem. The "spatialization" of sound he ascribes to post-Wagnerian operas does not depend on advances in compositional technique alone, but more importantly on advances in acoustics, which allowed the opera house or concert hall to constitute itself as a counter-geography to the world outside. The court opera of the eighteenth and early nineteenth century had been open to the world outside, not least because it implicitly replicated it—the theater evoked the *theatrum mundi*, both presided over by the sovereign. Once the bourgeoisie began erecting opera houses as monuments to its own ascendancy (for instance, the somewhat counterintuitively named Vienna *Hofoper* on the *Ringstrasse*), opera's theatricality entered into a different relation with its outside. The world was neither replicated nor simply continued in the opera house, but rather transfigured into something separated absolutely from the quotidian, temples of the autonomy of art. Acoustics was the central technology in transforming opera into a separate world explicitly opposed to whatever was external to it.

An analysis of opera based on its technological features proceeds from the simple fact that opera in the later nineteenth century constituted not merely an aesthetic problem, but rather a cognitive one as well.[16] Questions of attention, of audibility, of illusion were as much a part of Wagner's project as the integration of librettist and composer. Wagner's project rested on two codependent transformations of operatic form: for one, the old, disaggregated practices had to be fused into one coherent whole, what Schreker called "the problematic element of the opera as artform"[17] had to be resolved; for another, however, such unification was possible only in a particular kind of opera house, and alternately certain transformations of the opera house made sense only in light of a concomitant change in "opera as artform." The technological side of these transformations center around the construction of an artistic and artificial geography and the concomitant elision of the actual geography of the opera house: What had previously been primarily a semiporous sphere of attraction and distraction (e.g., the Italian or French grand opera) was in Wagner's *Fest-spielhaus* rapidly transformed into a darkened, autarkic place of contemplation. The doors locked, the lights turned down, all chatter banished, the opera house of the turn of the century resembled earlier ones as much as a modern airliner resembles the deck of a nineteenth-century steamer.

The nineteenth-century opera house took to disciplining its audience. Spectacle made demands on its spectators, turned them into observers who were expected to surrender entirely to the spectacle.[18] As we saw in chapter 3, when Arthur Schopenhauer fulminates against women who ruin man's concert-going experience by "continuing their chatter" even "during the most beautiful passages of the greatest masterpieces,"[19] the masculine "masterpiece" requires absolute silence and devotion. The technological reforms of Wagner form only one component of this disciplining of the audience. Consider, for instance, Wagner's scathing caricature of an Italian opera house:

> In the opera house of Italy there gathered an audience which passed its evenings in amusement; part of this amusement was formed by the music sung upon the stage, to which one listened from time to time in pauses of the conversation; during the conversation and visits paid from box to box the music still went on, with the same office one assigns to table music at grand dinners, namely to encourage by its noise the otherwise timid talk.[20]

The contrast to the (modern, Wagnerian) opera house is obvious: The audience, in its pitch-dark space, is being discouraged from any communication, even from looking at each other, except for occasional disciplinary frowns at accidental or thoughtless emissions of sound. The music, on the other hand, with its source hidden from view, becomes acoustically dominant, demanding constant, unremitting attention, visual or auditory.

As Crary points out, "Wagner completely eliminated the lateral views of older theater design to achieve a frontal engagement with the stage for every spectator,"[21] a development roughly analogous to the passage from a carnival-esque "cinema of attractions"[22] to the modern multiplex. What disappears in the pitch-dark space is primarily the fellow listener or viewer: Lateral views expose a scene comprised of spectacle and spectator, direct views leave the individual audience member in quasi-mystical solitary communion with the operatic event. The audience and their response are not part of a forming *sensus communis*, but rather distractions that a successful and discriminating viewer can abstract from his or her authentic experience of the opera itself.

Similarly, the operatic model of spontaneous applause and acclamations during a performance became increasingly frowned upon—most famously in the case of *Parsifal*. Fearing a disruption of the opera's somber mood, Wagner had decreed that no curtain calls would be taken between *Parsifal's* individual acts. Bayreuth audiences, confused by the master's instructions, thought they were not supposed to clap at all during the *Bühnenweihfestspiel*. Martin Gregor-Dellin reports a famous incident in which Wagner himself, registering his admiration for the flower maidens in the opera's second act, was angrily silenced by his own audience.[23] While Gustav Mahler fought most valiantly against bought applause (the *claque*) at the *Hofoper*, an editorial in the *Österreichische Volkszeitung* at beginning of his tenure there made clear that the *claqueur* was only the tip of the iceberg: Rather than chasing only the "hired clapper" from the opera house, the same should be done to "every theatergoer who gives loud expression to his delight without respect for the artistic quality of the performance," be this "a *tapageur* or clapper, a *rieur* or laugher, a *pleureur* or weeper, an encore caller or as a *chatouilleur* who tries to sweet-talk the audience."[24]

All of these types became, if not extinct, then at least endangered species by the end of the nineteenth century. It was this change in the operatic ecosystem that enabled the complex syntax of distance employed by Wagner, Strauss, and Schreker, and it was this change that gave this syntax its meaning. Of course it would be just as misguided to read Schreker's or Wagner's project in purely technological terms as it would be to reduce it to musical innovation alone. Investigating this connection requires constructing a dialogue between Walter Benjamin and Theodor Adorno, in particular of their respective deployments of the term "phantasmagoria." In Wagner, the project of a new kind of compositional practice and a new kind of theatrical architecture were two sides of the same coin. Wagner decided that traditional opera houses were simply inadequate to the revolution in operatic composition he envisioned, "that works whose originality alone already requires absolute correctness of presentation [*Aufführung*] in order to have the correct impression on their audience, cannot be left to this kind of theater."[25]

Given this twin origin of the Wagnerian project, its most salient feature, namely "phantasmagoria," asserts itself in the kind of "presentation" as well as the "kind of theater" Wagner envisioned. "Phantasmagoria" is the aesthetic equivalent of what Marx called the fetish character of the commodity: the tendency to regard what human hands have wrought in labor as something "naturally," perhaps even metaphysically, given. But what exactly it is that human hands have wrought and what it is that phantasmagoria obscures, was up to some debate among those that employed the term. When Theodor Adorno speaks of "phantasmagoria," he tends to mean that the compositional artifice inevitably associated with musical (let alone operatic) production is repressed in favor of a sound that wears the garb of the given, manna from heaven, like the boys' choir in *Parsifal*. For him, this repression asserts itself in Wagner's dissimulation of musical logic and development—rather than recognizable instruments combining in recognizable ways to present and develop recognizable motifs, Wagner opens his *Ring* with static harmonies indebted to narrative rather than musical logic, which abjure the instruments that produce them. The overall effect, according to Adorno, is a repression of historical development, modernity, and modern alienation. Coherent, metaphysical meaning is imparted, as though it were unproblematically and straightforwardly available in modernity.

When Walter Benjamin deploys the term, what counts as the means of (musical) production differs from Adorno's usage. Benjamin's means of production do not concern what composers, librettists, or conductors do, but rather something that architects, designers, stagehands, light technicians, and sound technicians conspire in. Accordingly, where Adorno's primary instance of phantasmagoric production is opera, Benjamin's examples (catalogued in the monumental convolutes of the *Arcades Project*) are drawn from modern mass culture and do not involve opera—world exhibitions, shopping arcades, train stations, and panoramas. And rather than providing a unified experience of the artwork, his phantasmagorias present a unified and static *sensory* experience, aesthetic in the sense of the eighteenth century rather than the modern one. But since opera after Bayreuth became an "aesthetic" problem in both senses—a cognitive project as well as one of aesthetic form. What then does a phantasmagoric experience of the opera house look like in this second, Benjaminian sense of the word?

THE DIALECTIC OF THE DOME

The silencing of the opera house, its emphasis on a new (and particularly modern) kind of sensory operatic experience thus moves our discussion of the concept closer to Benjamin's understanding of what constitutes "phantasmagoria." Benjamin follows Marx in reading phantasmagoria as fetishes that divest a world of commodities of its historical contingency and transfigure it into something universal, natural, inevitable.[26] But the suppression of labor in the fetish also translates into an elision of the world of industry in favor of *Feerien* (fairytales), preserved seemingly isolated from the industrializing world that made them possible in the first place. In a modern world characterized by fragmentation and alienation, where a unified experience is virtually impossible, phantasmagorias artificially recreate a sensory totality that suggests a level of (social, metaphysical and cognitive) cohesion that no longer exists in reality. They create, as Susan Buck-Morss has described it, "a total environment . . . that functioned as a protective shield for the senses" through the "manipulation of the synaesthetic system by control of environmental stimuli."[27] This system reintegrates sensory experiences that have become subject to shock, dispersal, and displacement "under conditions of modernity."

Benjamin never ventured too far into the musical realm with his technological concept of phantasmagoria. For him, this new kind of experience was primarily visual, and his catalogue of phantasmagorias of the nineteenth century concerns most often phenomena in which "dream images" suggest a false totality of *vision*. But Adorno picks up on Benjamin's use of the concept in his 1958 essay "Die Naturgeschichte des Theaters" ("The Natural History of the Theatre"). There, Adorno interrogates what is specifically modern within the (technological-architectural) place of performance by juxtaposing it with the atavistic ritual sublimated within it. He doesn't call the process he describes "phantasmagoria" reserving that term for "compositional technique," and instead refers to it as the "dialectic of the dome."[28]

The "dialectic of the dome" refers to the most material aspects of production: it connects the performative aspect of phantasmagoria to the technological conditions of its performance.[29] Benjamin, in his radio text on the "Theater Fire of Canton," discusses the theater as "not the pieces, that are performed [in the theater], or the actors . . . , but rather the audience and the space itself"[30]—it is precisely this sense of theater that the dialectic of the dome interrogates. Adorno's approach to this dialectic is to read production back into the aesthetic object—something he had done with respect to music in *In Search of Wagner* already. But "Die Naturgeschichte des Theaters" no longer conceives of production in terms of color and sonority, but rather attempts to describe, in a rather Benjaminian way, how architecture and acoustics conspire to produce a particular kind of synesthetic experience. I take this "dialectic of the dome" to stand metonymically for an entire range of applications that come to dominate the post-Wagnerian opera house. The dialectic of the dome inheres in the form of the opera house, but it is only the opera, the *performance*, that releases it.

What makes an opera house phantasmagoric in this sense? Firstly, of course, an opera house depends on shielding its audience from anything lying beyond the experience of the opera—and that anything, as both Benjamin and Adorno argue, is primarily the social world. The opera (like the autonomous artwork) is supposed to lie beyond the social and economic sphere—even in the very straightforward sense that any opera house worth the price of admission banishes the noise of the street and the bustle of the masses. But why is this experience that the opera house artificially creates "synesthetic"? Benjamin argues that any fully integrated perception of the human social world is necessarily shattered in the fractured conditions of technological and social modernity. We experience many things happening (often enough we hear one thing, but are forced to smell or see ten others), but paradoxically we are no longer capable of what Dewey would call "having an experience."[31] Our sensorium is as dispersed as the life world to which it is forced to attend.

Arthur Schopenhauer suggested that the shocks of modern life—noise and interruption—prevent the unification of the senses in what he calls "spirit."[32] Noise, on Schopenhauer's account, prevents the integration of sense data onto one point (an object), and from uniting that sense data in one point (a unified subject).[33] It is here that the connection between Benjamin's cognitive aesthetics of shock on the one hand, and the aesthetic project of the Gesamtkunstwerk on the other, becomes clear. Phantasmagorias technologically will into existence an artificial totality for a subject "for which the shock experience [*Erlebnis*] has become the norm,"[34] as Benjamin puts it; similarly, Wagner, for Adorno, wills into existence a total work of art unconcerned with the social preconditions of its theatrical production and the distractions of the social world outside. The meaningful and unified experiences increasingly impossible outside the opera house are artistically and artificially reinstated by the musical performance inside. Outside, we are "cheated out of experience,"[35] inside we are rewarded with an experience that is no longer really possible, but exists only as illusion.[36]

The dialectic inherent in the dome of an opera house lies in its double function as "dividing wall and reflector in one."[37] Neither ancient amphitheaters nor Shakespeare's Globe had domes; thus the ritual from which drama of all sorts descends could rise to the heavens (for which, as religious ritual, it was ultimately intended). The dome is, by its very existence, evidence of and index for the disappearance of this totality of sense and meaning. The modern spectators are fragmented, severed from any total sense or sense perception of their world. The dome is also, however, a "reflector." The sounds erstwhile destined for heaven do not go to waste today; instead they are reflected back toward us, the audience. They face us as a technologically produced nature—*our* sounds (the sound humans create) are as greedily consumed as the world outside is drowned out. What is more, the sound that reflects at us may even seem to us to come from heaven anyway—at which point we have mistaken human work, alienated by human means, for a hint of the divine. In fact, one prime factor in the vaunted acoustics of the Bayreuth *Festspielhaus* was the audience itself—the Bayreuth sound "from nowhere" could only be accomplished once the listeners' bodies had in some sense become part of the structure, the technology.[38] As a Bayreuth audience, we are among the very means of production the phantasmagoria hides from us.

One can see how this concept lends itself to the late Wagner's Christian mysticism—anyone who has seen a performance of *Parsifal* in which a light show and an invisible choir accompany the revelation of the grail has been witness to this technological, theatrical manna. Not surprisingly, too, the "dividing wall and reflector" is, in the nineteenth century as today, often adorned with a technological firmament, usually in the shape of a giant chandelier. Adorno's most striking example for this transposition of myth into the technology is nothing other than applause.[39] Applause, he asserts, obviously once had ritual function—maybe a call out for the Gods to honor someone, or, perhaps more sinister, a call for a sacrifice. Today applause comes back at us roaring in all its mythic force, yet disconnected from anything whole. What we experience is nothing but uproarious agreement with each other, a brief identity not with the cosmos but with a (select) crowd of our fellow men.

The opera house functions as what Adorno thematized throughout his philosophy as "identity," which Frederic Jameson has aptly characterized as "repetition as such, the return of sameness over and over again, . . . that is to say, neurosis."[40] The dome of the opera house stymies all forms of openness: firstly human openness to difference as present outside the opera house. It stymies secondly cognitive openness to any difference within the opera house, since it "collects" the sounds we are required to hear and subdues the manifold of buzzes and tingles into an experience. And thirdly it undercuts any awareness or differentiation of who is doing what (since any such awareness may eclipse the self-sufficiency of the hall) and gives us the illusion that what people have produced comes like manna from heaven. It blinds humans to the tautological claustrophobia of their "second" (cultural) nature, and to the very real differences and injustices that persist within it.

All of this, however, could just as well be said of any kind of roof over a theater or an opera house. Adorno's "dialectic of the dome" goes beyond theorizing the roof of the concert hall as "dividing wall and reflector in one," to consider also the specific construction of the dome, as man-made and technological. Identity requires work, and that work consists not merely of passively obviating but rather of actively bundling the elements of the phantasmagoria. The dome has been *made* to actively bundle: it functions as shock preventer and shock conductor, both in the sense of some*thing* passing something else along and in the sense of some*one* conducting a performance.

How can a dome do both? It is the job of the modern opera house to keep certain stimuli from entering the sensory field of each audience member and to amplify others. One might argue that a wall or a well-placed window may perform a similar task, and that is where the second sense of "conductor" comes in: The modern opera house, far from swallowing some sounds and allowing others to pass, is in fact actively (even uncannily) engaged in styling, modulating, and inflecting the sensory input of its audience. It carefully determines which stimuli are to reach the senses, when they are to do so and from where. It is only through this careful management of stimuli that the synesthetic can enter modern experience—only through active manipulation, in other words, can the senses be brought into congruence. For instance, the Bayreuth phantasmagoria is not just sonic and visual, not simply a matter of acoustics and hidden orchestra—it has been said that if you have the right seat at Bayreuth, you do not *hear* the first few bars of *Das Rheingold*, but you feel them as they travel up your legs. Both dome and phantasmagoria gather and order sensory data to suggest a coherent whole rather than a buzzing confusion. But because a real synesthetic experience is rarely possible "under conditions of modernity," as Adorno puts it,[41] the phantasmagoria produces a synesthetic experience technologically. It composes space, time, and sound in order to delude the spectators' sensorium into experiencing modernity whole, when in fact it isn't. Phantasmagoria has the purpose of shielding the subject from things that might unsettle a (false) unity of experience through newness, disruption, shock.

Since they provide a total experience in a fragmented world, phantasmagorias are as marked by what they leave out as by what they keep in. Their effect lies in the management of "shocks," as Walter Benjamin describes in his book on Baudelaire.[42] We are adapted to shocks by being systematically exposed to them in a technologically simulated environment. It is not so much that the phantasmagoric techno-totality is supposed to drown out the noise of traffic and people; it is ultimately supposed to attune me to them. After all, it doesn't combat noise by silence, but with more carefully structured noise. Not only

do phantasmagorias shut me off from reality, then, but they gradually and artfully reconcile me to reality, in spite of my very real alienation from it. This is
precisely how a modern opera house works: its greatest work goes into shut-
ting out the world beyond the "magic circle" of stage and audience; within the
space of silence thus created, the modern opera can lay out a new geography, an
anesthetic one. The conductor Bruno Walter relates the following story about
Gustav Mahler: On a visit, Walter expressed admiration of an alpine panorama,
to which the composer replied that there was no need to do so, since "I've
composed all this away already."[43] Composing means simulating and erasing
that which might lie behind the simulation. The anesthetic, particularly in the
case of Wagner, can be about as noisy as a helicopter attack on a Vietnamese
village, but it provides a composed assault as art or as entertainment, which
prepares the audience for the world outside, both because it hardens them to
it (makes them ready for it) and because it leads them to ignore it.

Of course, this cognitive autarky of the concert hall somewhat paradoxically
enables the unfolding of what Adorno elsewhere calls "symphonic space."[44]
Because the membrane between the concert hall on the one hand and the foyer,
the coat checks, in short, the building shell itself, have been rendered imperme-
able, music can now undertake to simulate distance within the confines of the
concert hall. Adorno claims that the New German school is guided by the idea
of a "distant sound," by which he means something very much like phantasmagoria, in which "music becomes static and spatialized."[45] Even on a purely
empirical level, the question of distance enters into the compositional, as well
as the technological, equation through Wagner. In Mahler's symphonies, for
instance, horns, trumpets, and other instruments routinely chime in from offstage, for instance the distant call of the *postillon*'s horn in the Scherzo of the
Third Symphony. The horn can be heard from the distance and launches into
a duet with the horns onstage; Adorno himself comments that this dialogue
"reconciles the unreconcilable [*versöhnt . . . das Unversöhnte*]"[46]—in other
words that it creates precisely some kind of falsely coherent (phantasmagoric)
space. Mahler's posthorn dialogue annihilates (real) space, only then to unfold
its own simulated space. Operatic eroticism becomes one of the few ways of
detecting the real space behind the simulated one.

FRITZ'S DISTANT SOUNDS: THE TOPOGRAPHIES OF *DER FERNE KLANG*

The simulated space within the silence opera house is of course most readily problematized in narrative forms. What holds true in Leroux's *Phantom*

of the Opera holds doubly in the case of opera: the tendency to problematize the space that both technologically produces the opera and is technologically repressed by the Gesamtkunstwerk asserts itself as a drive that propels the narrative beyond the confines of the stage. In many operas of the immediate Wagnerian aftermath, the narrative either explicitly thematizes the stage, the backstage area, or even the balconies of the opera house. It is above all Schreker's operas that make the repressed spaces of the opera house a target for erotic longing.[47] When *Der ferne Klang*, the opera Adorno turned to when it came to giving the very phenomenon a name, elides the real geography of the opera house and establishes a new, simulated geography, it does so to rather unique aesthetic ends.

Considering topography within *Der Ferne Klang* means focusing on aspects of the opera that Adorno himself seems to have been less interested in: When he charged Schreker with the phantasmagoric annihilation of specificity, Adorno is thinking of the overture, the various narrative arias, Grete's suicide attempt in the forest, and Fritz's death scene. The phantasmagoric creation of artificial specificity on the other hand, the simulated geography performed by the technological apparatus of stage and orchestra, is by contrast visible in several dynamic juxtapositions throughout the opera, often featuring diegetic music or "naturalistic" musical effects. All of them not only lay out a new totality across and beyond the stage, but do so with unsettling social undertones.

The first one of these occurs in act 1, scene 3: The stage is occupied by Grete's home, but from the distance we can hear the clamor of the seedy bar, where, unbeknownst to her, Grete's fate hangs in the balance. In scanning that distance, Grete notices the face of the witch ("die Alte") who is to discover her in the forest at the end of the first act; in other words, looking at one unwitting determinant of her fate (her father and his friends gambling for her), Grete sees an actual determinant of her fate—the old woman. At this point, the opera stages the *méprise* between Grete and her mother: "Who is that woman over there?" Grete asks, but her mother misunderstands her and replies: "Of course he is over there." The distant sound of the bar flares up as though in response—the bar, as Grete's mother explains, is where the family money now resides, with "the rogue, the scoundrel." The decisions for these women are made elsewhere, and fate rules over them by proxy—only insofar as Grete's father has given in to his addiction to game and drink does fate actually have control over them. It is the social relations of the marketplace from which they are excluded that lord over them like a force of nature—but the shape this supposed force of fate or nature actually takes is that of a bunch of men drinking. While topography is very clearly laid out, then, it is activated by the opera in highly contradictory ways—what distance figures for is anything but clear, but it is patently caught up in social difference, social flow, social position.

A second instance of "simulated geography" occurs in the opening of act 2. Here, Schreker's instructions make the scene's geographic aspirations explicit: "The following scenes should present a mélange of the different sounds drifting onto the stage (voices from above, gypsy music, gondola music, the count's serenade) in such a way that the listener gets as realistic an impression of the milieu as possible, and almost feels as though he was himself in the middle of the action." Although, much as in the more tonal or color-oriented segments of the opera, Schreker insists on a mixture (Adorno calls this phenomenon Schreker's "mixed drinks" and "elixirs"[48]), the mixture does not perform the work of *disorientation*, of pure libidinal suspension, but rather that of *orientation* or interpellation. In other words, the scene's different actors call out to the audience to place them vis-à-vis the goings-on, to make quite clear just where they are.

That this is done in service to "fidelity to the milieu" seems to highlight Schreker's debt to naturalism and verismo—however, the instructions go a lot further when they seem to insist that only by positioning the audience (which, note, is male-defined) as though they were themselves part of the scene, it can give the audience a "realistic impression" of the "milieu" (i.e., the social topography). The scene will not allow spectatorship from a safe and separate distance, implicating the spectator in the same mirror complexes "he" has been so comfortably left out of in the opera's opening scene; adding the fact that act 2 transpires within the confines of a whorehouse, this seems to implicate the viewer in the same "libidinal economy" as the events viewed. Phantasmagoria here tends toward the transcendence of its anesthetic function and toward an implication of the consumer in the stage economy.

The third instance of this kind of simulation occurs during the *Zwischenspiel* and in act 3, scene 9. Fritz's opera *Die Harfe* has turned out an unmitigated disaster; the composer has withdrawn into his study. Outside the study, which Schreker describes very carefully, birds are singing (indicated in the score as well), and while there is, in keeping with Adorno's point, no identifiable quality to these voices, they nevertheless create an overall impression. Most interestingly, Schreker's notes do identify the bird voices individually ("Soliste, Nachtigall, Amsel, Fink, Lerche . . ."), as well as the exact interior of Fritz's study, which as goes so far as to allow guesses as to how well-off Fritz is at this stage in his career ("vornehm, einfach"). The most telling detail, however, is the painting that hangs above the grand piano: Arnold Böcklin's *Der Eremit* is on display ("clearly visible"), a painting depicting a hermit playing his violin for a group of angels. While the clear layout of inside and outside (and the "distant sound" of the birds) is another example for the topographies I have been identifying, I would like to focus on Böcklin's painting: We find here, within the stage setting, a "framed framer"—while it may seem as though Fritz the bourgeois artist has acquired Böcklin's image of unalienated art, the very question of distance and of "here-now-ness" (the hermit faces a wall without any sign of anxiety) seems to reverse that order. The Böcklin painting frames the opera by providing the very distance Fritz desires, but which the painting's subject, the hermit himself, does not seem to desire. Fritz's world makes obsessive reference to distance, whereas that distanced painting seems to rest in itself without surrendering any of its life.

We see then in all three examples of "simulated geography" how spatial distance, in essence a position of difference, is co-opted in the very idea of the opera. The idea of utopian difference is reinscribed into spatial difference; the distant sound is of course a utopian symbol, but it is a spatialized one. It evokes *Ferne* (distance) only insofar as we can't reach it (except in death, a point to which I will return) and insofar as the bustle of the world distracts us from it. If we were to perform *Der Ferne Klang* under open air, we would probably not hear the sound at all—the opera, as we have said, depends on its very theme for the hermetic sealedness that modern technology provides. If we were not in an opera house, we would not hear the distant sound and we might assume Fritz is simply delusional. Correspondingly, however, Fritz *can't* hear the distant sound—he can't hear the distance, because of what is going on onstage. As he discloses in the opening:

> A lofty goal is before my eyes,
> But I must be free to achieve it—free!
> For I can find no rest for happiness and enjoyment,
> No rest for love and bliss—
> Till I find it and hold it,
> The mysterious, otherworldly sound,
> Which wafts over towards me.

There are two ways of reading Fritz's description of the here and the distant: On the one hand, we can assume that he will return (as he himself promises) to perform his duties in society (especially vis-à-vis Grete) once he has found his distant sound. As becomes evident toward the end, that is never actually possible—following the distant sound is rather a different beast altogether: Fritz leaves society because he cannot find peace, love, *Seligkeit* (bliss, salvation) and quests for the purely aesthetic experience of the "distant sound," even if it means his death. In fact, Fritz has much to complain about when it comes to society: the arias, the many songs and marches, which make their ways across the stage in the course of the opera (including his own!), combine to make it impossible for him to hear his distant sound.

Fritz's quest mirrors the one that has led the audience to the opera in the first place: To get away from the "socialized world" (Adorno's term) and to the "five o'clock world" (not Adorno's term) of aesthetic experience. To leave behind the noise and discontinuity of everyday experience and find the wholly different offstage. And yet, the fulfillment of this desire is always a return into the womb (for the opera-going public as well as for Fritz); it is death. The wish for the distant sound is nothing but the death drive. It is the movement away from the complexities of the world and into a unified artistic production. It appears that Schreker, who understood this drive quite well, interrogates and indicts it in *Der ferne Klang*, and finally offers something of an antidote to operatic phantasmagoria.

DISTANCE AND EROS

"From the distance, sweet sounds exhort me to hold you in my arms in close embrace."[49]

WAGNER, *Tannhäuser*

Gaston Leroux's classic *Phantom of the Opera* appeared in installments in 1910, at a time when the repression of the actual physical topography of the opera house had proceeded to such a point that it could haunt the operagoer as though from a parallel dimension. Leroux's Christine Daaés, much like Schreker's Fritz, is listening for a distant sound, that of the Angel of Music her dying father told her about when she was still a child. When a mysterious voice (identified simply as "the Voice" at first) starts to beckon her from the viscera of the building itself, she assumes that it is this Angel of Music that is speaking to her, and she sets about capturing not the origin of the Voice (the phantom), but its beautiful distant sound. In a bravura performance at an opera gala, Christine succeeds precisely because she has taken voice lessons from the Voice, has managed to bring the offstage distant sound onto the stage— and by embodying the otherwise disembodied genius loci (or *phantom loci*), she becomes a star. However, the condition of possibility for the phantom's seeming disembodiment, the Voice's ethereal existence as seemingly distant sound turns out to be architectural: Erik (a.k.a. the phantom) was one of the planners involved in the construction of the Opéra Garnier and was able to construct a secret maze of tunnels and trapdoors within the building worthy of Rube Goldberg.

Christine's erotic-nostalgic attachment to the Angel of Music whom she believes to live in the metaphysical offstage space, though he in truth occupies the physical innards of the actual building, points to a central factor that serves to distinguish the distant sounds of the German fin-de-siècle from the unmoored voices of earlier eras: In *Idomeneo*, for instance, the distant sound was that of a god, a *deus ex machina*, one character among many. In Wagner and especially after him, distant sounds focus erotic desire on something technological and depersonalized—very rarely do these distant sounds originate from clear and individual sources, nor are those sources usually offered up as straightforward potential object of desire. Rather, technology disperses both object and the desire that may attach to that object. This may have to do with the introduction of and fascination with phonographic technology—a technology that could elicit emotional reactions, amorous attachment, sensual fixation vis-à-vis an object that was not, or no longer, really there. The singer's body was available through the voice, but not present as such.

In 1922, Paul Bekker wrote an essay entitled "Klang und Eros," which he subtitled "Brief in die Ferne." Indeed, the essay is addressed to "a dear friend," who dwells in a "unknown yet familiar distance." "I do not know your name," Bekker writes, "but I firmly believe that you exist out there somewhere." Why would an essay on "sound and eros" be written as a letter to an unknown person in the distance? The answer has to do with the interaction of distance and sound: Sound is erotic because of the way it goes forth into the distance, a distance of which we don't know where it is but the existence of which we nevertheless have to count on. Just as Bekker's letter, or any letter, leaves the subject for an uncanny sphere of potential proliferation, interception, and promiscuity, so sound always directs itself toward an open list of recipients, namely whoever happens to be within earshot.

It is precisely this sonic promiscuity that the phantasmagoric "distant sound" seems to lack. The phantasmagoric opera house not only quite carefully determines who is in earshot, but controls obsessively where and how the distant sound meets its listeners. A letter into an uncertain distance this sound is not. Rather, under the regiment of the new acoustics every listener should feel beckoned and invited. Moreover, Bekker's distant sound is emphatically erotic: "From afar the song of a woman's voice drifts over. A strange, heavy perfume issues from it. Where does [the perfume] come from? Not from the mere charm of her melody, for if I repeat it for myself, its unique magic evaporates. Nor does her sound as a physical phenomenon explain the effect, since when replayed on the violin the impression is a different one yet." Bekker's answer is, "What sounds here is sex [*das Geschlecht*], we are in the immediate sphere of influence of human eros." Bekker here anticipates what Roland Barthes would later term the "grain of the voice": In the voice a human body expresses itself, the occult qualities of the former issue from the organs, muscles, sinews of the latter.

The "grain of the voice" is entirely opposed to Fritz's "ferne Klang," and the same goes for the vast majority of the distant sounds of the fin-de-siècle. Glockenspiels, horns, bases, boys' choirs—what drifts onto the stage from the pseudogeographic distance is almost invariably something disembodied, ethereal, never something as "grainy" as Bekker's female voice. Since Schreker follows Wagner's use of tone color, if anything heightening Wagner's tendency to "not tolerate the sticking out of any particular instrument,"[50] his "mixed drinks"[51] make it time and again impossible to say for certain which instrument it is exactly that sounds from behind the stage. Bekker says the violin cannot replay what the distant voice sings without changing it; in the distant sound, the opera as much as the phenomenon, on the one hand, and violin and voice on the other, tend to become indistinguishable.

And yet, the obsession with which Fritz pursues his distant sound is clearly erotic; however, it seems to be a different kind of eroticism. The erotic charge that Bekker claims for the female voice drifting in from afar derives from the body that produced the sound. This is what the phantasmagoric distant sound makes impossible. Since it has to deny that any body produced it, the eroticism that comes to attach to it does not aim for a body, but rather a disembodiment. Or, more exactly, behind the dialogue with the technology in a technologically produced distance lies nothing other than the desire for disembodiment. Fritz's search for the *Ferne Klang* is, as Schreker makes perfectly clear, nothing other than the "oceanic" feeling, an ideation of "limitlessness and of a bond with the universe,"[52] or perhaps better the death drive described by Freud, which always works toward "a reinstatement of an earlier situation," and which ultimately strives for a return into the womb, into an inanimate state.[53] Just as the child in Benjamin's *Berlin Childhood around 1900* which, while playing hide and seek, becomes "the wooden idol of the temple, whose four pillars are the chiseled legs" of the dining room table, the desire for the distant sound is a drive toward the inorganic, toward becoming inorganic. Ironically, then, the repressed theatrical geography behind the scenes reemerges as the covert object of the desire for the "distant sound."

The sense that to respond adequately to the demands of the modern "soundscape" may require becoming more like a physical object was a widespread one around the turn of the century, as Friedrich Kittler has suggested for media in general. Thus, the same was true for the carefully secluded technological environments in which modern dissonance was kept carefully managed. After all, the idea of modern acoustics could easily be understood as teaching the physical environment to become a better listener, so as to offset natural deficiencies of the human sensorium and attention span. The preternatural attention, concentration, and discrimination required by opera may in turn place a demand on the human subject to leave behind its limited sensorium, to push its sensorium past the point of what is humanly possible. The idea that both the inanimate performance space and the human listener could be taught to attend better to sound, and that the former might teach the latter to do so, was explored by famed Austrian architectural critic Adolf Loos.

In 1912, Loos was asked to write in defense of the Bösendorfersaal, a former riding school attached to the Palais Lichtenstein on Vienna's Herrengasse. Loos agreed, however, as he cautioned, not for "reasons of piety"—giants like Bruckner had seen some of their most famous work premiere at the Bösendorfersaal—but rather for "reasons of acoustics." A surprising reason, since, as Loos himself concedes, the Bösendorfersaal is not known for being ideally laid out; its design was faulted when it was first opened—no one, he claims, would build a Bösendorfersaal again in 1912. What mystery, then, accounts for the famed acoustics of this infelicitous space?

> Have our ears changed? No, the material the hall is made of has changed. For forty years, the material has consistently absorbed great music, and it was varnished [*imprägniert*] with the sounds [*klängen*] of our symphonists and the voices of our singers. These are mysterious transformations on a molecular level, such as have hitherto only been observed in the wood of the violin.[54]

Operatic architecture is no invariant, its acoustics cannot be studied scientifically, as Loos's own era had begun to do. Instead the sound it is bathed and lathered in all day, during rehearsals, and sprinkled with on performance nights transforms the physical space "on a molecular level." Just as Leroux's phantom allows the opera house and the soloist Christine to enter into a dialogue, so

Loos proposes that each time a pianist strikes a key in the Bösendorfersaal, the sound activates "the sounds [*töne*] of Liszt and Meschaert," which dwells in the halls wood, plaster, and stone.

If the Bösendorfersaal sounds better because it has been awash in beautiful and artful sound, it is capable of education much like a human ear. In a 1913 piece on "Die kranken Ohren Beethovens" ("Beethoven's Sick Ears"), he describes the human ear quite analogously: At the turn of the nineteenth century "the bourgeoisie" ridiculed Beethoven, "for, they said, unfortunately the man has sick ears. He hits on the most terrible dissonances."[55] But in the one hundred years since, our ears have become accustomed to those seeming dissonances—"they have all become sick. They all have Beethoven's sick ears." One hundred years of music has transformed "all anatomic details, all the ossicles, canals, eardrums and tubes" are transformed into those "sick" ones of Beethoven. The very architecture of the human ear can be transformed by a century of Beethoven. For Loos, the *Klang* of the opera house is a physical force; neither the architecture of the concert hall nor the human ear are acoustic invariants, both can be changed and deformed in their very physical constitution.

This also means that ear and concert hall become ever more similar: the ear can be bent and sanded like a piece of material; the hall not only hears the music that is played in it and even responds to the music's quality. On the other hand, the human being becomes an acoustic factor: As Cosima Wagner notes in her diary, the vaunted Bayreuth acoustics depend on the presence of an audience, their bodies absorbing and thus directing sound. In Loos, the material of the concert hall becomes a listener; in Wagner the listener becomes material. The human organ and the concert hall become identical. Like the *Arcades Project*'s detective, or the child "enclosed in the world of matter," while playing hide and seek, the listener sidles up to the material to the point of mimicry. The operagoer, like the playing child, is a fetishist and an animist, willing to bring to life dead matter and to reduce living flesh to an inorganic state.

Moreover, however, Loos's theory of the transformative power of *Klang* is subtended by its own fantasy of erotic entanglement of near and far, organic and inorganic. When it comes to describe what exactly *Klang* does with the objects it transforms, the German text is much less innocent in its choice of words than the English translation makes it sound. *Imprägnieren* means to cover something with a protective coat, but the process Loos describes places the word's meaning much closer to its etymology and its English cognate. For the "good music" the Bösendorffersaal has played host to does not so much coat the hall's surfaces, but instead penetrates its very substance and transforms its very molecular structure. A forming agent invades the dumb material and transforms it; the quality of the resulting new object depends not on the material so formed, but on the quality of the forming agent. This of course was the image of fertilization and gestation from Aristotle to the Romantics. Loos, fascinated with questions of generativity and degeneration, here propagates something like a eugenic theory of the concert hall.

For it is organic transformation that creates acoustically receptive space in either the opera house or the human cranium; any attempt to contrive such acoustics out of thin air is doomed to be unsuccessful—without imbrication of *Klang* and matter, it is undialogical, asexual, and ultimately barren. What motivates Loos's infamous indictment of the "ornament as crime" is not, as is often thought, a wholesale rejection of the ornamental element of art. Rather, ornament that has grown or become acquired by custom escapes Loos's ire, while invented, haphazard ornamentaion draws his criticism. The *Imprägnieren* of the Bösendorffersaal is precisely such subcutaneous emendation; and the attempt to rebuild the hall to reproduce its sound exactly is doomed to failure in the same way that a Roman pillar, reproduced in plaster on a *Ringstrasse* palace can only be gaudy and "criminal." The erotic-generative element in the *Imprägnieren* of the concert hall thus accounts for the good sound of the Bösendorfersaal—as in Bekker, authentic sound is sound in which the erotic expresses itself.

MUSIC FROM THE OUTSIDE

While, as Adorno has shown, the fascination with death is part and parcel of phantasmagoria, *Der ferne Klang* hesitates before embracing typical fin-de-siècle infatuation with death. After all, the shape Fritz's death actually takes seems far from mystifying. First, the distant sounds as musical motif makes its first full appearance (illustrating the equation of the distant sound and death), but then dies along with Fritz (rather than intensifying with his death, thus seemingly undoing the equation). Second, Grete plays the part of Isolde quite well until her final line, in which she is not only clearly surprised by Fritz's death ("ach Fritz—was ist Dir?"), but also seems anything but accepted. Third, what has seemed up until this point a *Liebestod*-pastiche is dirsrupted by a final, violent blow, which seems to achieve the opposite of transfiguration of the particular, the reconciliation of the individual in death—suddenly the music seems to insist that the opera's denouement is tragic.

The very last three bars of the opera's score break not only with the mystification of Fritz's death with which the opera has seemed to flirt; they also rupture the entire notion of the operatic with a violent exclamation. The opera ends with a scream of surprise and sorrow, rather than on any melodic note. The "distant sound" has developed itself out of existence with Fritz's death, and the opera seems to suspend its traditional musical means in the moment of death. Moreover, if it were not for the outburst of the final three bars, the opera could have ended as it began; it might have decrescendoed itself out of existence just as it slowly insinuated itself into existence in the overture. This return to the same is, of course, the mark of myth or fairy tale. *Der ferne Klang* proposes a fairy-tale or dream logic: The opening and the closing are identical, all is restored to equilibrium (or identity), the death drive has found its fulfillment. The opera has turned into one huge tautology, the travails of Grete and Fritz banished relegated to a dream, banished into equivalence by the recurrence of the overture and eventually drowned out by the applause.

Significantly, the overture and the final scene both play out in the distance, the former setting up the space in which the dream content of the opera will unfold, the latter rescinding that space. These positing and taking-back gestures are both accomplished via the "distant sound," in which, as Adorno remarked in the passage I quoted at the outset, music is spatialized, and social systems mystified into nature. The opera replicates through the fates of Fritz and Grete the operations that phantasmagoric mystification performs on the social totality: an abnegation of social agency, of the fundamental made-ness of human fate, of the injustice entailed in and yet eclipsed by abstract reason. Just as Fritz has to die by some cosmic law, just as the "distant sound" beckons as though a matter of metaphysics and not acoustics, the audience leaves the theater confirmed in their belief that they deserve to be watching the drama, while others are involved in producing the latter or building the former.

But of course Schreker's opera finally rejects this tautology. The sound travels precisely where it ought to, where metaphysical sound lives in *Parsifal*: up the dome, "dividing wall and reflector in one." And just as in *Tristan*, voice comes to die and get reborn in instrumental music, while instrumental music dies and dissipates in the highest reaches of the opera house: "The sound dies in the highest heights." But then something unexpected happens: "All music falls silent,"[56] but the voice reasserts itself, in a horrified, horrific, primal scream. The gesture of taking back the techno-totality just as it was granted in the opening bars, is disrupted by Grete's scream and the chord accompanying it. This chord is no longer distant, it is not static or timeless—it is instead a flash of historic time, emphatically despatialized. It no longer transpires within the spatial framework set up by the music and the phantasmagoric apparatus; it happens outside of it. Moreover, by insisting on tragedy over transfiguration, the final chord paints as tragic not so much anything particular that animates the story, but the story's movement as a whole. Rather than putting anything narrated into question, it interrogates the very form of the narration. It places a question mark behind the death drive, insists that what has been posited can never be taken back without an indivisible remainder of suffering. As such it is historicizing.

In other words, Schreker's opera critiques the drowning out of the distant sound by equating the distant sound with death. The only way to get beyond the "white noise" created by modern society and to reach something like pure aesthetic experience is to die; and in Schreker's formulation this sounds less like a neutral statement of a generalized human condition than an indictment of modern society. *Der ferne Klang* thus historicizes its own stasis, its empty dynamism. But Schreker would be something of a cheat if he simply ignored the spatial dimensions of the post-Wagnerian opera house, the "magic circle" woven by architecture, stage design and modern acoustics, in favor of an emphatically despatialized alienation effect. And indeed, Schreker's approach is to have his cake and eat it too: He tells the story of the alluring distance, exploits the technological capabilities of the post-Wagnerian opera house, while at the same time inquiring into its medial and technological a priori. This involves not simply refusing distance, but rather utilizing distance to critique distance and the silencing of the opera house that subtends it.

If the deathly embrace of ear and *Klang* inside the opera house is an abiding feature in operatic plots of the fin de siècle, the scene has its twin in scenes of what might be called musical *flânerie*—scenes, that is, in which we are confronted with the phantasmagoric "magic circle" from outside, from a vantage point that renders the erotic-acoustic production profoundly uncanny. Much like that of the all-consuming, world-constituting scene of performance itself, the scene is clearly one important to musical modernity, for we find it recapitulated even in the period's orchestral music: The first *Nachtmusik* (night music) of Gustav Mahler's Seventh Symphony, for instance, constitutes itself something like a flanerie past a concert hall.[57] In the words of Hans Heinrich Eggebrecht, "Mahler walks through the town in the evening and takes in all the music he can hear," including snippets of music emanating from an opera house and a music hall.[58]

This act of musical *flânerie* finds its theoretical expression in the work of those two thinkers who went furthest in outlining the opera house's "phantasmagorias," be they a matter of acoustic technology or compositional technique—Walter Benjamin and Theodor Adorno. In their theoretical oeuvre, both thinkers explore the value of "irresolution"[59] before the "magic circle" of the theater. In an excerpt from his 1958 lectures on dialectics, Adorno takes the flaneur to the opera, arriving late as a hermeneutic trick. It is a rare moment in Adorno where distraction becomes a "method of attention"[60] and where, as Edmond Jaloux, in a passage quoted by Benjamin in the *Arcades Project*, puts it, "the mere turning right or left already constitute[s] an essentially poetic act."[61] This is a step Benjamin's solitary wanderer never took: The *Arcades Project* discusses "the opera as center,"[62] and pays special attention to Hauss-mann's *Avénue de l'Opéra*, but stops short of the building itself. Benjamin does, however, discuss a visit to the opera in his *Moscow Diaries*, and applies to it an optic remarkably reminiscent of Adorno's tardiness. He describes a perfor-mance of Rimsky-Korsakov's *The Tsar's Bride*:

> The administrator greets us. [He] shows us through all the rooms (in the vesti-bule, quite a crowd has gathered long before the beginning of the performance, people who have come from their workplaces directly into the theater) and also the concert hall. In the vestibule, there is a extremely noticeable and unpleasant carpet. . . . Our seats are in the second row. . . . In one of the intermissions we go to the vestibule. But there are three. They are far too long and they tire Asja out. . . . At the end, retrieving our coats proves quite difficult. Two ushers form separate lines on the grand staircase in order to to regulate the flow of people into the tiny coat checks.[63]

The above citation edits Benjamin's report somewhat, but leaves its most baf-fling aspect intact: His visit to the opera includes a description of rows of seats, the carpet in the foyer and an exhaustive account of the intermissions—but it entirely leaves out "the performance itself." Adorno's *flâneur* similarly per-forms his "poetic act" by not heading straight into the concert hall, but rather loitering in the foyer, the grand staircase or the coat check. Adorno explains this purposeful tardiness as follows:

> I therefore performed the experiment of arriving at reflections, observations about music by something I called "music from the outside" [*"Musik von Außen"*], both in the literal and metaphorical senses, literally listening to music not as it sounds in an opera house or a concert hall, but as it sounds when you are late in returning to your box after intermission and you hear this noise from the outside, the feeling that this reveals a side of the music that one usually does not see, and, speaking more generally, I realized that describing a phe-nomenon involves seeing it as though from the outside and not just from the inside.[64]

In many respects, then, Benjamin's *Moscow Diaries* find him practicing something along the lines of "music from the outside"—the crucial difference being that he mentions nothing of even the most incidental sounds of the operatic performance. Adorno's aural *flâneur* on the other hand hears bits of music, noise, applause, the shuffling of feet, nothing particularly distinct, one imagines, but rather what the radio listener picks up, tuning in and out of different broadcasts.[65] In his studies on what he dubbed the "radio voice," Adorno claims that this approach is doomed to fundamentally misapprehend music; here, however, he seems to think there is something in music that the latecomer in the foyer may be better attuned to than those sitting diligently in their seats inside.[66]

What is it that makes this "experiment" of "music from the outside" theoretically productive, rather than a state to hurry through on the way to one's box? Benjamin and Adorno seem to value the late comer's vantage point precisely because it disrupts those elements of operatic architecture and acoustics that forced viewer and spectacle into one single and unbreakable "magic circle." Rather than the immanence of the phantasmagoria of music, harmony and acoustics inside, the latecomer encounters the means of production that enable that phantasmagoria in the first place. What is more, what Adorno calls "music from the outside" attempts to trace the scars of the great silencing in the opera house. What the latecomer gleans from the distant noises of the concert hall, what gives these distant noises their evidentiary quality is nothing less than the disciplining work, the technological effort that goes into the silent, darkened, acoustically perfect opera house in which sound can happen seemingly immediately.

Since, as we have seen, the post-Wagnerian opera house is "identitarian," that is, tries to preclude a plurality of readings, Adorno's and Benjamin's technique for reading this repressed or sublimated archaism takes the shape of a kind of "double vision." In a post-Wagnerian opera house many things happen at once, but none detract from the one unified, coherent thing we are meant to experience there. The way to dislodge this identity is via spatial and bodily dislocation—looking where we're not supposed, or physically moving to a place from which the techno-totality is revealed as a production. We might, as Benjamin does in Moscow, pay attention to the carpeting of the foyer. We might turn around and look precisely where we are not to look—Adorno amusingly picks out the gallery as the locus of a "second stage," from where, in a more natural theatrical environment, such as a saloon, someone might actually shoot the piano player. The latecomer is the natural ally of the *claquer*, the *pleureur*, the ladies or the Chinese who talk through the performance, the aris-tocrats, the Italians who insist on coming and going as they please.

If Schreker pushes this phantasmagoric dimension of opera, its magic-circle character, to its extreme, he also, as we have seen, partakes of the project of the silencing of the opera house in a highly refracted, self-conscious way. After all, *Der ferne Klang* puts the operatic audience onstage in the figure of Fritz—his chase for the "distant sound" is that of the audience; his erotic attachment to it is that of the audience; and the fatal surety with which his quest ends in his death serves as something of a warning to the audience. But Schreker also alle-gorizes the latecomer, the auditory *flâneur*, who is still patiently waiting outside for the right moment to reenter his box. Throughout the opera, Fritz is haunted by the titular sound, which always beckons offstage: at times it comes from the orchestra, at others the score indicates that it should emanate from backstage. In an attempt to capture this distant sound, to cleanse it off the racket of di-egetic song, dance and march, Fritz composes his own opera, *The Harp*.

In *Der ferne Klang*'s third act, we get to hear Fritz's effort from the distance. The action itself takes place in a restaurant near the opera house and bits of music float over, as do the applause and eventual boos:

> The garden of the *Theaterbeisel*. Across the way is a broad street. Not too busy, but intermittent traffic from trolleys, omnibuses, carriages, etc. On the street, clearly visible, the court theater [*Hoftheater*]. Brightly lit. From time to time one it emits muffled music and the sounds of applause.[67]

The scene unfolds entirely in a dialogue between the restaurant space onstage and the theater visible in the distance behind it: The discussions circle around the opera being performed there; spectators file into the establishment, bear-ing news of the performance as it unfolds; once it is over, one can hear the "gaggle of voices" as the operagoers leave the building, as their valets shout for carriages. While Schreker's stage directions do not make this clear, one can safely assume that the "trolleys, omnibuses, carriages, etc." called for in the score do not physically roll across the backdrop of the stage, but are mostly sonically present. The opera being played, it turns out, sounds exactly like the first act of *Der ferne Klang* itself and we are thus separated once more from the "distant sound" (phenomenon and opera) by a gulf of quotidian (and dis-tinctly modern) noise. Here, then, the audience is itself listening to itself from the outside—in a restaurant rather than the foyer, but outside the magic circle nonetheless.

While Schreker's third act in many respects recapitulates the spatial dynamics of the first two acts (in which the stage is really a sideshow while the main action takes place offstage), the particular geography Schreker develops here centers around the "magic circle" of the opera house itself. The dutiful opera-goer in his box is surreptitiously allied to the dissolute latecomer out by the coat check—and instead on beautiful performances and a pure Gesamtkunstwerk the listener is (at least in the distance) treated to those extrinsic experiences of operagoing that Benjamin describes in his Moscow Diaries. Just as among the audiences Wagner warned against and Benjamin celebrated, *Der ferne Klang*'s third act radically disperses presence. Rather than concentrating the presence of operatic performance only onstage, music and audience together come to constitute the operatic phenomenon. Whereas those in attendance at Bayreuth were only expected to surrender their bodies to the acoustics of the opera house, that is to become conductors of a *Klang* from above, here the audience's reactions are themselves an integral part of the opera's *Klang*.

In *Der ferne Klang*'s third act, the audience finds itself both inside and outside the phantasmagoric magic circle. In the previous acts, Schreker has insistently involved the opera's listener in the social and gender geographies laid out onstage—now he forces his listener to listen to himself listening. The boos, the applause reveal the atavistic investments so carefully concealed by smoking jackets and aftershave—but opera's atavism does not come about because we look where we're not supposed to; it unfolds instead on the stage itself. Music from the outside enters the magic circle, yet reminds the audience uncomfortably of that outside. This strange chiasmus of inside and outside, of presence and distance is characteristic for Schreker's ambivalent deployment of phantasmagoria in general. More so than any other post-Wagnerian, Schreker stakes out his own path out of Wagnerian phantasmagoria by having his cake and eating it too, recognizing both the political and aesthetic problems of operatic distance and the desire that drives the composer's pen and the listener's mind offstage, into the phantomic space behind the scenes.

CHAPTER 5

Congenital Blindness: Visions of Marriage in the Operas of Eugen d'Albert

One of the most famous anecdotes from the life of German opera composer Eugen d'Albert concerns a witticism on the subject of marriage. As legend would have it, an archaeologist remarked to d'Albert that our knowledge of the Assyrian civilization stems from but a few hundred pieces of broken crockery, to which the composer replied: "It seems that marriage is indeed an ancient institution." What seems significant about d'Albert's quip is not just the image of the "ancient institution" as nothing but a endless chain of domestic wreckage, but especially the composer's own bemused vantage point, surveying the marital mayhem with the keen eye of the archaeologist—a Benjaminian angel of erotic history watching in horror as the pile of broken crockery mounts before him.

The composer's oeuvre bears out the perspective he assumed in the little quip: Marriage and history are linked in his operas. Where his contemporaries tended to dehistoricize the erotic, d'Albert's operas deal with marriage rather than love, and they deal with it in explicitly historical contexts. D'Albert was married six times and marriage was one of the enduring themes of his operas. From the early musical comedy *Die Abreise*, the raucous *Tragaldabas, der geborgte Ehemann*, the frothy domestic comedy *Die Verschenkte Frau*, via the verismo operas *Tiefland* and *Liebesketten*, to the serious psychological works *Die toten Augen* and *Revolutionshochzeit*, and the blood-soaked spectacle *Mister Wu* that remained unperformed and unfinished in the composer's lifetime—marriage and its meaning, its genesis, and dissolution constitute a central preoccupation of d'Albert's operas, as well as the wide range of source texts he drew on for his libretti. D'Albert offers a unique opportunity for investigating both the sustained interest in marriage by opera composers and librettists and those aspects specific to fin-de-siècle operatic presentations of the subject.

On the one hand, d'Albert is very much embedded in particular post-Wagnerian moment, drawing on Italian *verismo* and the nascent new music, but on the other hand, he takes a historicist approach to his opera plots, importing the concerns and styles of earlier operatic and dramatic practices into the present along with his libretti. D'Albert drew his libretti from a wide range of German- and foreign language texts from various periods (running the gamut from Petronius, via the eighteenth-century comedian Steigentesch, to the expressionist poet Hanns Heinz Ewers), and there is consequently very little overlap from one opera's representation of marriage to the next. The function of marriage within the moral universe of its characters, their attitude to the institution and to institutions in general and the wider political ramifications of marriage are each left intact in translating them into post-Wagnerian German opera. Within their arc d'Albert's operas manage to encapsulate a history of German thought on marriage *en miniature.* When Paul Bekker described the post-Wagnerian moment as "the beginning of a historicizing, backward-looking age,"[1] he was referring to formal musical questions, but d'Albert extends this historicism to opera's erotics as well.

From the late Baroque celebrations of *amour gallante* to the Romantic metaphysics of marriage, to incipient psychoanalytic discourses—d'Albert and his various librettists trace the marital union in different guises and iterations, some proper to the fin-de-siècle, others frankly historicized. Among the post-Wagnerians, d'Albert's operas are uniquely eclectic in genre, theme, and form, when compared to such stalwarts as Siegfried Wagner, Richard Strauss, Hans Pfitzner, or Engelbert Humperdinck, and his treatment of marriage indulges a similar eclecticism, drawing on amorous philosophies that had long slipped from modern Germans' hermeneutic horizon. In d'Albert, marriage seems to be no longer thought of as one particular thing or problem (as it had been in Wagner, for instance), but rather radically historicized, repeated, and reflected upon.

That such erotic historicism was usually in league with a musical historicism should not surprise, given that Bekker's own (highly critical) characterization of this "historicist" age is replete with imagery of sex, reproduction, and heredity. In his description, Bekker emphasizes the importance of "reproduction," whether as simple "iteration" [*Wiedergabe*] or as "creative new formation" [*schöpferischer Umgestaltung*], speaks of (mostly unsuccessful) attempted "solutions to [opera's] hereditary problem" [*Erbschaftsproblem*] and the lack of "sufficient autonomous production" [*ausreichender Eigenproduktion*].² The historicist turn in operatic form is thus framed in terms of sexuality and heredity. If this generation of composers were so obsessed with their own provenance, he suggested, a lot of their obsession was owed to their musical heredity, their insecurity about their own hereditary material, and their uncertainty what to do with it. Why then should that form not turn to sexuality to work through the formal problems enumerated by Bekker? D'Albert's erotic historicism goes hand in hand with a musical historicism and is at times indistinguishable from it; their mutual constitutions and interrogations are the focus of this chapter.

OPERA'S MARRIAGES

Insofar as they go beyond the music and affect the plots and texts of d'Albert's libretti, one could object that these ideas aren't properly d'Albert's at all, but that they instead belong to his librettists, the sources they drew on, or a combination of both. Indeed, it seems foolhardy to pore over the libretti of a composer who wrote libretti for only his earliest operas, who moreover on occasion optioned libretti with only minor alterations, and whose libretti almost always drew on earlier texts. However, this seeming difficulty will be to some extent my point: D'Albert's contemporaries praised his "truly protean mutability, always in the service of his subject matter,"³ which makes his choice of subject matter so much more significant. And it is precisely the *choice* that matters: D'Albert freely chose to commit himself to the words of another person, to yoke himself to another person's understanding of the erotic, to subject years of his life to another's subjectivity. He chose to sign away some of his autonomy, to be to some extent outwardly determined.

"Autonomously chosen heteronomy," this is how we might render the famous definition of love provided by Ottilie in Goethe's *Die Wahlverwandschaften*.⁴ The erotic plays a clear role in the relationship between librettist and composer, as does the contract that reins in what we might term the librettist's promiscuity: traditionally, autonomous libretti were available for other composers, and were indeed set to music again and again. Iterability and mutual mobility are part and parcel of the traditional relationship between librettist and composer. As a result, seduction is a central part of their relationship as well: the libretto has to draw in the composer, and not by accident was Lorenzo da Ponte apprenticed in the art of seduction by none other than Casanova himself. The many negotiations involved in their relationship, their sustained collaboration over several operas, and their tendency toward unhappy unions combine to make composer and librettist less of an amorous couple, but instead a squabbling married one instead.

In this chapter, my contention will be that d'Albert utilizes the freely chosen dependence of marriage and the relationship between librettist and composer (and by extension the different media that make up the Wagnerian Gesamtkunstwerk) to have each depict and interrogate the other. Opera, like marriage, is irreducibly dual in d'Albert, an implicit rebuke to the Wagnerian model, in which, as Strauss seems to have realized after composing *Guntram*, the lone man left on the stage and the lone man composing the opera are similarly lost in their own hall of mirrors (see chapter 3). I argue that this self-delimitation, the irreducible relationality of both marriage and operatic production asserts itself in both the forms and the theme of d'Albert's marriage operas. The fact that these operas deal with marriage, in other words, is one piece with the fact that they are to some extent collaborative, not the projection and assertion of a single genius subjectivity. When d'Albert turned the story of the *Golem* into an opera, the libretto he chose (by Ferdinand Lion) presents the Rabbi who creates the Golem as an illusionist. His Golem is an extension of his spectacles, which are described as spectacular theatrical effects—but these efforts at creating a cohesive, seductive Gesamtkunstwerk culminate in the production of the all too real Golem. This creation, transgressing the proper sphere of illusion and representation, constitutes Rabbi Loew's tragic overreach, which at the end of the opera he is forced to undo.

Both the move toward marital, historicist eroticism and the move toward an irreducibly collaborative aesthetic of opera were thus intended as implicit rebukes to the Wagnerian model. Like *Guntram*, d'Albert's first three operas, *Der Rubin* (1893), *Ghismonda* (1895), and *Gernot* (1897), were much more heavily indebted to Wagner than his later output in terms of structure and tone—they were also the only operas on which d'Albert served as his own librettist. While the move toward collaborative work constituted to some extent a move away from Wagner, it is worth noting that it ushered d'Albert into collaborating with a fair number of Wagnerians—among his librettists were several authors of monographs about the master of Bayreuth, the editor of the *Bayreuther Blätter* and several music critics with strongly Wagnerian inclinations.

If d'Albert reconceived the role of marriage in the process of his reconsideration of the Wagnerian legacy, this went along with a newfound tolerance for difference and incommensurability in his operas. The picture of love that Schopenhauer and the Romantics had bequeathed to Wagner had insisted on complete unification. Those particulars that fell short of such exacting standards (the paradigm of which is the poor dwarf Mime, who demands a kind of love he cannot feel, inspire, or command) were condemned as inauthentic and degenerate. The libretti arrived at by d'Albert and his various librettists turn to marriage at least in part because it is different. Philosophy has tended to think of marriage as necessarily a juridical or doctrinal concept grafted onto a slippery biological basis. Marriage, like the unified work of art, is to some extent a mere desideratum, subject to subversion and slippages. It is this that d'Albert's marital productions on marital themes undertake to tease out.

But there is, of course, another aspect to the operatic Gesamtkunstwerk, as we saw in the previous chapter, namely the synesthetic demand put on the audience. As an audience we are not only invited to make the intellectual leap from sexual figurations to social formations, but instead are pulled into the same erotics of vision that hold the opera's characters in thrall. But it is this thrall that adds to the astonishing multiplicity of the marriage motif in d'Albert's work. For insofar as marriage allegorizes the work of art, d'Albert's operas perform something of a double marriage. On the one hand, marriage comes to characterize something about the coherence of the work of art, in particular the interactions of different media that conspire to create it; on the other hand, the faithful unity of marriage comes to signify the faith we as an audience necessarily have to invest in the spectacle. Kierkegaard's "leap" into marriage is precisely one that the audience is asked to recapitulate vis-à-vis the operatic production. This double deployment of marriage as that which unites the disparate media in the integrated work of art on the one hand, and as that which determines the audience's relation to the integration of media on the other, becomes the central preoccupation of d'Albert's second most famous opera, *Die toten Augen.*

MARRIAGE AND ITS SPECTATORS: *DIE TOTEN AUGEN*

According to Søren Kierkegaard, Christianity had to necessarily frown upon second marriages (or third, fourth, fifth, and sixth, in the case of d'Albert) because it "had to assume that repetition of marriage introduced a reflection upon it which made it inadmissible."[5] D'Albert of course not only repeated marriage in practice, he also returned to it again and again in his operas. What happens, then, when one takes the inadmissible step and indulges in the "reflection upon [marriage]" that Christianity could not permit? And what is the role of visuality in that reflection?

We begin our answer with a marriage bed as the scene of a crime. Goethe's 1808 novel *Die Wahlverwandtschaften* (*Elective Affinities*) presents a married couple that has fallen asleep after lovemaking, but when they awake the next morning "the sun seemed to shed its light upon a crime."[6] The "crime" that transpires is what Karl Rosenkranz called the two marital partners' "moral adultery"[7]—they sleep with each other while each imagining themselves holding a different person altogether. The events that are aided by the darkness and the lovers' overactive imaginations have been carefully scrutinized for two hundred years since the novel's publication. What has received less attention is the daybreak after the famous scene, when the sun reveals the scene of the crime. What is striking about that scene is, simply put, that it features a married couple doing what a married couple is supposed to do—they wake up next to each other, having fallen asleep after renewing their marriage the previous night. But Goethe's narrator insists that this awakening is different from the thousands that have preceded it—instead, waking up next to the person you have vowed to wake up next to for the rest of your life has become, by dint of the night's events, a crime. "Inadmissible" reflection has entered into what had previously been an immediate relation—and the institution, so seemingly natural, has attained a new metaphysical nicety.

It is this insistence on the profound uncanniness of the institution of marriage that dominates much of the thought on marriage in nineteenth-century Germany. Goethe's narrator seems to think that the marital lovers' "crime" consists in their transgression against their true imaginary partners rather than in their transgression against each other. Similarly, Johann Gottlieb Fichte had insisted in 1798 that a marriage without love was "concubinage" and should not be legitimated by state or ecclesiastical authority. For Fichte, as for the Romantics, the deontological account of marriage exemplified by Kant was based on a misunderstanding of the relationship between autonomy and feeling. For Kant, marriage was necessary to rid sexuality of its animal character and thus to the irrational heteronomy entailed in erotic attraction. Fichte, by contrast, posited that love (and by extension marriage) was essentially an effect of human autonomy and ultimately even of human rationality. Sex was not what swayed reason unjustly and thus had to be contained in marriage; sex (at least when it came to the male) was itself in accord with reason, and marriage was a mere extension rather than a reassertion of subjective autonomy. The only kind of marriage that, for Fichte and the Romantics, actually bullied the subject into heteronomy was the one made contrary to inclinations, be this for reasons of convention, convenience, or commerce.

The notion that there are certain nature-intended harmonies (or, in Goethe's terminology, *Wahlverwandtschaften*), while those couplings dictated by form, habit, and convention can produce only dissonance, naturally translated quite easily into the musical realm. It entered Romantic opera early (it clearly animates the rebuke to outmoded rules governing the union of lovers issued by *Der Freischütz*'s closing scenes), but was pushed to its apogee in the work of Richard Wagner—and even as his successors struggled to free themselves from his overwhelming legacy, they by and large maintained a juxtaposition of true love and marriage on the one hand and outmoded or aberrantly modern forms of either on the other. True natural feeling, as Wagner put it in "Über das Weibliche im Menschlichen," was to be kept free of the mandates of either tradition or commerce—"purposes entirely outside of itself,"[8] which degrade humanity "beneath the status of the animal."[9] When Fricka invokes the "sacred oath" of marriage in *Die Walküre*, Wotan rebukes her: "I deem unholy that oath, / that unloving oath; / and truly do not make me hold together / by force which [love] does not."[10] Concomitantly, however, this true natural love through which alone newness enters into the world ("Learn, what comes together of its own accord, / even if it never happened before"[11]) is juxtaposed with a love that cunningly reproduces the existing, exemplified through the *Ring*'s many characters incapable of love, but adroit in transforming their own selves into some new guise or form—Mime, Alberich, Fafner, and to some extent Loge.

As we saw in chapter 1, in Wagner, the kind of love decreed by tradition (Fricka) or financial expediency (Mime) is associated with "wit" [*Witz*] or "cunning" [*Verstand*]. The subject pursues amorous union with another the same way the capitalist seeks to exploit the vagaries of the marketplace. The deeper connection that ultimately points to self-denial and true union with another is connected to what the German Idealists knew as intellectual intuition—a kind of feeling cognition neither entirely discursive (it is too inchoate to understand manipulable causes), nor entirely instinctive (it is a kind of propositional knowledge). Among the German Romantics, this had been the distinction between contractual marriage dependent on a framework of social and ultimately commercial norms and a marriage that springs, spontaneously and autonomously, from the subjects themselves. It is a juxtaposition that maintained its charms well after Wagner, and accordingly the Wagnerian eroticism of intuition and *Verstand* made its appearance in the early operas of d'Albert as well—1903's *Tiefland*, written by Rudolf Lothar based on the Catalan-language play *Terra baixa* by Àngel Guimerà (1845–1924), d'Albert's first great success.

Tiefland tells the story of the villainous grandee Sebastiano who keeps the beautiful young Marta as his mistress, but, in order to be able to marry rich, schemes to marry her to Pedro, a hapless young shepherd from the high reaches of the Pyrenees. Resistant at first, Marta comes to love her husband, which in turn arouses Sebastiano's jealousy. In a final confrontation, Pedro kills Sebastiano and the two lovers escape into the Pyrenean highlands. *Tiefland*'s plot is structured by a rather straightforward dichotomy between the authentic world of the high mountains and the debased and venal lowlands, a dichotomy that asserts itself most visibly in the realm of love and sexuality. In the lowlands, love is conducted in amorous transactions. Marta's father trades the girl in for his mill, and, as Sebastiano explains, he exacts his ground rent in love: "And now you are the miller. / You pay your rent in love. / That is the way of law and business."[12] Pedro is drawn into precisely this kind of amorous transaction and Sebastiano seeks to barter off Marta the same way he purchased her. But when Sebastiano asks Pedro to enter into a contract with him ("Shake on it, my boy"[13]), Pedro raises a question that no other character has raised thus far in the opera: Is this trade right and how does it square with Marta's own wishes and attractions? "Should I? May I? Will she want me?"[14] Rather than as the object of contracts, or a commodity to be exchanged ad infinitum, Pedro treats Marta as a subject capable of desiring or not desiring him.

Although its account of Mediterranean love and extensive scenes of rural life owe much to verismo, *Tiefland* is profoundly Wagnerian in its treatment of marriage. While its sustained emphasis on Christian religion is of course miles apart from *Die Walküre*'s Fricka as an embodiment of marriage, the opera does not deviate from Wagner's, and in turn, the Idealists', theory of marriage. Love and marriage are not essentially distinct—to be married to someone that one does not love means to not actually be married—and true love does not require a sanction by marital bond. This gives love in *Die Walküre* a highly anarchic valence—it upsets the world of contract, of the machinations of instrumental reason, of conventional morality. D'Albert's opera maintains this opposition, allying the rule-bound, instrumental form of dynastic politics with the titular *Tiefland*, where a barter for love is "the way of law and business," and tying the profound, rule-transcending love between two individuals to the *Hochland*, the place Pedro and Marta elope to at the end of the opera.

While Christianity is new to this equation, *Tiefland* sidesteps any possible dissonance through a sleight of hand. While for Wagner, as for Fichte, the religious claim on marriage would very much fall on the side of conventional, instrumental, and contractual "abuse of marriage," which are simply "calculated to multiply property,"[15] d'Albert and Lothar simply move God into the other column. The *Hochland* stands for true love, freed from conventional pieties and contractual commitments, but somehow God (just like Wotan) smiles on it anyway. Those who hail from it constantly invoke God, the denizens of the contractually structured beaneries of the *Tiefland* almost never do.

Die toten Augen, which premiered thirteen years later, finds d'Albert and his librettist profoundly rethinking the relationship between religion and marital love. The old *Walküre*-style juxtaposition that structured *Tiefland* has disappeared, as has the legacy of German Romanticism. Instead, marriage becomes an intricate system of representations and misperceptions, all presided over by Jesus Christ, who has a less-than-salutory influence on the proceedings. As a consequence, d'Albert's later opera comes to put into question not only the nature of the marital relationship itself, but also the meaning of its religious dimensions. And unlike in Tiefland, where religion still furnished an integral part of a Wagnerian erotic metaphysics, *Die toten Augen* deploys questions of religion and marriage primarily to confront the form's strangely intermedial nature. What is the nature of the faith demanded in marriage and how does it relate to the kind of faith (or suspension of disbelief) that is demanded of an operatic audience?

Opera's ostentatious, overtly representational character emerged as a source of anxiety with critics and composers by the twentieth century, who feared that it made opera an anachronism out of step with its audience and the wider culture. And this anxiety gradually seeped into the plots and even the very form of post-Wagnerian opera. As we saw in chapter 2, for instance, the critic Paul Bekker worried that opera might be but "a paradox which we cannot really take seriously" any longer, a "social pursuit of a past age," "kept alive by sheer force of thoughtless habit." A social formation maintained by "sheer force of habit," an unsolvable "paradox" incompatible with modern life, an ancient practice always at risk of being secularized out of existence: the same worries were expressed about the institution of marriage in the late nineteenth century. And trepidations about the continued relevance for opera do not sound so different from questions about the justifiability of marriage. When Bekker worries that perhaps opera composers have for centuries wasted their best efforts on a genre "whose allure rested solely on the irreconcilability of its contradictions, and thus on the intractability of its constitutive formal problem,"[16] he echoes in essence the *Wahlverwandtschaften*'s worries about marriage.

D'Albert wrote *Die toten Augen* in 1912 and 1913, based on a libretto by Hanns Heinz Ewers and Marc Henry. Ewers (1871–1943), a political, cultural, and sexual dissident of the Wilhelmine era who turned to right-wing politics in the Weimar Republic, adapted the libretto from his frequent collaborator, French modernist Marc Henry. Henry had written the play *Les yeux morts* in 1897, but had lost his autograph. At Ewers's insistence, he penned a brief story treatment, based on the myth of Amor and Psyche (a debt that is explicitly referenced in the libretto), which Ewers then expanded into a new play, *Die toten*

Augen. As he was writing, Ewers felt that "the text cried out for music" and decided to turn Henry's play idea into an opera libretto.[17] Although Ewers was a jurist by training, his libretto is entirely uninterested in marriage and adultery from a legal standpoint; like Goethe's *Wahlverwandtschaften*, Ewers (a voracious reader of Max Stirner) is interested in erotic cognition, what perceptions form the conditions for the possibility of marriage.

The story, framed by an optional Arcadian scene of shepherds largely unrelated to the main action, concerns the Roman senator Arcesius. Although he is considered grotesquely ugly, his wife, beautiful and blind Myrtocle, believes him a ravishing young man. Her desire to finally see her husband drives her to seek out a traveling sage who has been known to cure the blind—Jesus of Nazareth. Jesus manages to heal her, but warns her that she will curse him for his gift before sundown. Unimpressed, Myrtocle hurries home and readies herself before the mirror for her husband. When her husband arrives, he does so with his aide Aurelius Galba in tow, who has himself long harbored feelings for Myrtocle. When Myrtocle's maidservant informs them of the lady of the house's miraculous recovery, Arcesius runs in terror and hides. Galba, however, stands transfixed by Myrtocle, who believes him to be her husband. She embraces him, and Galba, after initial hesitation, begins kissing her furiously. Arcesius, wounded to his core, leaps from his hiding place, throws himself upon his friend and strangles him, only to then flee from his own handiwork.

The maidservant finally informs Myrtocle that her husband is not the beautiful dead man lying on her lap, but the feral creature that killed him, "this monster born of Hades itself / this creature, limping, deformed."[18] Cursing Jesus's name, Myrtocle stares into the setting sun until she is once again blinded. Arcesius returns and calls out to his wife, who in turn pretends that she never saw her husband—"I saw so much—but I did not see you"[19]—and vows that she "will continue to live in the world of dreams / for you, my beloved husband, for you alone!"[20] As the sun slowly sets, Arcesius takes her arm and guides his once-again blind wife into their home.

"Then the two slowly walk into the house"—like Goethe's crime-scene snapshot, Ewers and Henry's libretto ends with a scene of ordinary domesticity that is nonetheless uncannily transfigured. What appeared (at least to the protagonists) as an immediate and natural relation has revealed itself as founded on illusion, projection, and artifice. And that artifice becomes less innocent and sustainable as the opera goes on: Myrtocle's blindness cannot undo the fact that she *has* seen Arcesius, what had begun as a union structured around blindness has become one structured around a lie. More generally,

however, the light-giving, sight-taking power of the sun has eclipsed Myrtocle's autonomous subjective power. At the end of the opera Myrtocle once
again requires her husband's guidance into the house—when the sun "burns
out the light of my eyes,"[21] Myrtocle's dangerous autonomy is recaptured, and
she is once again at the mercy of outside forces.

As in Goethe, what becomes visible in the cold light of day is the sacrifice
required in marriage, a cliché which *Die toten Augen* turns into a grotesque in
its climactic blinding sequence. "One must relinquish one's own happiness to
save the happiness of others," Myrtocle intones at the end of the opera, but the
monstrous conceit by which she does so gives this willing sacrifice an unsettling dimension. Moreover, just as in Goethe's novel, marriage depends on, or
is identical with, a sort of blindness—seeing her inner image of her husband
realized in the outside world, in the shape of Galba, leads Myrtocle to commit adultery. The return to the domestic scene in the opera's final moments
depends on Myrtocle's voluntary sacrifice of her eyesight.

Given the opera's emphasis on eyes, it is difficult not to think of another set
of *tote Augen* in German literature, those of the doll Olimpia in E. T. A. Hoffmann's *Sandmann*: In Hoffmann's story, young Nathanael falls in love with a
woman who turns out to be a mechanical doll. While the rest of the automaton
is deceptively lifelike, "only her eyes seemed to [Nathanael] strangely stiff and
dead."[22] Just like Myrtocle's, Olimpia's eyes, too, are dead because they cannot
see—"her eyes had something stiff about them, I would almost say, they had no
power of vision."[23] Of course, Nathanael convinces himself that her impenetra-
bility indicates hidden depths rather than an interior of gears and cogs, falling
madly in love with what is at long last simply his projection, the machine he
grafts onto the evil Coppelius's machine. One central such projection concerns Olimpia's power of vision, as Nathanael animates Olimpia's dead eyes
and convinces himself that they are not dead, but instead can see: "But as he
peered closer and closer through the looking glass, he felt as though liquid rays
of the moon dissolved in Olimpia's eyes. It seemed as if only now the power of
vision was ignited [in her eyes]; more and more lively glowed her gaze."[24]

Myrtocle, too, seems to think that being able to see changes the way one
looks to others: "Are you confused? Do you not recognize me? / Do I look
different, now that I see?"[25] she asks the man she believes to be her husband.
Her return of the gaze changes her appearance, disrupts the comfort of viewing her. In *Tiefland*, too, Sebastiano falls in love with Marta "for your beautiful eyes"; but those beautiful eyes themselves constitute a threat, at least for
Pedro who worries that "she might find that I am ugly," and is humiliated when

"she fled when she saw me." Again and again, then, d'Albert's male characters want to see without being seen. A dialogue of gazes has something profoundly threatening about it. Women are offered as objects of barter and spectacle, but they have an unsettling way of looking back at the barterers and spectators, thereby disrupting traditional ways of dealing with, and of spectating femininity.

In Sigmund Freud's seminal reading of Hoffmann's story, the sandman's threat of taking young Nathanael's eyes becomes a cipher for castration anxiety. In that sense, *Die toten Augen* can easily be read as the story of the emergence of a phallic woman who ends the opera with her own voluntary castration and, by that logic, refeminization. Woman can enter marriage only through a lack (of sight); plenitude, full vision destroys her ability to function in a marriage and the surfeit of vision is tantamount to adultery. Like in *Die Wahlverwandt-schaften*, the problem in *Die toten Augen* is simply that Myrtocle's projection of her husband is identical with someone who is not her husband. Projecting turns out to be necessary to a successful marriage, but projection has to some extent to be taken on faith—the wish to confirm the reality of the projection (implicit in the notion of projection itself) reveals it as a sham and destroys it. As such, marriage becomes a trope for the suspension of disbelief required of an operatic audience: turn up the lights, look too closely at the romantic lead, ask too many questions; and the spectacle dissolves into the "irreconcilability of its contradictions," as Bekker put it. For opera, as for marriage, we must will ourselves to live "in the world of dreams."

However, the author of Myrtocle's fatal clairvoyance is of course none other than Jesus of Nazareth—"the man, who gave me light, who shattered my happiness."[26] "Who gave me light"—there is something Promethean, perhaps a bit of Lucifer about *Die toten Augen*'s Jesus of Nazareth—except of course Jesus "brings light" only very reluctantly and knows full well that it will destroy Myrtocle's marriage. Light and vision are for Jesus and for the audience; the spectacle which they witness, the marriage at the center of the plot can be illuminated only to outsiders if it is to endure. Myrtocle and Arcesius' marriage thus constitutes the perfect spectacle, viewable only for and demanding to be seen only by those who are not part of it. It is interesting to note that the role of Jesus, and by extension that of religion, is thus precisely not that of mystification and make-belief; instead, the opera associates Jesus with a cold and brutal clarity before which eroticism is ultimately doomed.

It is a clarity, however, that everyone but the lovers possesses from the very beginning of the opera. Blindness is essential to the stage action: the spectacle of the mismatched couple is as obvious to the onlookers (onstage and in the audience) as it is invisible to the two lovers implicated in it. It is precisely the spectacle of Arcesius that Myrtocle wishes to espy: "Beautiful is my husband, and all [others] can see him [*und alle ihn erschauen*]," she complains, "and therefore I want to see him!" Of course, that spectacle turns out to be of a very different kind—Arcesius is of spectacular ugliness, which all but Myrtocle can see. Unlike Goethe's marital partners, then, who encounter both their illusory partners and the reality of their actions the next day by themselves and in private, both the illusion and the reality of the relationship between Arcesius and Myrtocle are necessarily referred to a public of spectators. This public—which can see the irony at the heart of their marriage, can see both the logic of Myrtocle's wish for eyesight and her eventual sacrifice of vision—consists of characters onstage, the audience, and most prominently Jesus of Nazareth himself.

Jesus himself, however, remains invisible to the members of the audience as well. The opera's tenth scene, in which Jesus heals Myrtocle of her blindness, is entirely narrated "teichoscopically" by a throng of onlookers ("What is he doing?" "He's speaking to her"), who themselves seem visually impaired when it comes to the scene—their incessant "let me see [*Lasst sehn, lasst sehn!*]" directly mirrors Myrtocle's demand. But of course the horde of onlookers also blocks the audience's visual access to Jesus—we are as blind as Myrtocle when it comes to the King of Kings. But like Myrtocle (and like the mob), we wish to see—at least partially because we are given the voice of Jesus without his body.

SCENE ELEVEN
Suddenly deep silence. And through this silence

A VOICE
O woman, truly, I say unto you:
Before the sun sets, you will curse me!

ELFTE SZENE
Plötzlich tiefe Stille. Und durch diese Stille klingt hell

EINE STIMME
O Weib, wahrlich, ich sagt dir:
Ehe die Sonne zur Neige geht, wirst du mir fluchen!]

Unlike the invisible choirs of *Parsifal*, which are emphatically disembodied and arouse no desire (other than one born of interest in staging, stage technique, and dramaturgy) to discover the bodies behind the voices, Jesus's voice puts us in the position of the mob, clamoring *Lasst sehn, lasst sehn.* Jesus's voice is accessible to all, his body, however, is subject to an always already frustrated asymptotic approach. This has little to do with an operatic prohibition of graven images (Wagner's *Jesus von Nazareth* draft has Jesus both appearing and singing onstage[27]), but instead everything to do with blindness, desire, and visibility. For the very blindness that structures the audience's relationship with Jesus also defines Myrtocle's marriage to Arcesius. It is after all not by accident that, at the end of the opera, a once-again blind Myrtocle entrusts herself anew to her betrothed's beautiful voice: "The sound of your voice envelops me / like a warm rain in May."[28] The opera's climax thus finds Myrtocle moving from the position of wanting to see to basking in the sonorities of the voice alone, just as the audience is asked to content itself with "a voice" instead of the live body of the Savior.

The audience's blindness to Jesus is not an invention of Henry's. When Ewers adapted Henry's original story, he complained that "of course [the story] was entirely impossible for the stage, since the main role was that of Jesus of Nazareth, whom the censors will allow in oafish peasant plays [*in tölpelhaften Bauernspielen*], but not in beautiful, deep creations of art."[29] It is this paradoxical situation—in which a making visible of Jesus in turn makes him invisible for an audience and bars him from the world of the stage—that Ewers's peculiar staging of Jesus's vocal presence dramatizes. Unlike in Henry's original story (or in its source, the legend of Amor and Psyche), this implicates the audience in *Die toten Augen*'s oscillating play of blindness and insight.

When Walter Niemann charged that the composer's post-*Tiefland* output "poetically coarsened verismo to mere cinematic drama," he not only took aim at a kind of spectacularization of d'Albert's opera, but rather also made a point about the visuality of an operatic practice aimed at "the cinematic public of our time."[30] "Cinematic public," a pejorative term in Niemann's vocabulary, was not intended to accuse d'Albert of cheap populism—Niemann is clear that d'Albert does not mean to appeal to "the public that is raised by the cinema," "the modern war- and mass public."[31] Instead, the cinematic aspect that Niemann finds so problematic seems to reside in the emphasis on the visual, in particular the visualization of "sexual difference as central motif."[32] Cinematicity inheres both in the relationship between the sexes as staged in the drama and the audience's relationship to its staging.

SYNESTHETIC MARRIAGE

Wagner's *Tristan* concludes with the perfect unification of the lovers in death, and with them, the love plot transubstantiates itself into the purity of absolute music. Absolute marriage and absolute opera require the unification of the lovers in death. While the wide range of genres, styles, and source materials in d'Albert's oeuvre makes generalizations difficult, it is clear that love and marriage in his operas receive no such absolution. Marriage remains inherently bipolar and does not transcend its duality into either Fichtean "unification" or Wagnerian death drive. Wagner's erotic unity served to usher opera into the complete unification of the total work of art—in refusing erotic unification and insisting on an irreducible difference within the loving couple, d'Albert simultaneously rejects the remainderless unification of different media in opera. D'Albert's plots, by sidestepping the rapturous unification of lovers, recapitulate that other strange personal union his operas are marked by: the tentative, provisional and sometimes disharmonious union of librettist and composer.

Ewers's decision to add music to a dramatic plot that allegedly cried out for it is highly significant in this regard. For Bekker's worries about the mongrelized opera form derive precisely from a (for Bekker, Wagner-influenced) tendency among opera composers to simply put theater to music. For other observers, this raised another, opposite problem: that Wagner's influence prompted composers to strengthen the union of the different media hitched together by the Gesamtkunstwerk to the point of identity. Just as d'Albert never allows his lovers to become one, but spends the entirety of his plots conjugating their relationship, so his operas themselves never allow themselves to assume, stipulate, or mandate the identity or even coincidence of their constitutive media.

This is why *Die toten Augen* centers around a scene that is "impossible for the stage"—the sensual nonsynchronicity of hearing without seeing serves to unmoor vocality from staging, all the while dramatizing the desire for their unification. In a review of *Tiefland*, the music historian Richard Batka (1868–1922), who would later serve as d'Albert's librettist himself, extols this as d'Albert's primary virtue. Batka points out that d'Albert's orchestra as well is more autonomous from the drama onstage than in Wagner and his successors: "In modern opera, even if a needle falls to the ground, the orchestra has to take notice of it. No change in mood is possible, not the slightest change of heart can take root within the heroes, without the instruments following it and betraying it."[33] D'Albert, Batka argues, is different: He allows different media to ignore each other, or to eclipse each other momentarily.

In *Die toten Augen*, the visual and the vocal slide constantly vis-à-vis each other: the voice makes both Myrtocle and the audience pine for the visual, but the visual threatens to destroy the vocal. The opera's final scene has Myrtocle luxuriate in an intoxicating synesthesia, predicated of course on her blindness. "So well attuned is my ear that the rhythm of your steps / sends shivers into my heart."[34] His voice feels like "rain in May," the pressure of his touch "like a delicate coat" on her skin, her ear "drinks the sound of his voice."[35] Myrtocle is enveloped by a synesthesia even more comprehensive than a Gesamtkunstwerk—taste, touch, rhythm all conspire, but the phantasmagoria to which she thrills is nothing other than her husband. And it is the voluntarily chosen blindness of the "dead eyes" that allow her other senses to cohere, to banish the dissonance of seeing her "husband" and realizing it is Galba, of seeing a feral creature and realizing it is her beloved husband.

Marriage thus essentially models the awkward synesthesia of opera, its attempt to merge and unify separate media into a seamless whole, be this the Gesamtkunstwerk, or simply the acoustic and visual bundling that becomes increasingly important as opera houses grow quieter and darker. However, this effort doesn't just involve new technologies or compositional techniques, but most importantly an audience that is being differently conditioned—and that has to some extent amplify and modify the kind of make believe that is necessarily involved in any successful viewing of an opera. As we saw in the preceding chapter, both of these factors are part of the operatic experience as it emerges around the turn of the century: an ever more sophisticated technological and compositional apparatus putting ever greater demands on the audience, soliciting a leap of faith, a commitment to a generic contract much more stridently artificial than those required by other arts around the same period. Where Schreker's metaphysics of operatic distance often elide the fissures and ruptures, d'Albert's marital operas try to think through them. While d'Albert is of course anything but alone in reflecting on these medial transformations, he is most persistent in connecting them to the guiding metaphor of marriage—the illusion that is naturalized in Schreker becomes a matter of faith, a matter of effort in d'Albert. Not only does marriage come to stand in for the unification of different media onstage, but it also comes to serve as a site of reflection on the audience's relationship to the new modes of "intermediality" onstage—the audience that hears voices and says *lasst sehn!*

As I argued in chapter 2, in post-Wagnerian opera personal ugliness comes to represent imbalance among opera's individual features, and Myrtocle's blind forbearance vis-à-vis such ugliness is to some extent asked of the opera audience as well. An entirely different relationship between viewership and ugliness comes to the fore in another of d'Albert's operas, *Der Stier von Olivera* (premiered in 1918). The opera takes place in Spain, where Napoleon's troops are quartered in the Olivera castle, led by the exceedingly ugly French general Guillaume. When the noble family displaced by the invaders attempts to assassinate them, the general decides to have them executed. The family's oldest daughter, Juana, asks for clemency for her youngest brother, and Guillaume barters the boy's life for Juana's promise of marriage. To avenge her family, Juana schemes to ruin her new husband's life, first by cuckolding him, then by trying to rouse him to open rebellion against Napoleon. Eventually, she goes too far, and Guillaume sees through her schemes. In a rage, he stabs Juana. When Napoleon arrives at Olivera castle, Guillaume is charged with treason due to Juana's influence, but when the emperor sees Juana's corpse, he pardons Guillaume. When Spanish rebels threaten to cut off the emperor's retreat, Guillaume tells Napoleon to take his carriage, while he sacrifices himself by riding the emperor's carriage straight into a rebel trap.

Der Stier von Olivera presents a marriage diametrically opposed to that of *Die toten Augen*: it is a marriage of perfect vision, entirely cynical and emptied of all illusion. She is bound to him through blackmail of the most brutal kind; he is bound to her through obsession and sadomasochistic humiliation. Marriage becomes the proverbial "battlefield" of cliché. The "bull" of the title never actually appears in the opera: When the action begins it has been slaughtered, not in a traditional Spanish bullfight, however, but rather much more prosaically as food for Napoleon's troops. The absent bull, however, structures the actual opera plot in two central ways: It provides a last straw for the Spaniards to decide to murder their French oppressors; and it provides a metaphor for Juana's revenge on Guillaume, who becomes the harried bull that she is attempting to slaughter. The analogy between bullfight and married life becomes most explicit in the opera's climactic scene: Juana hands Guillaume a dagger to murder Napoleon with, but he plunges it into her breast instead, shouting "The bullfight is over, Madame!"[36]

If blindness in *Die toten Augen* comes to stand for the kind of projective, fantastic work that is a condition for the possibility of marriage, then ugliness stands for the reality of imbalance, for cruelty, asymmetry, and one-sidedness that it turns into. Even if in *Der Stier von Olivera* this focus on the sadistic streak in marriage becomes less observant and instead begins to smack of cliché, the overweening *corrida* metaphor illuminates the semiotic promiscuity of the marriage metaphor in general, a promiscuity that d'Albert himself seems to have taken note of. Among the questions d'Albert's long gallery of marital vignettes seems to be asking, a prominent one concerns precisely the amazing malleability of marriage as source or target of metaphor. How many things can be said to resemble marriage, and how many things marriage can be said to resemble becomes itself an issue in the opera d'Albert composed immediately following *Die toten Augen* and *Der Stier von Olivera.*

"YOUR MARRIAGE IS A SYMBOL": THE PRICE OF UNIFICATION IN *REVOLUTIONSHOCHZEIT*

In Johann Gottlieb Fichte's deduction of marital right in *The Foundations of Natural Right* (1796), marriage is posited as the "complete unification" of two persons, "which is its own end."[37] In Friedrich Schlegel's *Lucinde* (1799), the protagonist Julius sees in the lovers' embrace an "allegory of the completion of the male and the female into complete humanity."[38] Such formulations continued to be championed throughout the age of Romanticism (usually against Kant's infamous formula of marriage as a "contract" for "life-long reciprocal possession of their sexual faculties"[39]), influential to the point that not only the Romantics recurred to the formula, but even their opponents. Hegel's *Foundations of the Philosophy of Right*, written more than twenty years after Fichte's book, understands marriage as the agreement between two individuals "to become one person, to [each] surrender their natural and individual personality into that unity, which is in this respect a self-limitation, but insofar as they gain substantial self-consciousness, is actually a liberation."[40]

Liberation through unification continued to be understood as not just constitutive of marriage, but as also the defining feature of *modern* marriage. For behind the idea of a freely elected unification into a larger suprasubjective whole lay a bourgeois claim to political autonomy—the love that effected the "unification" of marital partners could bind larger agglomerations of people as well, independent of tradition, monarchy, or ecclesiastic authority. The charge was, as we saw in the previous sections, that those unions dictated by force rather than autonomy were incomplete unifications—heterogeneous and disharmonious assemblages at war with themselves, from Hegel's bourgeois "animal kingdom of the Spirit" to Tönnies's atomized *Gesellschaft.* Of course, music's ability to merge individual performers into larger harmonious wholes made it a highly popular sensuous analog for such fantasies of unification[41]—an analogization that became if anything more direct once Wagner sought to further drive operatic performance toward a unified whole in which the particulars "surrender their natural and individual personality." In this way, the fantasies of the Gesamtkunstwerk, which, as Adorno has shown, were antibourgeois in their ideological thrust, actually coincide with bourgeois conceptions of democratic unification.[42]

D'Albert's relationship to this ideological baggage is uniquely fraught. Although his roots are firmly in the German musical tradition, his operatic oeuvre drew largely on styles (above all verismo) and on forms (the comedic one-act opera) openly antithetical to Wagner's project. What holds true on the level of form goes for his opera's marriage plots as well. The main problem in *Die toten Augen* is not the role of illusion or projection in eroticism; what seems to have drawn d'Albert to Ewers's libretto and the many others that deal with marriage, is that illusion, projection, and misunderstanding, as in Goethe's *Wahlverwandtschaften*, always preserve the duality of the lovers. Wagner's lovers, be this Tristan and Isolde, Senta and the Holländer, or Siegfried and Brünnhilde, have a dangerous tendency toward unification, a unification that is of one piece with the Gesamtkunstwerk in which their unification is celebrated.

D'Albert, leery of Wagner's influence and given to emphasizing the collaborative in the process of operatic production, keeps the different media of opera similarly semiautonomous. Like the marital partners of his plots, they may converge or squabble, support or betray each other, but neither "says again what the other has already said,"[43] as Adorno has characterized music and text in the Gesamtkunstwerk (see also chapter 5). And, like marriage (and unlike the sexual love that overpowers feeble contractual marriage in Wagner's view) there is something constitutive and legalistic about their interrelation: the parties united are to become one, yet they enter the contract separately and the very contractual nature of their relation recalls the remainders of autonomy that cling to the individuals supposedly alloyed so fully in the marital relation. By insisting on conjugating rather than eliding synchronic and diachronic difference, be this in the plots he relies on, in the music he sets them to, or the way he combines both, d'Albert struggles to break free from metaphysics of absolute sexuality and absolute music.

This struggle becomes most explicit in d'Albert's *Revolutionshochzeit*, based on a Danish-language play by Sophus Michaelis (1865–1932). In turning Michaelis's play into an opera, d'Albert used an adaptation by Ferdinand Lion (who also wrote the libretto to d'Albert's *Golem*), apparently based on Marie Herzfeld's translation. D'Albert wrote the score to *Revolutionshochzeit* in 1917 and the opera premiered in October of 1919 in Leipzig. The story of the opera takes place in 1793. The young noblewoman Alaine is to be wed to the young man she was promised to, an *exile* who returns to France with foreign allies. Revolutionary troops descend upon their chateau almost immediately after their nuptials—however, realizing that they have interrupted a wedding, the young officer Marc-Arron asks that the newly minted husband's execution be delayed until the lovers have spent their first night together. At night, Marc-Arron, who has fallen in love with Alaine, offers to exchange clothes with her husband, allowing him to escape. Overwhelmed by the depth of his devotion to her, Alaine falls in love with Marc-Arron as well. They spend a night of passion and united go to their deaths in the morning.

Revolutionshochzeit is at its core a drama of unification: Its central metaphor, *Hochzeit*, brims with unifying pathos (a clear legacy of German Romanticism), suggesting that the marriage unites into one more than just two people—it represents the unification of revolutionary France and the émigrés, the merger of two separate spheres, bourgeois and aristocratic, public and private, earnest and frivolous, eighteenth- and nineteenth-century. As a contemporary review of *Revolutionshochzeit*'s first performance by the musicologist Adolf Aber noted, "Two different cultural worlds are confronted in this drama: the age of the rococo and that of the French Revolution. Only one power can unite the two: love. With a fine sense of humor, d'Albert first sketches opposition and unification of these two worlds."[44]

When however those two worlds confront each other once more in the two main characters, Marc-Arron and Alaine, the opera "also opposes two musical worlds: the minuet on the one hand and the through-composed recitative on the other."[45] Not just the opera's libretto, then, tells of unification and harmonization, so does the music—it increasingly merges eighteenth- and nineteenth-century practices, charted by the erotic progress of its star-crossed lovers: "Alaine herself initially moves in the musical sphere of the minuet, until (in the second act) her love to Marc-Arron teaches her his language, musically defined by stern, declamatory pathos."[46]

Once again, then, the marital union and the musical integration of an opera are explicitly identified. For Aber, the "marriage" being effected in *Revolutionshochzeit* is ultimately that of different musical styles or eras, styles that are themselves implicitly gendered: the high pathos of the revolutionary nineteenth century contrasts with the effete playfulness of the eighteenth. Indeed, historical signifiers and gender signifiers are liberally intermingled in d'Albert's score—or at least were so in the mind of the contemporary public, as Aber's review makes clear:

> Even in the forms of instrumentation, we can distinguish these two worlds. The Rococo is made colorful thanks to the liberal use of celesta, harp, triangle, xylophone and glockenspiel, while tympani, drums, strong brass and deep strings make sensible the revolution.[47]

Unifying two worlds through different instrumental groups is something d'Albert had practiced in a 1905 *Lustspiel* already: In *Flauto Solo*, d'Albert and his librettist Hans von Wolzogen tell the story of a martial Prince (*Fürst*) who tolerates only German marching bands and is particularly fond a group of six bassoons, while his son prince Ferdinand loves Italian music, speaks French and plays the flute. The opera's comedic and love plot (involving both princes only marginally) plays off "the pathos of the opera seria" (as the composer's directions in the score make clear) against supposedly autochthonous German forms, yet ultimately serves to unite these two different realms, reconciling the two musical worlds and the royals that represent them: Germany and Italy/France, tradition and modernity, utility and beauty, duty and *joie de vivre*, philistinism and aestheticism. The entire plot, focusing on two rival musical directors and a fetching singer rather than on the royals, draws on and reconciles these organizing dichotomies.

There is even a hint of erotic worlds being reconciled—throughout the opera there is a marked conflict over the prince's "flute mania" [*Flötenwut*]. Although Wolzogen (1848–1938), himself a Prussian aristocrat, of course doesn't make this clear, the two feuding royals seem to be modeled on King Frederick William I (the famed "soldier king") and his son, the later Frederick the Great, who was indeed an accomplished flutist, an activity his father hated. As a young man, Frederick was incarcerated by his father after attempting to run off with a close friend and possible lover, an event musicalized in *Flauto Solo* by having the old Prince forbid his son from playing the flute, on account of it being "overly precious, overly womanly, overly soft [*Verfeint! Verweibt! Verweichlicht!*]," although the young prince continues to play the flute in secret.

It is likely that d'Albert was aware of this prehistory—among his acquaintances, Hanns Heinz Ewers (librettist of *Die toten Augen*) had written extensively for *Der Eigene*, Germany's first publication for gays; and Richard Batka, another librettist and a music historian by trade, explicitly references the Friedrich connection and seems to allude to the monarch's homosexuality in his review of *Flauto Solo*: "Eventually the prince . . . is arrested and his flute is confiscated."[48] Whether or not they were aware of this particular dimension of his story, d'Albert and Wolzogen once again clearly gender the two opposing spheres—the hypermasculine sphere of the king and the effeminate one of the prince. Whether or not its prince is gay, *Flauto Solo*'s metaphorics are strictly heterosexual.

Just like *Flauto Solo*, *Revolutionshochzeit* analogizes the unification of two worlds by musical means and the way love harmonizes Marc-Arron and Alaine; music can perform unions the way marriage does. However, the libretto that d'Albert uses as the carrier of this analogy treats not just marriage, but the very analogization of marriage as highly problematic and ultimately a form of violence. In other words, the unifying pathos Aber's review identifies in the opera may be less positive than he seems to think. Lion's libretto is as explicit as Michaelis's original stage play in its metaphorization of marriage; however, since that metaphorization is constantly thrust into the foreground by the characters themselves, and since it is so explicitly foisted upon Alaine, the very insistence with which the political and the personal are (musically and metaphorically) hitched together becomes itself questionable.

The opera's opening scene (taken almost verbatim from Michaelis) constitutes a moment of double unification: Ernest has returned to France to reclaim France for the King and to marry his fiancée. Alaine is reunited with the man to whom she was promised "while still in the cradle"; and France is to be reunited with its rightfully appointed aristocratic rulers. In the play's first scene, Alaine worries that it might be egotistical ("sinful") to be concerned with her own marriage while the wider unification unfolds around her; but Abbé Copin reassures her that she is anything but egotistical, since "your marriage is a symbol."[49] The libretto thus stages an opposition between an egotistical, self-referential marriage (marriage for itself) and marriage as referencing or representing something external. According to the Abbé, "it is France that is once again betrothed to its lord. You, my child, are yourself the land itself."[50] Not only is the libretto perfectly explicit in its organizing image, the opera's bride welcomes not just her husband's authority, but also the weight of signification into her life on her wedding day.

Not surprisingly, the libretto's characterization of this signification is not entirely positive, but instead shot through with a disturbingly violent streak. That violence inheres both in the signified (the violent return of the exiles to France) and in the signifier (the marital union of Alaine and Ernest)—but it seems to extend to their very representational connection as well. Alaine's maidservant Léontine speculates about Ernest's "appetite," "a twenty-year old hunger which he must satisfy in a single night," refers to her husband "plucking [your] small ripe berry" and ominously jokes that "your hour has come [*Ihr Stündlein schlagen hören*]."[51] Not only is Alaine's marriage ceremony something of a bellicose conquest *en miniature*, her fiancé's "comrades in arms [*Waffengefährten*]" decide to "create a triumphal gate made of our blades above your path to the altar," thus infusing an obtrusively phallic militarism into a ceremony that, according to the Abbé was supposed to be only symbolic of a war.

As such, not only do war and marital unification become increasingly assimilated, but the encroachment of one upon the other in the guise of the symbol is itself presented as something violent: Just as the difference between the metaphorical conquest of marriage and the real conquest of France becomes ever slimmer, so escalates the violence with which the marriage is seized by that which it is said to represent. The Abbé Copin explains his rhetorical alliance between France's conquest and Alaine's in some detail: "I unite in you France's earth with its rightful owner. It is France that is betrothed to its lord." The Abbé thus explicitly connects the rapaciousness of Alaine's prospective husband with his own rapaciousness in claiming Alaine as a signifier for "France's earth." Both are forms of domination: one dominates woman *like* the French earth, the other dominates woman by *likening* her to the French earth.

While the libretto thus stages a concatenation of compounding unifications, bringing together eras, instruments, political camps, sexes, and musical styles, all bracketed together through metaphor of marriage, it seems to understand marriage as a profoundly disturbing and violent affair. In fact, it is the very unification of two separate things effected in metaphor and analogy that rouses the opera's suspicion. Not only does the likeness of marriage and matters aesthetic and political come into question in *Revolutionshochzeit*, but so does the very act of likening. If *Die toten Augen* and *Der Stier von Olivera* staged the spectacle of ugliness in marriage, then *Revolutionshochzeit* stages the spectacle of meaning: Marriage is obsessively referred to universals here, to a sensus communis that cannot let a pipe be a pipe. In the first act, Alaine's prearranged union with Ernest is freighted with a weight of signification that Lion's adaptation of Michaelis's play purposefully imbues with a highly aggressive hue—making marriage signify is essentially cast as a rape. In the third act, however, the love union of Alaine with Marc-Arron is similarly freighted with signification—the two need to unite (and die uniting) the warring factions of revolutionary France. Whether this remetaphorization is meant to be less violent, because autonomously chosen rather than traditionally ordained (in terms rather redolent of the Wagnerian erotics of *Tiefland*), or whether it is simply a second iteration of the first act's metaphorizing violence, is perhaps less clear.

What matters perhaps more in the case of *Revolutionshochzeit* is just how much unification is piled onto three individuals in two couples. In general, then, the case of Eugen d'Albert illuminates the manifold ways opera was expected to cohere after Wagner, and which ideological importance attached to such coherence, just how much its ersatz totality was supposed to repair; at the same time, d'Albert's oeuvre consciously registers just how impossible the onslaught of historicism, eclecticism, and modernism made any such attempt.

D'Albert's erotic historicism thus paradoxically serves to trace the outlines of the composer's alternate modernism. When seen through an erotic lens, d'Albert's eclecticism loses its air of arbitrariness; rather it represents a careful, if fitful and ultimately abortive, attempt to think through the legacy of Wagner's sexual metaphysics while taking the hereditary problem of opera seriously.

CHAPTER 6

Occult Legacies: Eroticism and the Dynasty in Siegfried Wagner's Operas

When Siegfried Wagner was born in 1869, his proud father composed what came to be known as the *Siegfried Idyll*. This piece would go on to become an important building block of the opera that—like the infant—bore the name of Wagner's hero. Young Siegfried Wagner's arrival very quickly became part of his father's work product. Although the *Siegfried Idyll* had no singing part and no text, its score was, upon publication, accompanied by a short poem by the composer's hand dedicated to Cosima Wagner. "It was your noble will ready for sacrifice," we read there, "that gave my work its sanctuary." Of course, Cosima had just proved her will to sacrifice for a very different kind of work product—namely the boy whose name graces the idyll. The project of producing an heir and the project of producing the *Ring* were thus entwined: Cosima provided sanctuary to the work, while her giving birth to Siegfried inspired and structured the completion of the great work that bore his name.

In 1918, with that great work seriously threatened, with Wahnfried and its family in financial disarray, and with the *Festpielhaus* effectively shut down as the war sucked up money, men and material, Siegfried composed the *Wahnfried Idyll*. Unlike the *Siegfried Idyll* which was scored for a small orchestra (strings and woodwinds), the *Wahnfried Idyll* was a piece of chamber music, written for piano and soprano—"a composition for children," as Nike Wagner has put it.[1] Just as the idyll occasioned by Siegfried's own birth, the *Wahnfried Idyll* celebrates the Wagner dynasty, occasioned by seeing his mother Cosima with his first-born son, Wieland.[2] The text reflects the perspective of the boy, nearly two at the time, but other members of the Wagner clan (Siegfried's sister Eva, his wife, Winifred, his daughter Friedelind, and their nanny) appear in the song. Siegfried maintains a childlike tone throughout ("Kugeli! Kugeli! Dudel-dazwi!"), as the boy wakes up, wakes up his parents, urinates, takes a bath, and visits the "Omama" Cosima next door.

In the judgment of posterity, the second dynastic idyll failed to live up to the first one. The catalogues of Siegfried's works did not list it as one of the composer's works until well after his death. But while judgment of the piece has been almost invariably harsh, few have remarked on the fact that the piece is spectacularly poorly suited for a direct comparison with Wagner père's idyll, even as its genre and connection to the house where Wagner's "Wäh-nen" found "Frieden" seem to demand such comparison. Jacques Lacan's spelling of "perversion" as *père-version* has never seemed more appropriate. As the Great War grinds on and threatens to engulf the last vestiges of the Wagner clan, as the Gesamtkunstwerk is bereft of its means of production and the theater built for it lies dormant, Siegfried returns to his father's aesthetic-political project, and more importantly to his own role in it. What becomes of the two legacies Wagner left behind—the family of *Wahnfried* and the work performed at Bayreuth—hangs in the balance.

But this turn to the father is itself perverse—this time in the everyday un-derstanding of the term. Where Richard's *Idyll* became a great orchestral in-terlude, a building block in his towering aesthetic edifice, Siegfried produces a rather traditional ditty, and the "idyllic" character Richard's piece gave to the orchestra to unfold is asserted explicitly, a school song of a third-rate boarding school or a football team's fighting song. Where Richard's *Idyll* became a pro-ductive pause from the existential drama that flanks it, Siegfried's text is idyllic only in its limitation, in its childish, even ditzy naiveté. Siegfried's insistence of adding words, moreover his own, is of course itself a nod to his father—un-like Richard, Siegfried was otherwise fairly content to set at least songs to the words of others. Here, he dons the cap of the poet composer, and delivers fairly embarrassing (and altogether untranslatable) lines like "Drum Kugeli kugeli Dudeldazwi! Ruft mit dem Gockel: Kikeriki!"

Between them the two idylls speak to the younger Wagner's tortured rela-tionship with his father, and more importantly with his own part in carrying on his father's legacy. Throughout his career Siegfried evinced a perverse com-pulsion to invite comparison with his father, and to come out lacking in the pro-cess. To be sure, his musical idiom owed much more to his teacher, Engelbert Humperdinck, than to his father, and yet his operas are littered with moments like the *Wahnfried Idyll*—moments that solicit our judgment, knowing full well how it will turn out. As Heinrich Schenker, no friend of the elder Wagner, put it in an otherwise genial essay, "The non-genius son of a genius father" "sought out the father's art, to see and feel in it the father again and again, as well as to satisfy the inherited drive."[3] Throughout his operas Siegfried seems haunted by the specter of illegitimacy, just as public debates and even lawsuits over the legitimacy of his continuation of Richard's legacy roused his self-doubt and sense of persecution. For Schenker "the spectacle was, both with respect to its human and artistic aspects, as funny as it was sad."[4]

Siegfried's unease with the dynastic task bequeathed onto him in the *Siegfried Idyll* has often been read in terms of the composer's homosexuality. And indeed, the fact that the man who was to carry on the bloodline of Bayreuth was perhaps less than enthusiastic about procreative sex was an irony that failed to escape notice even at the time. Unusually candid were the allusions and intimations both within the world of Wahnfried and outside it. Siegfried's sister Isolde, the black sheep of the family, seems to have tried to blackmail her way back into the clan by threatening to expose Siegfried's orientation.[5] In June of 1914, the journalist Maximilian Harden, who specialized in what we would today call "outing," wrote an exposé about the situation in his journal *Die Zukunft* under the title "Tristan and Isolde," which gleefully alluded to Siegfried's homosexuality. It was this crisis that convinced the powers that be in Wahnfried (which pointedly did not include *Fidi* himself) that Siegfried had to marry and sire an heir.[6] This is how Winifred, the dedicatee of the Siegfried's song, entered the idyll.

But Siegfried's sexuality itself plugged only into a wider narrative, one of an heir unable to live up to his heritage, even as the work he was called upon to safeguard obsessed over questions of lineage and heredity. This put Siegfried in the unenviable position of having to rely on those very topoi in order to defend himself that would serve to doom him. As we shall see in the next section, the fact that Siegfried's defenders were obsessed with the same logic of heredity and degeneracy as Richard Wagner had been, meant that they persistently drew the "young *Meister*" into dynastic narratives that ended up making him look the worse for the comparison. These dynastic narratives always concerned two things at once: the Wagner name and the aesthetic project associated with it. Did Siegfried Wagner's own oeuvre, and indeed his person, fall short of the exacting standards of the total work of art?

CRITICISM THAT "COMES BY ITSELF"

Houston Stewart Chamberlain, Richard Wagner's son-in-law, remarks in his 1892 book on Richard that "Siegfried Wagner has grown up with the work of Bayreuth; with him may it prosper and impart a new long life to Germany's great poet!"[7] How Siegfried succeeded in carrying on that legacy was a fore-most concern among Wagnerians, and often a source of ridicule for those who disliked the clan. Chamberlain had attained fame not so much as a writer on music, but as a propagandist of the most vicious kind of racism. His *Founda-tions of the Nineteenth Century* (1899) had obsessed over questions of hered-ity, decline, and degeneration. Chamberlain's hopes about the continuation of the "work of Bayreuth" depended on a felicity of inheritance that has to be very much understood in the biologistic terms of the late nineteenth century: Siegfried had to have the right genetic material, if the Wagner project was to continue—dynastic and aesthetic project were thus, if not one, then at least closely aligned.

In 1911, Carl Friedrich Glasenapp, Richard Wagner's biographer and glow-ing acolyte, decided to publish a book about "the young *Meister* of Bayreuth."[8] The book, *Siegfried Wagner und seine Kunst*, appeared at a time when the composer had completed six of what were to become his twelve finished op-eras, and Glasenapp acknowledged in his preface that his presentation came perhaps a bit early. In justifying his own early arrival, Glasenapp contrasted the ever-growing literature on Richard Wagner, which arrives "*post festum*" and is thus in some way parasitical to a work that can stand on its own without it, with his own attempt to present Siegfried Wagner's art "*ante festum* or *pro festum*," which "leads us to the great feast [*Fest*] of art and prepares us for it."[9]

Glasenapp cited the *Meister* saying that writing about a work would "come by itself," and distinguished two kinds of such "coming by itself." There is, for one, that efflorescence of commentary, hagiography, and critique that emerges almost necessarily from a towering work. But there is another that does not fol-low so logically from a work, that instead attaches itself to a work in the process of becoming, but which "comes by itself" in a different way: It emerges spon-taneously from an encounter with the work of art and doesn't seek to attach its fortunes to the luster of an already established corpus of classics.

Glasenapp never makes explicit the irony that he is disparaging the *post festum* character of Wagner idolatry, while idolizing a man whose very name points to his own *post festum* character. The idea of being "post" the main event haunts Siegfried's oeuvre—"non-genius son to a genius father," as Schenker had put it. Siegfried himself remarks in his 1923 *Erinnerungen*: "There are those who would make me into a tragic figure." "How the weight of your fa-ther's fame must weigh you down," he imagines them saying, "and that you have the temerity to try to become an opera composer and the naïveté to think you'll get on like that!"[10] He insists that he does not "regret" having the father, mother, and grandfather that he had, any more than he regrets his sisters or children. Would a man so beaten down write these memoirs? he asks. But those memoirs, which eschew the grand narrative sweep of Richard's *Mein Leben* for a few vignettes from early childhood, travels in Asia and Italy, and a few humorous observations, betray that Siegfried himself did not think that a continuous story of House Wahnfried could be told. The *Wahnfried Idyll* and his *Erinnerungen* suggest that Siegfried seems to have been aware of the fact that carrying on the legacy of Bayreuth would by force tell a story of disjuncture and decline. He was a caretaker of a legacy, not a continuation of that legacy: his memoirs were remembrances—looks back to Bayreuth's heyday, not accounts of "my life." And his own operas were worth one paragraph in it—for more information Siegfried directs his readers to Glasenapp.

From his correspondence, we know that Siegfried was not always so content to respond to slights against his person, both the perceived and the actual ones, with good humor—and Bayreuth's defenders could easily strike a much more hysterical tone when defending Richard's legacy in Siegfried. Glasenapp is a case in point: *Siegfried Wagner und seine Kunst* is a highly paranoid book. Its author provides synopses and brief discussions of Siegfried Wagner's first six operas, reprints some of his previously published studies on those operas, but throughout dwells obsessively on their reception. Since that reception, with the possible exception of *Der Bärenhäuter*, was fairly toxic, Glasenapp spends an inordinate number of pages chronicling slights, bad reviews, and other mistreatments of the different operas. To hear Glasenapp tell the story, shadowy cabals of *Intendanten*, critics and "jealous" composer colleagues conspired against the spawn of Wahnfried from the beginning and were able to convince the public that Siegfried's works could be safely ignored or mocked.

Although he is at pains to defend Siegfried against all manner of "enemies"— Glasepnapp does not use the term "critics," because for him the charges leveled against the "young *Meister*" were "in intention usually not criticism but rather hateful attacks"[11]—in his defense a number of anxieties about Siegfried and his art come through all the more forcefully. The prime anxiety attaches to Siegfried's status as "dramatic artist" (i.e., Siegfried's ability to write music and poem, and to integrate the two successfully). Siegfried's "enemies," Glasenapp writes, attack the composer by pulling apart poem and music, finding nice things to say about the music while deriding Siegfried's libretti. But Glasenapp insists that Siegfried is not a "composer of pleasing music" set to "meaningless shrubberies of words"; he is "not an aesthete and literary man who accidentally wandered onto the stage"; he is not "a scenic-theatralic poet and musician,"[12] a label that, Glasenapp thinks, is usually "meant to imply suspicion" of Siegfried's art.

For a preface to a monograph celebrating the art of a fairly successful composer, Glasenapp spends an almost sadistic amount of time ventriloquizing these sorts of "attacks" on his subject, protesting far too much, and again and again calling on his readership to arrive at their own judgment. But why is it the issue of Siegfried's libretti that Glasenapp returns to so obsessively? The charge that incenses Glasenapp so, and the fear that animates his nearly endless list of what Siegfried is not, thus has to do with Richard Wagner's command that poem and music be completely integrated. Siegfried stands accused not of being a bad composer or a bad librettist, but a bad Wagner, "*post festum:*" a decline from a pinnacle rather than its continuation.

But there is more at stake here: Siegfried's status as poet has been overlooked not because he represents a decline from Richard's prose, but rather because the standards of poetry have declined between Richard's day and Siegfried's. Symbolism and other poetic movements, by their "sentimental and often thoroughly un-German word artifice [*Wortkünstelei*]," have "poisoned the public's sense of taste." Now every time a new work by Siegfried Wagner appears, the critics "pick out a few beauties of unique expression and denounce them as word-ogres [*Wortungeheuer*], idiosyncrasies [*Schrullen*], monstrosities, and mannered freaks [*Mißgeburten*],"[13] when in fact it is the critics' "artifice" that represents a degeneration of German poetic art, born instead of "mulatto aesthetic instincts." It is not true that Siegfried constitutes a decline vis-à-vis the past, specifically vis-à-vis Richard; his present fails to understand him because it itself has degenerated since Richard's day.

While Glasenapp's discourse here traffics in the common tropes of fin-de-siècle declinism, his confident narrative of decline in the wider culture contrasts with his somewhat more anguished insistence that no such decline has taken place within the Wagner family. And while he frames his comments on Siegfried's art in terms of the aesthetics of the Gesamtkunstwerk, his indictment of the wider culture makes clear that the decline he has in mind is biological—that is to say, degenerative in nature. Modern German poetry is biologically inferior—misbegotten, monstrous, and mulatto—because of its heredity. It has debased its own genetic material, as it were. The very dynastic infelicity Glasenapp denies in the case of the Wagner clan, he diagnoses in the world's judgment of it.

At stake in that diagnosis is nothing less than the ideology that regarded Wagner's aesthetic project as the spontaneous expression of a Germanic essence. For them, Siegfried was not simply carrying on an artistic legacy, or managing a "brand" (as Nicholas Vaszonyi has recently put it[14]); he was carrying on his father's unique connection to truly Germanic art. And that unique connection, his fans believed, Siegfried had inherited biologically from his father. In his 1918 *Geschichte der Musik*, Karl Storck described Siegfried's "true sense of folk [*Volkstümlichkeit*]" as "part of nature's dowry [*Mitgift*]" to Richard's son.[15] Richard did not pass on his skill, or his instincts to his son, as far as Storck is concerned; rather, he passed on the ability to create a holistic work of art that arises organically from the spirit of the people. "Siegfried Wagner's precious inheritance from his father is his ability, to inhabit our treasury of myths and fairy tales to such an extent that it reveals itself to him in all is essential element."[16]

THE IMP OF THE PERVERSE: EROTICISM AND THE GESAMTKUNSTWERK IN SIEGFRIED WAGNER

Siegfried himself seems to have been all too aware that his claim to legitimacy rested on factors that, in the eyes of the world and the press, served to undercut it. Siegfried himself invoked the language of breeding and degeneration to explain why he wrote the kind of operas he wrote (representing "the soul of the German people, the only antidote to the pestilence of the metropolis"[17]), and he was aware that the scorn and derision his work had aroused was not infrequently tinged with those same questions. Siegfried thus interpreted the attacks on him as signs of degeneracy (what he, in that noxious habit inherited from Cosima, termed "Jewish"), but those attacks themselves applied the same biologistic logic to his works.

In a letter to Clemens Strauss, Richard Strauss relates an encounter in Berlin's Hotel Adlon. Siegfried, who had repeatedly applied to Strauss the thinly veiled moniker of "stockbroker," sneered that "business seems to be booming." In his letter, Strauss says he wishes he had replied "at least I live off the fruits [*Erträgnis*] of my own store, and not just manning my daddy's."[18] A look at Siegfried's operas suggests that Strauss was right in not wasting his breath—the object of his scorn was perfectly well aware that he was manning someone else's shop. Siegfried's operas turn out to be shot through with dynastic concerns, often allied with questions about how legitimacy is transmitted through generations. That means that Siegfried's operas rely on a picture of love far more complicated than those of his father, and even many of those of his musically more advanced contemporaries. At least those serious operas Siegfried thought he drew from the "soul of the German people," but what he found there seemed to put the lie to the kind of natural and immediate instincts Richard had implanted in his characters—and had hoped to inspire in his audiences.

The opening act of *Der Friedensengel* (1914) is a case in point: The opera introduces an existing family on the verge of crisis. Willfried and Eruna are married, but their marriage is loveless. The first scene of act 1 presents his mother's three attempts to make sense of that lovelessness. Her first guest is the philosopher Balthasar, who propagates free love, the second a pastor, who insists on morality; finally, a doctor arrives whom Eruna consults to find out what is wrong with her husband. He decides to perform craniometric measurements on Willfred, and promptly diagnoses him with a mental illness. Richard Wagner's operas rely on natural attraction, which does not have to be consciously contemplated (e.g., in the "Winterstürme wichen dem Wonnemond" duet in *Walküre*), to move along their plots and to integrate opera's constituent media. His son begins with the mystery of a mismatch, a union that does not function automatically or instinctually, but which requires investigation and justification.

While it is of course tempting to read especially the phrenological investigation into Willfried's inability to love Eruna in terms of the writer/composer's homosexuality, the formal ramifications are perhaps more significant. Science, religion, morality are all brought in to buttress a situation that in Richard Wagner's oeuvre constitutively had to stand on its own in order to count as authentic; what used to be automatic (at least among the right kind of people), requires reflection, interrogation, support. The erotic has transformed from being an ally of operatic form to being deeply problematic, a source of anxiety rather than coherence. For Siegfried in Richard Wagner's opera, overcoming Mime's false maternal love in favor of a genuine erotic relation (to Brünnhilde) led from the defective world of fairy tale to the all-encompassing world of myth, and from inauthentic operatic practice to *Originaltheater* and Gesamtkunstwerk. This transcendence was utterly natural, brought about by Siegfried's burgeoning awareness of himself and of the erotic.

In *Der Friedensengel*, love becomes a medical issue instead: Things do not come together naturally in Siegfried Wagner's operas more generally, and once they come together they rarely seem a good fit. In *Das Sternengebot* (1906), Agnes, the daughter of emperor Konrad, is fated (by the titular "command of the stars") to marry Heinrich, but she loves young Helferich von Lahngau. At the end of the opera, she consents to the fated marriage, but tells her intended that she will never love anyone but Helferich. "Above the command of the stars, there is a second, higher one: that of the heart." Agnes's decision represents a rebuke of Richard Wagner's insistence that inclination and destiny (the "command of the stars") were one and the same.

In act 2 of *Die Walküre*, Siegmund and Sieglinde understand changes in nature as approving reflections of their incestuous union (in the duet "Winterstürme wichen dem Wonnemond" mentioned above). Morality might frown upon their loving union, they reflect, but the universe clearly does not. When confronted by an incensed Fricka, Wotan makes much the same point: "What horrible thing did that couple make, / which springtime united in love? / The magic of love enraptured them; / who would atone for the power of love?" Because dictated by the power of nature, the love between the twins should be celebrated rather than condemned. For Siegfried Wagner, no such prestabilized harmony between destiny and inclination exists: you can be *bestimmt* to love one person (by divine command, or, which amounts to the same thing, by Richard's), but be drawn to another.

As I have argued in previous chapters, much depends on the naturalness and inevitability of the self-transcendence Richard Wagner describes here. When Siegmund and Sieglinde give in to a law higher than that made by man (or even the gods), when Siegfried instinctively senses that he is part of something larger than the odd couple in Mime's forest, their erotic self-transcendence is supposed to mirror, or even enact, the transcendence of individual arts in the Gesamtkunstwerk. For Wagner, this transcendence is not dependent on will; it rather responds to instinct. Just as for the German Idealists and Romantics, "transcendental intuition" of the absolute did not require schooling, but instead lurked inside any authentic human being, so for Wagner the path to the totality of arts was ideally an automatic one. In pointing out that love can be a strange and unstable thing, that fate and sex can be very much at variance, Siegfried thus strikes at the very heart of the erotic ideology of the Gesamtkunstwerk.

This connection becomes clear in one of Siegfried's more comedic efforts, *An Allem ist Hütchen Schuld* (1917). The opera's characteristically convoluted but uncharacteristically strife-ridden plot, eventually comes to involve even Siegfried Wagner himself (in a speaking role). Its complications are revealed to derive entirely from the machinations of the invisible imp Hütchen. The opera montages together no less than forty separate fairy tales and myths— Siegfried's way of proceeding is here very much reminiscent to Richard's, but the sheer number of ingredients makes this opera a deliberately baroque and ridiculous concoction. Hütchen, the imp of the perverse, is the master of ceremonies who brings together these often rather disparate motifs and insists on grafting them onto each other in one plot. When Jacob Grimm, the inveterate collector of fairy tales, appears on the scene to accuse Siegfried Wagner of "brewing together forty fairy tales" in his operas, then, well, once again it's Hütchen's fault.

Hütchen is also behind the opera's love plot. In *An Allem ist Hütchen Schuld*, the star-crossed lovers, disapproving parents, and all the other traditional trappings—turn out to be nothing but effects of Hütchen's meddling. The fact that Frieder's and Katherlieschen's love takes on operatic form at all is Hütchen's fault. Hütchen engineers the misunderstandings and crises that at different points in the opera keep them apart. Where Richard Wagner's operas again and again take opera and the erotic to be naturally in league, Siegfried Wagner pits them against each other. The spirit of the opera intrudes into the central relationship and disrupts the erotic. If the opera's personages try to live normal, nonoperatic lives, Hütchen is the force pulling them again and again into ostentatiously artificial plots, be they melodramatic or comedic. Hütchen's meddling represents opera intruding upon real life; it does so to render perverse what would otherwise be a perfectly straightforward and straitlaced relationship. Opera perverts eros—or, more accurately, the Gesamtkunstwerk perverts eros.

For the libretto makes clear that Hütchen in many respects functions as the spirit of the Gesamtkunstwerk. Hütchen strings together a huge number of narrative elements, and he does so by way of synesthesia. Hütchen, who in fact has a *Tarnkappe*, much like Siegfried has a *Tarnhelm*, stitches together the opera's disparate elements by playing with what the opera's characters perceive and what its audience perceives. Hütchen is invisible to the opera's characters, but visible to the audience, in the shape of a "child of about twelve." But that "child of about twelve" is audible only to the characters onstage; the actor himself remains mute. For most of the opera, Hütchen does not sing, but just silently tickles, snatches, and otherwise manipulates objects onstage. He does not however sing, but only screams. When Hütchen reveals himself, the soprano singing the part is placed behind the scenes.

Figuring out that "it's all Hütchen's fault" thus requires quite a bit of work. While not as onerous as the deductive demands placed on the opera's characters, Wagner thus asks of his audience a transposition: voices that aren't present in the stage world are of course all too common in opera (villains singing about their nefarious schemes in earshot of their victims who are nevertheless none the wiser), but the absence of bodies is another matter entirely. Similarly, voices that have no location on the stage abound throughout the operatic canon—voices that have a supposed location, but move vis-à-vis that location are far rarer.

Of course, Hütchen's *Tarnkappe* is a much more ostentatious legerdemain than the kinds of dramatist's tricks Richard Wagner availed himself of—the magic hats, love potions, and potions of forgetfulness that so embarrass the elder Wagner's more serious-minded defenders. Siegfried Wagner generally wants the seams between opera's source materials and its constituent media to show. Richard's attempts at montage were owed at a desire to reconstitute a lost plenitude of genuinely German art. While Siegfried at times claims to carry on that legacy, he is far too content to let the artifice of such reconstitution stand—to the extent that it seems doubtful he ever believed in the vaunted authenticity of the source material to begin with. The *Gesamt*-ness of his operas (and here *Hütchen* is only the most outré example) is ironic and ironized—just as his erotic plots make love seem a difficult effort rather than a natural reservoir of authenticity, his operas wear on their sleeve the fact that they are self-conscious assemblage with no claim to organic form or an origin in the life of the *Volk*. Whatever Siegfried Wagner's *völkisch* politics, he seems to have found himself incapable of being a *völkisch* composer.

At the same time, Siegfried is after something quite serious with Hütchen: In English we translate glibly that "it's all Hütchen's fault," but the German "Schuld" weighs far more heavily. What the opera's characters are supposed to come to understand is the question of guilt, debt, culpability. Siegfried's operas tend to raise questions of debt and guilt explicitly in connection to questions about the medium of opera itself. Moments that connect the two abound in Siegfried's other works as well—most of them much less lighthearted than *Hütchen*. *Rainulf und Adelasia* (1922) is as far from a *Tristan* plot as can be imagined. Its two central figures are married, but they are married as part of a deadly intrigue and are at all times antagonists. Rainulf, younger son of the Count of Alife, has robbed a monastery and pinned the blame on his elder brother Osmund. Adelasia is in love with Osmund and wants to prove his innocence, and much of the plot becomes something of a whodunit, as Rainulf and Adelasia seek to outwit each other at every turn. But while Adelasia indeed manages to outsmart the murderer and clear Osmund's name, this happy ending does not extend to her. Osmund has from the first been in love with Beata and lives with her, while, in what can only be called the classic Siegfried Wagner ending, Adelasia retreats into the mountain to dedicate herself to another one of Rainulf's victim—another *Liebesopfer* in the name of an unattainable love object.

In the second act of *Rainulf und Adelasia*, Adelasia finally manages to trick her hated husband. Arnulf wants the wise woman Sigilgaita to put Adelasia to sleep, so he can finally consummate their marriage, but Adelasia turns the tables on him. She has Sigilgaita tell Rainulf the story of Daniel and the judgment *mene mene tekel upharsin* he alone was able to decipher. In order to become master of both his wife and his kingdom, he needs to be able to decipher his own future. The only way he can do it, Sigilgaita tells him, is under hypnosis—only then "will I disclose the truth to you in a dream." Rainulf at this point almost lusts after the truth more than after his kingdom or his resistant wife. As he puts it, "I want to enter into that foreign country! / Raze the wall that separates me from it!"

This demand, that the "wall" that separates him from the "foreign country" of dreams disappear, seems to point to the operatic itself. Throughout the scene Rainulf behaves as though he is attending a performance, or indeed an opera: "I see the curtain open again! Do we not have another play [*Schauspiel*] to hope for?" Just as Parsifal's attempt to understand the grail ceremony, Rainulf's wish to decipher his future is an allegory of spectatorship: what drives Rainulf's thirst for dreams is the thirst for the erotic (he wants to possess Adelasia); the fusion he seeks with that "foreign country" beyond the curtain is that sought by the average operagoer rushing late to his box.

But the "foreign country" Rainulf enters is of course no grail castle; he is being lured into a trap. The wish to see, so rarefied an undertaking in *Parsifal* that the young man fails at it once before he can finally get it right, is here a dangerous lure. In his trance, Rainulf encounters his mother and confesses all his transgressions to her. When he wakes, he scornfully dismisses what he has seen as "doubtful ambiguous drivel [*zweifelhaft, zweideutiges Zeug*]," but privately worries whether he has made his confession aloud and "become a traitor to myself." Rainulf's worry constitutes yet another, rather witty moment of self-reflexivity: opera characters by their nature have to sing out their most private thoughts and rely on the unwritten rule that their surroundings will miraculously be deaf to them—except, of course, for the audience, which giddily keeps the character's secret. Here, however, an opera character worries about what he has vocalized and how it has been received.

As we saw in chapter 1, in Richard Wagner's *Siegfried* Mime falls victim to a similar breach of generic contract, as he cannot but betray his dastardly plans to his ward Siegfried. But Rainulf understands full well that he has been lured into a realm of representation and now can no longer be sure of the status of his discourse—has he sung his confession to the audience, or also to the characters onstage? "Dastardly witch . . . ! I, who wanted to investigate have become the

object of investigation!" The drive toward the *Schauspiel* of truth has turned
Rainulf into a *Schauspiel* of his own. Just as in *Hütchen*, then, the operatic in
Rainulf und Adelasia is a mode of self-betrayal, a way of giving away too much
of oneself. Again, Siegfried's homosexuality cannot be unconnected from this
idea: The sense that the erotic might open one up to betrayal runs through
Siegfried's operas; *Rainulf und Adelasia* adds another layer to that anxiety: the
erotic might lead one to betray oneself. The medium of betrayal in either case
is the opera: Where the sense that the erotic and the Gesamtkunstwerk might
help one overcome betrayal runs through Richard's operas, his son seems to
turn that confidence on its head. Desire and operatic form no longer constitute
linked projects—rather, operatic form threatens to betray and pervert desire.

THE OPERA AND THE FAMILY: *DER KOBOLD* (1904)

Even a most cursory glance at the plots of Siegfried Wagner's operas reveals
something that sets them apart from virtually all other operas of the period, and
it is this difference that seems to vex Glasenapp and inspire his protectiveness
vis-à-vis the composer: Siegfried's operas are the least streamlined operas imaginable—where his father, his contemporaries, and his teacher, Humperdinck,
proceed with a pronounced economy in introducing plot points, backstory,
and characters, Siegfried is absolutely profligate with all of them. *An Allem
Ist Hütchen Schuld* (1917) has twenty-one individual singing parts (and two
additional speaking parts); *Herzog Wildfang* (1900), *Das Liebesopfer* (1917),
and *Der Schmied von Marienburg* (1920) each have twenty; *Der Kobold* (1903)
has fifteen; and *Der Friedensengel* (1914) has sixteen. This is partly because
Siegfried's operas are rich in tangents and digressions, the titular "kobold"
or "duke" of *Der Kobold* and *Herzog Wildfang* spend a comparatively short
span of time on the stage. There is something baroque about Siegfried's use of
fairy tale and mythic motifs, which are often piled on so thick as to lapse into
self-parody.

But there is a reason for the staggering lack of economy in Siegfried's operas, and it has to do with their erotics: Whereas most of the period's post-
Wagnerian operas are organized around a central relationship that emerges
early, Siegfried's operas present much more refracted erotic plots. In the most
expansive of Siegfried's operas, these plots play off the individual love story
against a wider dynastic frame that inflects and in most cases complicates
the straightforward love plot. In the libretto of *Wernhart*, a revision of *Das
Liebesopfer* Siegfried drafted in 1929 but never completed, the love between
Irene and Hans is undone by the fact that Irene's father has made a deal with

the devil; in *Schwarzschwanenreich*, Liebholt loves Hulda, but her guilt over having killed her illegitimate child eventually dooms them both; even in the far more comedic *An Allem ist Hütchen Schuld*, the lovers are forced to rely on the devil's own grandmother to return them from hell.

Often enough, the presence of these framing characters shades into the demonic—dead siblings, aborted children, buried uncles, and paternal pacts with the devil disrupt, and in many cases undo, the plot that is ostensibly the opera's focus. But what sets Siegfried's operas apart is that these demonic dynasties that stand behind the nuclear couple at the center do not stand against it—their power over the loving couple is portrayed as altogether legitimate. Whether through obligation, through guilt, or through money, they have a claim on the main characters that the lovers disregard at their own peril. The debts the lovers feel they owe, they indeed owe; the deeds that burden them with guilt are indeed heinous; the obligations they feel they have, they have. The question of *Schuld*, debt or guilt in German, thus enters the very structure of the opera, even though only the title of the frothy *An Allem ist Hütchen Schuld* makes that fact explicit. Guilt and debt enframe all of Siegfried's operas; and the central relationship is not just threatened—it is delegitimated by its dynastic frame.

Again and again, Siegfried's plots revolve around families that owe their stature or even their structure to heinous acts, and where guilt behaves like an inheritable trait. In *Das Liebesopfer*, Wernhart is an impoverished farmer anguished that due to his poverty he cannot let his daughter marry the man he loves. The opera's villain suggests a remedy: Wernhart's wealthy uncle lies buried with all his gold—just the cash injection the young people's romance requires. Wernhart digs up the dead uncle's loot, but matters go awry: first he destroys the roots of his life tree that grows from the uncle's grave, then he is surprised by his daughter's other suitor and feels he has to kill him. Before long Wernhart has taken a lover and dissolved his previous marriage; his prospective son-in-law stands accused of the suitor's murder, and Wernhart is too much of a coward to clear his name. By the end, Wernhart is dead and the two young people have decided not to marry, sacrificing their love to atone for the sin that was committed to make it possible—the *Liebesopfer* of the title.

Again and again these kinds of sacrifices are made necessary by guilt and debt that travel from generation to generation. Consider for instance *Der Kobold* (1903), which spins a rather complicated love plot between a count, a countess, a young peasant girl, and two members of a theater troupe. This plot intersects another one, in which children, who have been murdered by their mothers, haunt the living as invisible kobolds. The main plot is held together by a stone, which allows one to bind one's lover to oneself for eternity. This stone the peasant girl Verena receives from the kobold *Seelchen*—who is in fact the soul of her brother, whom her mother killed while still a baby. One of the actors meanwhile, who steps out on his wife while on the road with his troupe, has a wife back home who in desperation has also slain her newborn, another kobold to whom she tends full of guilt. In the end, Verena sacrifices herself for the actor, and saves her dead baby brother's soul.

As this brief synopsis makes clear, the goblin from which *Der Kobold* derives its title has a very marginal role to play in the opera. *Seelchen* instigates the plot, but is otherwise altogether supplemental to the story—any stone, regardless of its provenance, could bring about the events of the opera, and *Seelchen* and its stone drop out of the plot of the third act entirely, until it is time for Verena to sacrifice herself and invoke her brother's name while doing it. The kobold story thus functions as a frame that puts the central love plot into a new and fairly disturbing context, a frame that is, moreover, never fully glimpsed by the main characters. At least the opera's central character is dimly aware of this wider frame as a nagging feeling of contingency. What Verena swats away in her opening dream ("Laß mich! Laß mich!") is nothing other than the knowledge of her own illegitimacy and contingency. Verena was allowed to grow up and *Seelchen* was not, and since the mother's crime is never explained, we are denied any sense of why.

This intrusive and manipulative frame again and again bears the signature of Richard Wagner. The very first strains of *Der Kobold*'s prelude start with a set of chords highly reminiscent of the overture to *Lohengrin*—no accident, given that Siegfried dedicates the score to "The Grail Knight Hans Paul Freiherr von Wolzogen." During these opening bars, as the libretto tells us, the stage is enveloped in "a thick fog, so that the scene is initially invisible to the audience." Only then do "tiny figures" appear, the kobolds. And only now is their main theme heard, an eerie, almost ominous little motif. What came before the main action is thus musically introduced as a quote from the elder Wagner—and it only paves the way for a theme associated with ghostly apparitions, spirits who cannot find peace and haunt the living.

In *Der Kobold*, the young count feels cursed by his provenance—by the fact that his father was nothing but a usurper and a usurer; particularly damning is the fact that Napoleon raised him to his current status. Several times references are made to his father as a "Falschgraf," a fake count. And while the count protests that "It was him, not me," he understands his successes as the legacy of his father's crime. At one point a girl raises that accusation that "your father was a wizard" and one of the actors protests the old count's innocence—but then adds "silently": "And if it were so, would the son have to do penance for it?" The issue of *Schuld* is the central theme of *Der Kobold*, invoked ad nauseam—and the word occurs only in two contexts: Verena's abortion and the count's legacy. For the count, then, guilt is identical with an overwhelming paternal legacy he is powerless to alter—he has to live with his inherited guilt, just as Verena has to live with the effects of her own deed. The ghost of Richard Wagner, wizard and pretend aristocrat, clearly looms in the background here.

At the end of act 2, the goblins fight the "little hangman" (*Galgenmänn-chen*), a creature born from the seed of a hanged convict, for control of the magic stone. As they insult him, they turn to the fantasy creature's provenance, "a bastard birth," whose father is "the gallows" and whose mother is "the grass." Their invective bears scrutinizing in German: "Pfui, Du schäbige Schandgeburt! / Schuftiger, weg da!" In insulting hangman's heredity, Siegfried's libretto turns to *Stabreim*, the rhyme scheme associated like none other with his father's poetic output, and fairly rare in Siegfried's own opera texts. In fact, allusions to Richard abound throughout *Der Kobold*, in particular where questions of reproduction, descent, and legitimacy are concerned. Here, the possibility of a "bastard birth [*Schandgeburt*]" is raised in Wagnerian idiom. The dynastic frame, which disrupts the lives of the onstage characters with an overwhelming and ineluctable *schuldlose Schuld*, guiltless guilt, is nothing other than the legacy of the Wagner name and the kind of art it stands for.

CODA

When Claude Debussy heard *Herzog Wildfang* in 1903, he remarked that it resembled "an exercise by a pupil who has studied under Richard Wagner—but one whom his teacher didn't consider very promising."[19] This was a common assessment of Siegfried among the more progressive musicians of the age—if both he and they had learned much from his father, he seemed to have internalized exactly the wrong lessons. And indeed, when it came to operatic erotics, those composers following in Wagner's footsteps sought to replicate or radicalize the sparseness of *Tristan*'s erotic plot—lovers became loving types, detached from wider social or familial context. Siegfried, perhaps by necessity better attuned to the way large families complicate and subvert the kind of nuclear typicality sought by the likes of Schreker and d'Albert, pushed in exactly the opposite direction.

But it would not go far enough to suggest only autobiographical reasons for Siegfried's turn to the dynasty, which made for his messy plots and strange dramaturgic choices. Rather, when the tidy and spare erotics characteristic both of his father's operas and those of most of his contemporaries dissolve under the pull of the dynastic, that pull more often than not bears the finger-prints of Richard Wagner. Siegfried's operas thus probably don't represent just a working through of the overwhelming paternal legacy, but rather an as-tute interrogation of Richard's aesthetic program. The son, burdened with the demand that he continue the line in spite of his homosexuality, seems to have understood only too well the erotic investments of the father's operatic project. He seems to have realized that the total work of art had an erotic; and he perceived the demonic side of the totality that impinges upon the individ-ual. Eroticism for him could shape and contour the total work of art—but, like d'Albert, he was only too keenly aware of the price.

The Power of the "Verfluchte Lohe": (Post-)Wagnerian Redheads in *Das Rheingold, Fredegundis,* and *Irrelohe*

What is the color of Siegfried's hair and how do we know? We know that Emma Bovary has black hair, "whose two bands seemed as though they were each of one piece,"[1] that Alyosha Karamazov has "dark brown"[2] hair, and that *Oliver Twist*'s Fagin has a face "obscured by a quantity of matted red hair."[3] But the novel as a form tends to be spendthrift with details, while an opera score has much less room for a wealth of detail, and much less use for it. What composer and librettist tend to give an audience to work with has usually to do with vocal or musical, rather than exclusively visual cues. Sometimes we can hazard a guess *ex negativo* at the author's inner picture—for instance, if a supposedly ravishing young Senta turns out to be a bit more corpulent than one might have suspected on the page or on CD. Librettos and stage directions tend to be silent about physical appearance—they list actions, the inflection of those actions, and the actual physical environment in which those actions take place.

Hair color thus tends to become definite rather than left up to the vicissitudes of staging, casting, and makeup only when it becomes a matter of plot, or if characters directly refer to it. It is so that we learn that Wozzeck's Marie has black hair, for instance. More importantly, there are characters whose hair becomes a matter of central importance either to the plot or the metaphors of the story, or even comes to impinge crucially on the music its characters produce. It is at this moment that cultural attitudes come to powerfully influence the deployment of seemingly extraneous details like hair; the detail has to mean more than Emma Bovary's black hair, cannot be part of an *effet du réel*, but instead has to stand in dialogue with the artifice that required its deployment.

The telling detail, which librettist or composer decree independently of staging, becomes fraught with significance; hair has to tell a story the music cannot tell, or cannot tell on its own.

Another factor, however, is seemingly peculiar to red hair. Blondes may be identified as such in a libretto, but a redhead may become obvious through the metaphors that attach to redness. One of the most spectacular examples of a redhead who reveals himself metaphorically is Loge in Wagner's *Rheingold*. We know that Loge was a redhead when first portrayed by Heinrich Vogl (in both the 1869 and 1876 premieres); Wilhelm Moor, for instance, wrote at the time that the god "appears on the stage . . . in a red skirt and yellow mantle with fox-red hair and beard."[4] This redness, however, is not actually in the score; nothing is said about Loge's hair, even though the Old Norse Loge of course famously cut the (blond) hair of Sif, wife of Thor. Wagner never thematizes Loge's hair, yet his association with metaphors of flaming and fire indicates quite eloquently what color of hair the god may have. When Donner, for instance, thunders angrily that "Damned flame, I'll put you out,"[5] he is not simply referring to Loge's area of divine responsibility, or to the etymological proximity of "Loge" and flame ("Lohe")—the list of Loge's attributes points to his hair color as well.

What makes operatic redness unique, in other words, is that it comes always already with a set of semiotic associations in tow, a set of associations that becomes spectacularly visible and whose seductiveness is somehow tied to its character as spectacle. Unlike other hair colors, operatic redness cannot but stage its own status as symptom, as symbol or as metaphor—and any erotic allure it exerts is profoundly self-conscious. In fact, unlike blonde hair, which always carries the potential that it is deployed with reference to the racial, biological, or characterological connotations it carried in the nineteenth century, red hair turns out to refer ultimately to referentiality itself. Rather than *a* signifier for some outside thing, it becomes the signifier that signifies signification, not least of all musical signification. For Wagner's "Fire-Loge has the job of giving us our first musical warmth,"[6] as Moor claims in his review of *Rheingold*'s premiere. And indeed, Loge's fiery redness is rather insistently signaled in *Rheingold*'s music as well.

This is particularly significant since Loge, a character of major importance to the plot of *Rheingold*, disappears in the *Ring Cycle*'s following days, or rather disappears into his element, into the fire magic of *Walküre* and the all-consuming fire of *Götterdämmerung*. He accomplishes this transformation musically, as the flickering semiquaver motif that signals Loge's arrival in Valhalla in *Rheingold* transforms into *Walküre*'s *Feuerzauber* motif and a whole slew of fire motifs after it. Loge the singer, the onstage actor no longer appears in the cycle—his motif and his name survive and intervene into the stage action. Importantly, however, Loge's dissipation into the purely motivic-elemental aspect of the musical drama and his complete disappearance from the embodied drama constitutes a promotion rather than a demotion: Motivically, Mime's lies, Alberich's intrigue, and *Götterdämmerung*'s scheming Gibichungs owe a debt to the Loge of *Rheingold*. Loge's disappearance thus leads to a motivic proliferation along metaphoric axes: the unsteadiness of fire becomes the unsteadiness of lying; the flickering semiquavers (already a indicator of the vanity of the gods of Valhalla at the end of *Rheingold*, according to Carl Dahlhaus[7]) leave behind their ties to fire and come to signify undoing, subversion, and destruction *tout court*.

As Sven Friedrich has pointed out, both the Norse god Loki and Wagner's Loge are etymologically related not only to the Greek *logos*, but also to the German word *Lüge* (lie).[8] Like the other messenger god, Hermes, Loge thus has to do with signification. But, in keeping with his divine attribute of fire, Loge is accurate messaging that can take place in signification (the subject of hermeneutics), but instead everything to do with the deception and distortion that can plague the signifying process. Accordingly, Loge is the most difficult to decipher among the *Ring*'s actors—hermeneutics, the art of Hermes, fails before his flickering inconstancy. While he is physically onstage, he represents neither *ratio* nor the senses, neither the law nor anarchy, at least not with any degree of stability. Once he disappears into the ubiquitous fire, he becomes even more contradictory, contaminating, protecting, purifying, destroying, often at one and the same time.

At first glance, it may seem strange to discuss Loge's red hair in the context of Wagnerian eroticism. After all, his red hair is no one's erotic object, nor is there a sense that the trickster god has any interest in matters erotic, dynastic, familial. When Freia is borne off by the giants, he alone is unaffected. "Home and hearth," he claims, "do not suit me," Wotan's palace he regards with skepticism. But in the sexual-dynastic world of the *Ring*, Loge is almost unique in his isolation from the erotic. He neither renounces the erotic in frustration like Alberich, nor extols its disseminating power like Wotan; he seems to manage it with the same unconcern and fleet nominalism with which he treats everything else. Loge's red hair, his flame-like quality turns sex into simply another sign, something to be exchanged, bartered, and substituted. As such, he both grounds the *Ring*'s erotics and remains indifferent to them. He drains the erotic object of its particular essence and renders it exchangeable; but he is himself, and his red hair signifies, that very exchange relation.

Loge remarks that "in the depths and the heights my inclination drives me; home and hearth do not suit me: Donner and Froh, they are the ones who think of roof and timber [*Dach und Fach*]." In German, something is *unter Dach und Fach* when it is safely stored away, secured in place, when it has a home; Loge, god of the "depths and heights," is profoundly *un-heimlich*, at home nowhere, possessing no essence or location, but rather dealing in constant changes, substitutions, and trades. In the first volume of *Das Kapital*, Karl Marx jokingly proffers Henri IV's assertion that "Paris is worth a mass" as a paradigmatic exchange, in which Paris and a mass are stripped of their particularity and abstracted into tradeable equivalents. Loge's task in this scene is to engineer precisely such a switch: He has to persuade the giants to substitute gold for Freia (*Ersatz für Freia zu suchen*), a substitution that seems to recapitulate Alberich's substitution of gold for love in the opera's first scene. Loge recounts that he traveled far and wide, "in water, earth and air, I asked much and inquired with all, where power stirs and seeds develop"[9]; however, no one seems to be willing to sacrifice "love and woman" for anything, and Loge faces only "scorn for my inquiring ruse."[10] Love, it turns out, is not worth a mass of gold.

The *un-heimlich* substitutions in which Loge traffics hit a limit when it comes to sexuality, which seems to surprise the god himself. A "born leveler and cynic," always ready to exchange anything for anything, Loge seems flummoxed by the fact that no one is willing to trade Freia's charms for something else. Loge's mutability, his cynicism is of course of one piece with his flame flicker: Just as his cunning proceeds from the inherent contingency of signification (that nothing necessarily means only one thing), just as his machinations depend on the premise of the basic commensurability (and exchangeability) of all things, so his ever-changing motifs seems to be ready at all times, as Marx suggests, "to exchange itself body and soul," to transform itself, divest itself from Loge's body and become a ring of flames, the luster of a palace, or the inferno of the *Götterdämmerung* itself. As we saw in chapter 1, such willingness to transform without respect to essence is for Wagner the opposite of sexuality itself—and indeed Loge seems genuinely surprised by the hold eroticism has over the world. Exchange, as abstraction, is unerotic, even antierotic. To facilitate exchange, to prostitute the particular, means rejecting the erotic as master signifier. It is for this very reason that Wotan turns to Loge—the fire god is to assist Wotan with such trickery as the erotically overactive god himself is incapable of: "To make the enemy's need our advantage, that we learn only through craftiness and wit, as Loge practices it slyly."[11]

If Loge is a master of substitution, of the deferral of meaning, then his willingness to undergo transformations does not so much deconstruct the coherence of Wagner's attempt at a Gesamtkunstwerk—it is rather its *conditio sine qua non*. Without Loge's willingness to doom (for whatever individual reasons remains unclear throughout *Rheingold*) the project of the gods of Valhalla, Wagner's own project would risk incoherence. In this respect, too, asexual Loge spawns a surprisingly large group of descendants in post-Wagnerian opera—characters whose fiery, flickering, semiotically overdetermined red hair has to bear the burden of the opera plot's coherence, and not infrequently that of the opera's music as well. Red hair is braided into the coherence of the total work of art, and in tracing it we trace, strangely enough, nothing short of a history of operatic coherence after Wagner.

SIGNIFICATIONS OF REDNESS / THE REDNESS OF SIGNIFICATION

In *Rosso Malpelo*, a short story by Giovanni Verga (who also provided the source material for Mascagni's *Cavalleria rusticana*), the main character "was called Malpelo because he had red hair, and he had red hair because he was a mischievous rascal who promised to turn out a real knave."[12] As so often in the nineteenth century, causation travels along paths the early twenty-first century is unaccustomed to—from the metaphysical mystery of character into the ends of the hair and from there into human action. Of course, hair, like faces, hands and bones, was an open book for the nineteenth century, and readable in a way altogether different from our own era's favorite reads, double helixes, fingerprints, and retinas. Rather than safeguarding the continuity of the particular subject, via "facial recognition," there was no *re*cognition involved in the characterological approaches of the nineteenth century. Instead, the expert could divine the nature, character, disposition, and pathology at first glance—to the initiated, the shape of the hand could speak of a past of degeneration and a future of criminality.

Hair was one of the many signifiers nineteenth century bodies had at their disposal for betraying themselves. Hair could decipher provenance and foretell a future as "a real knave." The para-sciences of physiognomy and phrenology, which held, as Hegel scathingly put it, that "the Spirit is a bone,"[13] descended from the art of animal husbandry: The gaze that attempted to divine the "knave" in the redhead was the same gaze that had attempted to diagnose the character of an animal before purchasing it, or selecting it for breeding. And unlike in human beings, where hair color exists in all manner of mixtures and shadings, horse breeders recognized four distinct types of fur color—white, brown, black, and red—and believed that a horse's character was tied to the pigments in the animal's coat. According to the "science of the exterior," black horses were choleric, white ones cold (melancholy), brown ones are reliable (phlegmatic), and red-coated horses were said to be "sanguine." Since this schema drew on classical humorism which sought to categorize *human* character and disposition, it is not surprising that a similar matrix seems to have operated for human hair. Accordingly, then, redheads were supposedly characterized by a vivacious, flighty, and overly sexual temperament, an association that long outlived the actual theory of humors and was increasingly dressed up in fashionable scientific garb as the nineteenth century wore on.

Cesare Lombroso's *L'uomo delinquente* (1876), for instance, one of the founding texts of nineteenth century positivist criminology, was not concerned with the color, but rather with the amount and thickness of hair, which supposedly constituted atavistic remnants, and thus an index of an evolutionary backslide.[14] Yet when it came to mapping the physique of Italy's population, his questionnaires asked specifically for red hair as well.[15] This was because red hair was not important in the (mostly violent and felonious) "criminal *men*" Lombroso compiled in *L'uomo delinquente*, but was a major trait charted among *female* (mostly sexual) offenders. In the book's companion piece *Criminal Woman*, Lombroso points to a "predominance of blond and red hair among women offenders against chastity"—of the sample given in the book, 48 percent of the "criminal" women were redheads, as opposed to zero percent of the "normal" female population.[16]

Red hair was thus readable, or worth reading, in women only, and there it seemed to indicate almost automatically a pathological or criminal disposition. What is more, however, the crimes the red-haired *donna delinquente* is always already suspected of by virtue of her hair are *sexual* in nature and *sexual* in etiology. Red hair not only points to malfeasance, but it also points up and down the family tree: up, because it points to an "atavistic" throwback, a family history of cretinism, sexual licentiousness or insanity; and down, because in the fevered imagination of positivist criminologists, the red-haired delinquents were busy begetting more unfit offspring, and in fact the majority of their crimes revolved around sexual intercourse and reproduction.

But while red hair was thus an eminently recognizable part of a biologistic matrix of signification, it also uniquely transcended such easily diagnosable systematization. When the artists of the pre-Raphaelite brotherhood made their Ladies of Shallot, their Salomés, their nymphs redheads, they did not do so because they wanted to convey either sanguinity or consanguinity. As the Victorian writer Mary Eliza Haweis wrote in *The Art of Beauty* (1878), there was something deliberately perverse about the pre-Raphaelite championing of red hair: "Red hair—once to say a woman had red hair was social assassination—is the rage."[17] The reason, as Elizabeth Wilson has pointed out, is that the pre-Raphaelites had uncoupled beauty and nature.[18] Red hair, pale skin, green eyes were beautiful because they were unnatural, perhaps even contrary to nature. Wilkie Collins gave "horrid red hair"[19] to the impostor and murderess Lydia Gwilt in *Armadale* (1866)[20] and there was something of a natural imposture, of automatic artifice to the redheads the pre-Raphaelites adored.

This artificiality was of course heightened by the fact that, as Haweis's remark makes clear, fashion in this case could not, as Walter Benjamin showed in many others, wear the guise of nature—here was something that had been "social assassination" not too long ago, but was now, by the vagaries of fashion, "the rage." Red hair was stridently artificial; like the color mauve, it wore its character as signifier proudly and displayed it spectacularly. Its artificiality referred ultimately to the artificiality of signification itself. Just as in the case of Loge, however, this signification was intimately bound up with questions of lawlikeness and free spontaneity—Loge is the eccentric god, always in an ambivalent relationship to the elaborate systems of rules set up by Wotan. In Schmidt's *Fredegundis*, in its incarnations as book and opera, makes red hair a marker of hereditary autonomy—in the opera, the heroine's red hair even becomes a *mechanism* of that autonomy. In Schreker's *Irrelohe*, on the other hand, red hair instead functions as an index for the heteronomy entailed in heredity, the way calamitous traits born of sexual misdeeds long past in the ancestral line can determine the individual's life. Red hair is densely interwoven with the madness passed down in the titular family, triggers that madness and alerts the outside world of the vagaries of the cursed alleles. In either case, however, red hair is emphatically introduced as a sign to be read and interpreted—and the autonomy and heteronomy *signified* by red hair in either opera come to stand in for the autonomy and heteronomy of the sign, the signifier itself.

DEHISTORICIZING REDNESS: FRANZ SCHMIDT'S *FREDEGUNDIS*

Walter Frisch has emphasized the great importance of opera for fin-de-siècle German nationalism.[21] As Benjamin Curtis has pointed out, opera was one of the central channels through which questions of national identity could be made musical—because it could draw on a national literature, on national characters, plots and myths.[22] It also offered a way of linking questions of national and sexual identity (see chapter 1). Franz Schmidt's (1874–1938) opera

Fredegundis is peculiar in that it does not seek to anchor national identity in the safely distant past, but rather unsettles that past by reading the prenational Germanic tribal lands as an analogue to the unsettled character of nationhood in modernity. The opera's modernity rests almost entirely on the shoulders of the opera's main character, the villainous, alluring and thoroughly modern Fredegundis who rises from a lowly station to become Queen of the Franks. Fredegundis, a historically documented woman of the seventh century, was rediscovered for fiction in a novel from the early years of a unified German Empire, and was picked up by Schmidt a few years after its end.

What will concern us in what follows are the transformations Fredegundis and her story undergo in that time span. Most critics have understood Fredegundis as a typical fin-de-siècle femme fatale, something of a more vicious older sister to Salomé or Lulu.[23] However, when one takes into account the opera's source material, matters are more complicated: The opera's libretto suppresses much of its source material's wider-ranging concerns over nation and modernity, condensing them in its alluring heroine and above all in its heroine's red hair. Schmidt wrote *Fredegundis*, his second opera, between the years 1916 and 1921. After had bad experiences with the libretto to his first opera, *Notre Dame* (premiered in 1914), Schmidt cast about for a suitable libretto for years, eventually settling on a libretto penned by Bruno Warden and Ignaz Welleminsky. After a troubled writing process and a disastrous production process beset by problems, *Fredegundis* premiered in 1922 in Berlin to overwhelmingly negative reviews.

Fredegundis is based on the most unlikely of texts, a voluminous novel of the same name by the German historian and popular author Felix Dahn (1834–1912). The novel was published in 1886 as part of his twelve "short novels from the Period of Migrations [*Völkerwanderung*]," all of which manage to run over six hundred pages in length each. These twelve novels belong, alongside Dahn's most famous work, *Ein Kampf um Rom*, to a subgenre peculiar to late nineteenth-century Germany, the so-called *Professorenroman* (represented mainly by Felix Dahn, Gustav Freytag, and Georg Ebers), long historical epics dedicated to historical accuracy, indebted to positivistic historical *Wissenschaft* and meant to educate the public about ancient (usually German) history. With their immense casts of characters, extreme temporal sweep, and pronounced disinterest in the poetic and aesthetic aspects of the novel form, these texts would seem to make uniquely poor templates for an opera.

In adapting Dahn's seven-hundred-page tome into three and a half hours of opera, Schmidt and his librettists necessarily had to make extensive cuts, condensing much of Dahn's plot into a few signature scenes. Even so, it was generally agreed among the opera's critics, listeners, and even those involved in its production that the opera's libretto remained less than successful. A famous incident involved Richard Strauss allegedly telling Schmidt that "I would have made four operas out of" Dahn's book.[24] The action takes place in northern France during the Merovingian period, around the year 650. Schmidt's opera opens on a bluff overlooking the River Seine near Reims, where Fredegundis, servant in the king's household, hides herself in the branches of a tree, where her long red hair catches the rays of the setting sun. Landerich, a young squire infatuated with Fredegundis, comes searching for her; she rebuffs his advances, pointing to her far greater ambitions. A fanfare sounds and suddenly a ship bearing Chilperic the king and his bride passes on the Seine. As the ship passes the tree, Fredegundis captures Chilperic's attention.

When a rainstorm nears, Fredegundis sings an invocation to the Wild Huntsman, a pagan figure—but the wild rider who finds and rescues her is none other than Chilperic who takes the maid downriver on his boat. The second act opens on the private chambers of Chilperic's queen Galswintha several months later. It is night and in the moonlight Fredegundis can be seen sneaking into the room. We learn that Chilperic has been keeping Fredegundis as a courtesan, a relationship Duke Drakolen, Chilperic's advisor and father to Landerich, disapproves of. As Drakolen and Landerich, now bishop of Rouen, wait for the queen to take her to morning mass, Fredegundis, wearing a veil, enters the queen's bedchamber and stabs her to death. Alerted by his mistress's scream, Drakolen tries to stop the fleeing assailant, but is stabbed as well—however, in the struggle he tears out a bushel of her red hair from under the veil. Duke Drakolen indicts Fredegundis as the queen's killer, but Landerich, still in love with Fredegundis, attempts to deflect blame from her.

The opera moves directly to Chilperic's wedding to Fredegundis. Landerich is highly conflicted about having to crown queen the woman he loves yet knows to be a murderess. His father Drakolen appears at the wedding ceremony clutching the bushel of red hair, once again renewing his accusations against Fredegundis. After Fredegundis whispers to Landerich that she still harbors feelings for him, he wrests the telltale hair from his father's grasp. Fredegundis declares Drakolen a traitor and has him blinded. The third act opens on the queen's bedchamber many years later. Fredegundis, who has a child with the king that is by now dangerously ill, calls upon Bishop Landerich, asking him to pray for her child. Landerich, now impervious to her charms at last, declares he will do so only if she will renounce the crown and confess to the murder of Galswintha. Fredegundis pretends to comply, but actually fixes a poisoned drink for the bishop. Just at this moment Chilperic returns and drinks from the poisoned cup—Fredegundis' husband and her child die at the same moment.

The opera's last scene takes place in Rouen cathedral, where Chilperic's open sarcophagus is on display—Fredegundis appears and, finding prayer to no avail, performs an incantation to the pagan gods to reawaken her dead husband. By accident, she knocks over the sarcophagus and her hair is trapped under its heavy lid. By the first light of morning, Fredegundis, her hair turned snow white, expires by her husband's side, accepting the divine justice of her fate and renouncing her pagan inclinations. By and large, Schmidt and his librettists maintained the rough outlines of Dahn's novel (which is itself patched together from accounts of the life of Frankish king Chilperic II and his third wife Fredegundis, who appears to have started out as his maid), and he maintains the source material's outré misogyny. However, the obsessive emphasis on the red hair, which functioned as one pagan-Germanic signifier among many in Dahn's novel, is that of the librettists and the composer.

Where does this emphasis stem from? *Fredegundis* invites readings in terms of its composer's autobiography, more specifically in terms of sublimated guilt. The central murder of *Fredegundis*, the scene in which the opera's antiheroine stabs the queen Galswintha, seems to reference two women in Schmidt's life. The first was his wife, Karoline, who struggled with mental illness throughout their marriage and eventually was confined to the famous mental hospital Am Steinhof (setting of Thomas Bernhard's *Wittgeinstein's Nephew*). The second woman in Schmidt's life at the time was Augusta ("Gusti") Hasterlik, scion of a prominent Jewish family in Vienna, accomplished musician, and former student of his[25]—the affair began after the onset of Karoline's mental illness, but before her confinement to the Steinhof. Gusti had long, flowing red hair, a fact Schmidt remarks upon in his (only recently rediscovered) letters to Hasterlik, commenting that he "think[s] I see in you the embodiment of my red-haired heroine Fredegundis."[26] In light of such comments, it is hard not to read the murder of the queen (and subsequent usurpation of her position) in *Fredegundis* as a reference to the relationship between Karoline and Gusti. In letters to Gusti, Schmidt accordingly called the opera "our child," "a product of this love."[27]

Given Schmidt's psychic investment in his heroine's red hair, it cannot surprise that what in Dahn's novel was one signifier among many becomes in Schmidt's opera something of a fetish. It does so in a double sense, a Marxian and a Freudian fetish, since Fredegundis' red hair (a) almost magically brings together seemingly contradictory registers in a common signifier and (b) comes to eclipse rather than express the social conditions that form the framework of Fredegundis' rise to power. It becomes an index of Fredegundis' erotic ambition, as when she kills a red robin lest his beautiful red coat eclipse hers, but it also serves to indicate that for her desire and ambition are not really distinct: her desire is a demand that everything submit to her. The robin's threatening redness thus becomes an index of the fact that her demand always threatens to fall short—whether she is indeed the reddest of them all is always a matter of uncertainty, and her hair is thus both a master signifier *and* a signifier that indicates the lack of the thing signified—namely dominance. It is of course precisely this ambivalent signifying relationship that makes an object a fetish in the Freudian sense.

Not surprisingly, the heroine's hair retains its uncanniness when separated from her body. The image of father and son wrestling over a lock of Fredegundis' red hair points to the strange power her hair exerts over the men in the story. Of course, the lock of red hair means entirely different things for father and son, even though their competition over control over Fredegundis' fate has clear erotic overtones. For Landerich the lock fetish represents the desired yet unattainable love object, whereas for Drakolen, the lock represents "the truth" of Fredegundis and the anchor of his entire belief system (his devotion to his king, the illegitimacy of the upstart Fredegundis). Once again, then, the luster of Fredegundis' hair collapses two registers—in this case, power/knowledge and eroticism. Her hair, it seems, not only means many things to many people; like any fetish, its meaning can never be single, its registers must always be multiple.

What has of course changed once Landerich and Drakolen get their fingers on Fredegundis' hair is her level of autonomy: Red hair in Schmidt's opera manages to both point to terrifying female autonomy, to independence from the dictates of men, *and* by that token turn woman into an object that a father and son might wrestle over, a heteronomous object to be seized, understood, and possessed. In this sense it is important that Fredegundis is vanquished by nothing other than her long, flowing hair, which gets caught and traps her under her husband's sarcophagus. Lombroso associated an overabundance of hair with atavism and sexual availability, signified by a woman's head that is literally pulled back by the weight of too much hair.[28] Similarly, Otto Weininger tied woman's flowing mane to her supposedly unintellectual disposition: "The longer the hair, the shorter the understanding."[29] Weininger understands this hoary misogynistic bromide literally, that is to say that long hair indicates a preponderance of sensuality and receptivity over the intellect and autonomous spontaneity. That is precisely the dialectic of red hair in *Fredegundis*: Her red hair shows the heroine's independence from the strictures of family, dynasty, class, her unsettling, modern mobility; but this very autonomy makes her, like Verga's *Rosso Malpelo*, an object *of* her own hair, a rogue because she has red hair—which in turn makes her an object for others to comprehend and possess.

It may well be this psychic and biographical overdetermination that saps much of its potential energy from Schmidt's child with Gusti Hasterlik. What Schmidt's opera loses vis-à-vis Dahn's novel is more than mere plot: Dahn's Fredegundis is a Janus-faced entity, whereas Schmidt's is an essentially atavistic one, a hold-over from the pre-Christian world in the mold of Wagner's Ortrud. Dahn's creation on the other hand is much more ambivalent in this regard: Her seductive magic hearkens back to pre-Christian, Germanic sources, but her design also points forward toward a kind of instrumental reason and capitalist modernity. For it is not merely Fredegundis' barbarism that has her view the Christian system of sin with suspicion; her understanding of it (especially as a child) is shot through with monetary considerations. Since the rich and powerful can buy their way out of sin, she reasons again and again; all one needs to do is accrue wealth to atone for one's sins. Dahn's Fredegundis, in other words, combines a kind of atavism redolent of the *Kulturphilosophen* of the time with what would soon come to be known as "the Spirit of Capitalism." The political turmoil of the *Völkerwanderung*, to which Warden and Welleminsky's libretto gives short shrift, functions as a cipher for the disaggregating influence of modernity—an influence that makes itself felt in the novel by Fredegundis' family situation and her status as a woman that emerges from it.

For Fredegundis lacks a father and a liege, but it is not her status as orphan that matters for Dahn; instead she lacks a male to represent her in the order of things, consigning her to invisibility before the law. In 1881, Dahn had detailed the status of women in the time of the *Völkerwanderung* in a lecture entitled *Das Weib im altgermanischen Recht und Leben*. In this text, Dahn attempts to sidestep the pervasive tendency to romanticize the ancient Germans as "noble savages," insisting that the "raw but morally pure" kinship structures ascribed to the Germans by Tacitus in *De Germania* and uncritically repeated since were products of a desire to critique Roman kinship structures, not accurate representations of an actual state of affairs among Rome's northern neighbors. He places particular emphasis on the Langobard concept of "sexual representation" or *Geschlechtsmuntschaft*. The idea that one sex may speak for or represent the other is central to Dahn's novel as well. However, Dahn points out, this *Muntschaft* does not originally refer to the mouth (*Mund*), but rather to the hand (Latin *manus*).

In the novel's opening scene, young Fredigundis lectures Landerich, who has taken her to task for her ambitions, that he is "not my Muntwalt."[30] Warden and Welleminsky's libretto drops this rather arcane reference and instead has Landerich insist that "I am your master," to which Fredigundis offers no reply. And while the libretto offers some evidence as to Fredigundis' tenuous legal status ("Have never known my parents / born unfree, poor and lowly, subject to anyone's will"), it is not nearly as clear as Dahn's novel that Fredigundis' project is to reassert the self-control and self-representation she is denied legally in the sphere of sexuality. In a rather disturbing turn, Dahn's Fredegundis offers a smitten Landerich her amorous attentions in exchange for him teaching her to read and write, for, she explains, reading and writing, alongside her ancestral witchcraft will put "the world at my disposal"[31]; she schemes to become her own *Muntwalt*, to sexually self-represent. In Dahn's novel, then, Fredegundis seems to treat money, autonomy, and sex as fundamentally coterminous. In Schmidt's opera, this equation drops out; no more mention is made of money or ambition. Instead, all is condensed into representation, into sex appeal, or, more precisely, the appeal of the red hair.

The seductiveness of the signifier of the red hair thus extends well beyond the opera's characters. Its phantasmagoric allure manages to pull the socioeconomic, historic, and gender political valences of Dahn's original into its symbolic orbit, making sensual Fredegundis' autonomy terrifying without making it legible in a larger context. In Warden and Welleminsky's libretto there is nothing to be deciphered about Fredegundis—her motivation, it seems, flows almost from her red hair. In Dahn's novel, the red hair functions as a cipher of disenfranchisement—Warden and Welleminsky reframe it as a symbol of general unmooredness from dynasticity, of an anarchy without specific reference to the changing moral and legal world picture in which Dahn situates his antiheroine. To be sure, the libretto retains the Janus-faced symbolism of the red hair: Fredegundis' red hair ties her to the ancient Germanic world as much as to traditional representations of Mary Magdalene. But where Dahn's Fredegundis mobilizes the different registers of Christianity and paganism, of law, power, and sexuality quite knowingly, Schmidt's Fredegundis, again like Verga's *Rosso Malpelo*, is at the mercy of her red hair—the moment her red hair turns pure white ("Das Grauen bleichte ihr das Haar"), she is cleansed. Dahn's Fredegundis has a genuine grievance against her world—she is unable to represent herself; Schmidt's Fredegundis is motivated solely by an ambition that appears to be its own end.

In fact, most reviewers of *Fredegundis'* abortive Berlin run identified the lackluster psychology of its central character as the opera's central problem: "The authors did not notice," remarked a review by Julius Korngold, "how their heroine . . . lost all her psyche and psychology."[32] Schmidt had originally meant to adapt Karl Schönherr's *Das Königreich*, but the negotiations with the writer came to naught. Interestingly enough, Schmidt recognized that Schönherr's piece was not ideal, but contended that "its problems as a drama are its advantages as a libretto,"[33] since "the music has to say everything here."[34] What, then, is it that music has to say in *Fredegundis?* All the complexities that the libretto winnowed away from the plot of Dahn's novel (whose lack constitutes the core of *Fredegundis'* "problems as a drama"), in particular those complexities attending to the heroine's character, have to be shouldered by the music—the phantasmagoria of the heroine's seductive red hair must become audible rather than visible. How, then, does one make hair audible?

As Gerhard Winkler has pointed out, the answer is mapped out in the opera's first scene, where a theme representing Fredegundis is first offered in innocent A major.[35] The theme reoccurs when Fredegundis, enraged by a red robin whose beguiling redness she perceives as competition to her own red hair, kills the bird with a stone—however, it is already transformed and "sinister," as Winkler puts it. It occurs a third time once Fredegundis has laid eyes on the king and has decided to begin her climb to power. Here, the theme has transformed itself even more dramatically: Accompanied by the same insistent triplets that accompanied the killing of the robin, the theme has shriveled into a hurried, barely identifiable figure—a figure that "probably characterizes Fredegundis' red hair."[36] The first scene thus charts the heroine's development, or rather devolution from ingenue to cold-blooded social climber. Each of the stages of this development is bound up with the young woman's red hair: the first iteration of her motif finds the girl hiding her hair childishly in the foliage of a tree; the second iteration has her petulantly picking a fight with a bird over their respective allure; the third, finally, arrives when her intoxicating hair has at last caught the king's eye.

The qualitative leap in what Winkler has identified as the young woman's *Bildung* in this first scene doubtlessly arrives with the killing of the robin.[37] "Oh, how his feathers glow in the sunlight in most beautiful red," Landerich exclaims when Fredegundis points to the bird—and as his voice trails off, her red hair, it seems, takes over. Once Fredegundis has ended her line on the word "red," a curious substitution takes place. Immediately after her line is over, the orchestra begins a quick run of triplets into the highest registers, culminating on an F6. It is at this moment that, as the score informs us, Fredegundis "picks up a stone and throws it after the robin." A quartet of triplets, modulating down in half steps, accompany, perhaps somewhat predictably, the bird's fall, as Landerich rushes to retrieve the murdered animal. Melodically, then, what goes up must come down; however, what goes up is not the same as what comes down. What rises to the highest registers of the orchestra is not the proud bird, but rather the beautiful, overpowering word "red" that has aroused Fredegundis' wrath; what falls, however, is the bird, bested and—as Winkler suggests—a first victim of Fredegundis' own fall from grace, and of her mad climb to power.

It is the word "red," the redness of Fredegundis and her jealousy over the robin's red, that outlines the ambitious young woman's fall from the innocent theme in A major that opens the opera to the cryptic little figure at the scene's climax. But it also introduces a number of equivalences, where a rise is equal to a fall, a bird's coat is a threat to a woman's hair—that is, the central fetishism that structures the opera's plot. The musical material manages to suggest this fetishistic compression and the developmental logic (in which the red hair seems to unfold its power almost independently of the woman who wears it) that alone makes it possible. Just as in Loge's motionless flicker, Fredegundis' thematic material (and its orchestral accompaniment) seems to suggest static equivalences, in which plot and musical development only serve to spell out what musically was always already predetermined.

In discussing the ancient Germanic concept of the *Muntwalt*, Dahn points to the link between gender and private property, and remarks that the link is less straightforward than modern observers would imagine: Among the Germanic tribes, women were able to own and inherit private property, but there was an original hereditary stock (*Erbgut*) which men alone could inherit. Fredegundis, in trying to lay claim to being her own *Muntwalt*, or trying to grapple with the absence of a *Muntwalt*, moves into the political realm, where alone she can accrue *Erbgut* to pass on. Another opera of the same era uses red hair not to map out an attempt to inaugurate a new, autonomous hereditary line, but instead to map the obscure trap of hereditary traits of an entirely different nature—rather than dealing with judicial concepts, this opera is interested in *Erbgut* in its other sense, as genetic material, material that (unlike among Dahn's Germanic tribes) particularly women translated from the past to the present. As such, *Irrelohe* by Franz Schreker (1878–1934) sees red hair as a matter of hereditary traits, as a symptom not of genetic autonomy and modernity, but of genetic heteronomy and beholdenness to the past.[38]

THE REDNESS OF METAPHOR: FRANZ SCHREKER'S
IRRELOHE

By and large, theater follows opera in its reticence to provide too much detail about its characters, including hair, unless that hair becomes of central importance to the plot. There was, however, one nineteenth-century theatrical movement that delighted in introducing characters with so dizzying a range of details that one wonders how any theater troupe is supposed to find actors to fill the role: "Friebe is short, a little hunched already, bow-legged, with a receding hairline [*Glatze*]. His small, extremely mobile monkey face [*Affengesichtchen*] is unshaven. His hair and beard are a yellowish grey hue [*spielen ins Gelblichgraue*]."[39] For the naturalist school of German dramatists, such detail was essential for a very simple reason: It helped make visible, even spectacular, a (primarily biological) determinism—often "the catastrophe of a family," as Gerhart Hauptmann subtitles the play just cited (*Das Friedensfest: Eine Familienkatastrophe*). In Schreker's *Irrelohe* red hair traces not just family resemblances, it also inaugurates a metaphoric proliferation, a semiotic family tree of its own.

Irrelohe tells the story of the eponymous castle and the *Familienkatastrophe* of the family that has its seat there. Due to its occult provenance, the family is cursed with a history of mental illness that asserts itself in sexual violence. Thirty years ago on his wedding day, the old Count of Irrelohe forced himself upon the young Lola, set off by her "curly red hair."[40] Lola gave birth to Peter, a grown man by the time of the action. The new master of Irrelohe, Count Heinrich, sits isolated in his keep, terrified that his clan's hereditary madness will claim him too. The forester's daughter Eva, object of Peter's desires, falls in love with the reclusive count and agrees to marry him. Christobald, Lola's erstwhile groom who fled Irrelohe after his betrothed's debasement, arrives in town camouflaged as a wedding musician, with Fünkchen, Strahlbusch, and Ratzekahl, three arsonists, in tow. He has been returning to Irrelohe each year on the anniversary of the old count's outrage, setting fires around town with his accomplices. At Count Heinrich's wedding, Peter, in the throes of the old Irrelohe family madness, attempts to force himself on Eva; in the ensuing struggle, Heinrich kills him and immediately recoils, horrified that, despite his every effort, the family curse has staked its claim on him after all and forced him to kill the half brother he did not know he had. At this moment of profound despair, Eva reaches out to her betrothed and invites him to leave the town with her. As the castle burns, the lovers leave behind the town and the fate that ties them to it.

Unlike in *Fredegundis*, where the red hair served to set its bearer apart from outside structures, in *Irrelohe* red hair and its attendant metaphors (especially fire and madness) indicate dependence and determination from without. Red hair, as the trigger and the mark of rape, becomes indicative of hereditary madness and the heredity of guilt itself. This is the deterministic logic of naturalist drama. While Hauptmann had a pronounced distaste for Lombroso and his ilk, fulminating against them in both his letters and his diaries,[41] his early dramas aim to sharpen much the same gaze upon the body on the stage as Lombroso sought to develop in criminologists. We are given an intricate description of Friebe, because there is supposedly something to be gleaned from his physiognomy, and that something is heredity, usually hereditary illness, atavism, or vice. *Irrelohe*'s concern with hereditary madness, sexual violence, pyromania, and family resemblance (Peter's to the dead Count, Peter's to Heinrich, etc.) come from much the same source. And yet, it is less redness's power to transport biological meanings that animates *Irrelohe*—it is rather its capacity to transport meaning *tout court*.

Schreker's opera was largely written around the same time as *Fredegundis*, between 1918 and 1922. In his essay "On the Genesis of my Libretti (*Über die Entstehung meiner Opernbücher*)," Schreker claims to have discovered the title for his new opera before hitting upon its plot. On a railway journey, he writes, "it seemed to me as if the conductor called the name 'Irrelohe.' ... And I looked out and made out the station name of the place, which was indeed called Irrelohe. It was then clear to me that this name, about whose no doubt prosaic etymology I had no wish to inquire, carried the seeds of a drama within it. And so it was. The opera on which I am now working bears that name; the libretto was finished in three days. *Irrelohe*—flames of madness!"[42] While an artist's account of the genesis of his own works may seem suspect at best and irrelevant at worst, Schreker's letter does point to the fascinating compactness of *Irrelohe*—indeed the title's imbrication of fire and madness and its various permutations trace out almost the opera's entire plot, and the title is invoked directly or alluded to almost incessantly in the libretto. *Irrelohe*'s nonmusical drama is all there already in the opera's title.

While *Irrelohe* musically finds Schreker's style in transition, Schreker the librettist retreats further in the direction of his literary influences. The legacy of the Gothic literature, of Edgar Allen Poe and of German literary realism, is much more pronounced in *Irrelohe* than in any of Schreker's previous efforts—and what Hailey detects as traces of expressionistic fervor is probably better understood as an inheritance from naturalism.[43] This inheritance is not limited to the libretto's obsessive use of dashes to dismember its characters' discourse, nor to a proclivity for incomplete senses liberally sprinkled with exclamation marks otherwise unusual in Schreker's texts—most importantly the entire plot seems culled from naturalist drama. In fact, the opera's story, right down to the ambiguous happy ending, which finds the lovers suspended between having to reenact their genetic fate and striking out to make their own fate, resembles rather closely some of Gerhart Hauptmann's early dramas, in particular one we referred to earlier, *Das Friedensfest* (1890).

Naturalism was at the time of *Irrelohe*'s writing historic rather than avant-garde; what is more, since Schreker's one-word inspiration becomes in the opera the name of a castle and the family that owns it, the thematic nexus of fiery madness and sexuality becomes less concerned with the Freudian question of drives (as in *Der Ferne Klang* and *Die Gezeichneten*) and instead with the naturalist question of heredity. Not what tangled webs eros weaves in the fate of men is the focus of *Irrelohe*; instead it is what biological fate (i.e., heredity) does with human eros. *Irrelohe*'s characters are, as Hailey points out, "not driven from within, but burdened from without,"[44] and the mechanics of their desire owe more to Lombroso and Weininger than they do to Freud. Schreker's libretti had hitherto been fraught with hints of scandal and modernity, but *Irrelohe* returned to concerns and plots characteristic of the earliest stirrings of European modernism. Whether or not this constituted a failure of nerve on the part of its author, its effect is to heighten the self-enclosedness and self-relationality of *Irrelohe*'s poem. It is unclear whether the opera is concerned with fate, madness, or sex at all, or whether those variables do not simply derive, in an almost analytic manner, from the opera's title.

Given its genesis as essentially a play of language, the plot and libretto of *Irrelohe* create a downright dizzying metaphoric echo chamber centered around redness, fire and madness. Not only does almost every person come to invoke fire and madness at one point, but the libretto also delights in shifting the metaphorics of redness, madness, and fire from one invocation to the next: The flames of mad passion set the opera's calamitous events in motion, and the flames of pure love resolve the plot; red hair (invariably metaphorized as *Flammen*, "flames") becomes an index of sexual violence and that which triggers sexual madness in the violator; flames become expressions of madness ("the throbbing glow"[45]), but madness itself becomes combustible ("flames came out of a madness"[46]).

To say that a red thread runs through *Irrelohe* would be an understatement. Virtually all its themes and imagery rely on the semantic field of fire, the sun, blood, and red hair. It is characteristic for Schreker's metaphorics that the libretto often deploys this semantic field in seemingly contradictory or paradoxical ways: For instance, redness and fire both cause the outrage that occasions the plot and they help to resolve it—fire becomes a symbol for a crime and its punishment. On the old Count's wedding day, he notices a group of young dancers, "among them a girl with curly red hair."[47] Her red hair turns his head (and perhaps even his hair) red: "And suddenly—blood shot into his forehead—red, red his head, flames jumped from his hair."[48] Red hair thus provokes madness and signifies that madness once provoked. But the redness of the flames is not doused by water, flames in *Irrelohe* are put out by more flames: "Only fire can make piece, fire must eat what flames birthed,"[49] the three arsonists Strahlbusch, Ratzekahl, and Fünkchen intone. But their controlled burn turns into a metaphor for the all-consuming nature of revenge: "If we could do magic, brothers, all the world would be in flames soon."[50]

From the very beginning, the extreme metaphoricity of the libretto's action seems much less elegant than claustrophobic: In one of the opera's guiding metaphors, redness ("flames shooting from his head"[51]) refers to passion, to hot-bloodedness; the concern with blood in turn stands in for heredity itself, and a hereditary madness which announces itself through fire: "My blood is whipped into a frenzy—my blood is whipped into a frenzy—it burns and bristles—its flames flicker to the sky"[52]; and heredity is once again indicated by the unique genetic feature of red hair. The strangely airtight metaphorics of the libretto become the opera's organizing phantasmagoria: red hair becomes the medium through which the opera's every dramatic conceit emerges as essentially tautological—it becomes impossible to isolate one thematic strand without picking up all the others. This, however, also robs fire and redness of any role in furthering or deepening the opera's plot instead; fire functions as "a crackling prop," as Hailey puts it.[53]

The magic circle of interconnected metaphors is first established in *Irrelohe*'s first scene, in which Lola sings two songs that are formally self-contained closed forms, but are in each case subject to uncanny openings and subterranean interconnections. These interconnections, both textual and motivic in nature, all partake of the semantic field of red hair and fire. The opera opens on a strikingly placid note, with a straightforward little ditty in which Lola vexes fondly over her erstwhile beauty. Her reminiscences (and the music that channels them) become unsettled once the trauma of her rape (provoked by her beautiful red hair) enters her stream of consciousness. The second is a ballad, in which Lola tells her son the story of Irrelohe castle and its family. This ballad is similarly undercut by echoes of themes and motifs that intrude from outside of Lola's own discourse.

In each case, then, Schreker's music recapitulates the position of the subject in the opera's tightly wrought determinist logic: Just as the opera's characters fancy themselves individuals, but are in fact mere expressions of deterministic heredity, so the seemingly self-contained forms they utilize to express themselves in the first scene gesture already toward the larger context of which they are unaware, against which they are powerless, and which they are doomed repeat. This is in keeping with Schreker's tendency to give the orchestra the role of subconscious undercurrents subtending his stage characters' discourse, but the motifs are associated not with projections of those characters' individual psyches, but instead with supersubjective forces that determine them from without. In *Der ferne Klang*, for instance, the orchestra served to articulate the main character's drives (most centrally in the shape of the distant sound itself); in Irrelohe's first scene, the music subverts the characters' discourse—outlines their doom, hints at their salvation, without their having any awareness of it. As Janine Ortiz has recently pointed out, Schreker leaves this ballad without the closure that (at least in the German tradition) is usually associated with the genre, for the simple reason that the end of the story told in the ballad can only be provided by the opera itself (something that is famously true for Senta's ballad in *Der fliegende Holländer* as well).[54]

This strange open-ended ballad further extends a network of references to the opera as a whole. Unike Wagner, Schreker tends to leave diegetic music comparatively intact and detached from the *durchkomponierte* whole, often radically altering instrumentation or moving that instrumentation onto the stage to signal the break (see chapter 6). Not so in *Irrelohe*'s first scene, where several motifs from the overture vie with one another—one that seems to simply belong to the Irrelohe castle and family, another that the opera connects with the hereditary curse that afflicts said family, and a modulation from D minor to D major in the ballad's second strophe that anticipates the lifting of the family curse at the opera's resolution. What holds all these together is the same element that allowed for Loge's multiform iterations in the *Ring*—flames. The text is replete with references to fire, flames, the sun, and redness; and the music melds texts and motifs through an insistent string figure mimicking flickering, consisting of eighth and sixteenth notes.

Like Loge's flickering flames, it would probably go too far to call this figure a motif. Like Wagner, Schreker uses the flames as pure accompaniment—Ortiz speaks of an "ornament."[55] However, while none of the singer ever picks it up, while it never occurs without the aid of other motif, this seeming musical parasite actually holds the ballad together, as the musical equivalent of metaphor. The flame "ornament" is not extraneous, but rather allows for the programmatic likening of madness, fire, and redness—it is the medium, the *fluidum* that enables the amazing compactness of Schreker's dramatic conception, as well as its musical coherence. Flames are the emblem of universal exchangeability—where Schmidt's *Fredegundis* deployed redness as a substitute for psychological motivation, *Irrelohe* deploys it as a sign of the a priori substitutability of all psychological motives/motifs.

In his discussion of Wagner's *Walküre*, Theodor W. Adorno remarked on the similarity of Wagner's phantasmagoric music and *Walküre*'s magical fire, which "although flickering incessantly does not move."[56] As I have argued elsewhere, Schreker's operas are at best ambivalently phantasmagoric (see also chapter 6)—Schreker pushes the phantasmagoric, self-contained, and self-referential elements of his operas to a breaking point and then steps outside of what Adorno describes as phantasmagoria's "magic circle."[57] In this sense, one could think of *Irrelohe*'s red threads as "verbal phantasmagoria," a closed loop of references that always undulate from one register into the other without ever actually going anywhere. They delimit a space of claustrophobia, of overintegration and excessive referentiality, a semiotic "magic circle" which in the operas' final bars the characters at last step beyond.

CODA

While written over the same five-year period, and united in their hesitant and ambiguous modernism, *Fredegundis* and *Irrelohe* differ greatly in their deployment of the motif of the redhead, and by extension in their deployment of sexuality more generally. *Fredegundis* (much like Schreker's earlier operas) treats the salient detail (in this case the main character's red hair) as a phantasm, as a projection, as an object or expression of longing. *Irrelohe* on the other hand understands red hair as an index of suprasubjective forces of heredity, not emanating from the individual psyche of the opera's characters (such as Fritz's "distant sound" in *Der ferne Klang*), but rather shaping that psyche from without. As such, as the preceding section made clear, *Irrelohe* constitutes Schreker's move away from Freud. That in relinquishing a psychoanalytic position Schreker would turn to a picture of sexuality that had gained currency before Freud, namely the naturalist focus on determinism that reached its apogee in the 1890s, should not obscure the fact that Schreker's move coincides with what many in the 1920s began thinking of as the next step forward.

After all, the culture surrounding Schreker underwent a rather similar shift in the early 1920s, rejecting the mysteries of individual psychic cathexis in favor of the eroticism of the mass, of the movie screen, of the commodity. Tiller girls, movie stars, shop windows, streetwalkers—the intellectuals of the 1920s tended to be interested in erotic phenomena that were public rather than private in nature, caught up in social states of affairs rather than the privacy of the unconscious, emphatically modern, commercialized and gleefully alienated rather than neurotically romantic. *Irrelohe* partakes of the eroticism of Alfred Döblin, Bertolt Brecht, Siegfried Kracauer, in short of New Objectivity (*Neue Sachlichkeit*). In these and other writers, love, loss and longing were detached from the subjectivism of Anna O, Little Hans and the Wolfman and became instead that of Erich Kästner's 1928 Poem "Sachliche Romanze" ("Objective Romance"):

> When they had known each other for eight years
> (and we can say: they knew each other well),
> they suddenly misplaced their love.
> As other people do their walking stick or hat.[58]

In texts such as Kästner's, love is depsychologized and objectified—it is moved into the realm of competence of sociologists, statisticians, and accountants rather than psychologists. This cultural shift (chronicled in Helmut Lethen's famous book on *Cool Conduct* in Weimar Germany[59]) affected opera's erotics perhaps more fundamentally than that of any other medium. Musically, Schreker was opposed to this movement, speaking of it as an overreaction "which the serious artist was forced to find just as ridiculous as all that had preceded it."[60] When it came to operatic eroticism, however, the mid-1920s saw Schreker moving much closer to the world of new objectivity.

Throughout this study we have seen that operatic eroticism after Wagner was centrally coupled with concerns of operatic form. What is noticeable about the shift in Schreker's erotics of the 1920s, however, is that they failed to produce a concomitant shift in operatic form. In a 1928 essay, Arnold Schoenberg claimed that he and Schreker had followed the same trajectory among the critics, being first derided as *Neutöner* and then consigned to the dustbin of *Romantik*. It is the label of (late) Romantic that, according to Carl Dahlhaus, "did so much to damage the reception of Schreker"[61]; undeserved and unfair though this cliché may be on the whole, when it came to the post-Wagnerian coupling of operatic eroticism and operatic form Schreker indeed remained too indebted to Wagner to count as genuinely modern. Schreker thus provides a limit case: a composer who seems to have realized the outmodedness of Wagnerian erotic philosophy and moved away from it, but

failed to reflect on that outmodedness's ramifications for the formal constitution of the opera.

Irrelohe is a "work at the crossroads" in Hailey's phrase, not only because
Schreker experimented with new forms of instrumentation, different sonorities, and techniques, but also because the opera was understood by its contemporaries as a sign whether Schreker was still "modern" or whether whatever
was "modern" had moved well beyond him—whether the erstwhile revolutionary had become 1924's orthodoxy.[62] But, as we have seen, the opera stands
at an erotic crossroads as well: The eroticism the opera traffics in has changed
fundamentally since Wagner, but the formal entanglements that authorized
that eroticism in the first place have been sidelined. As chapter 6 showed, operatic phantasmagoria depended on a particular operatic erotics—in *Irrelohe*,
Schreker heightens the phantasmagoria, but abandons the erotics. The plot
gets ever more integrated, until it becomes nothing but the analytic elaboration (in a Kantian sense) of what is already contained in one central guiding
metaphor; the music becomes metamorphosized too; Loge's flickering semiquavers become not the indicators of vanity and insubstantiality, but rather of
the airtight compactness of the operatic Gesamtkunstwerk and the ultimate
fungibility of its particulars.

But what integrates and unifies plot and music both internally and between
one another is not the unification of two lovers in death, in marriage or erotic
bliss—instead, the phantasmagoric compactness seems to preexist the particulars that are supposed to erotically enact that compaction onstage. Unlike
Wagner's shape-shifting cast of characters, *Irrelohe*'s individual actors do not
have to metempsychotically merge in order to effect the identity and totality
of the Gesamtkunstwerk; instead, they matter by and large only as the car-
riers of red hair, which alone binds and structures the opera. It is the story
of fire, fate, and madness, held together by the strands of red hair—it is the
story of two lovers only secondarily. What is more, to escape the Irrelohe curse
the lovers must escape a *Liebestod*, must refuse the kind of closure that had
dominated German musical drama since Wagner and which Schreker's earlier
operas had trafficked in. Instead, the lovers end the opera by committing the
overintegrated, hypercompact, airtight, fated construct to the flames, and step-
ping away from it. It is a step away from the Gesamtkunstwerk. After Wagner,
for forty years the operatic Gesamtkunstwerk depended on the destruction
wrought by the love union; in *Irrelohe*, that love depends on the destruction of
the Gesamtkunstwerk.

CODA:
"I'M A STRANGER HERE MYSELF"

A number from Kurt Weill's *One Touch of Venus*, premiered at the Imperial
Theater in New York on October 7, 1943, would probably be one of the last
places we would expect *Tristan* to cast a shadow. And yet, when the hapless
window dresser Rodney Hatch kisses a department-store mannequin and
brings her to life, she turns out to be the goddess Venus herself and sings a
song penned by Ogden Nash entitled "I'm a Stranger Here Myself"—and the
viewer can espy with a certain effort the most extreme tip of that long, elusive
shadow. It is precisely its distance from the object, precisely the faintness of
the shadow, that makes it an instructive last vantage point onto the Wagnerian
legacy in the erotics of German opera.

It was Weill who was initially drawn to the story, and he went through
several teams of writers until he arrived at a story line and song numbers he
liked. Weill was likewise very involved in shaping the musical during production—too involved, as far as the director, a pre-Hollywood Elia Kazan, was
concerned.[1] Even though *One Touch of Venus* was a characteristically collaborative effort for Weill, the final shape of this Broadway production nevertheless manages to shed light on a musical world thousands of miles away from
Broadway—Weill's world, which had meanwhile vanished under jackboots
and carpet bombings.

Given that it is a story of dislocation and culture clash, championed by a
composer who had become intimately familiar with both, it might be surprising that it is *Venus* who finds herself on Fifth Avenue, and that it is in the sphere
of the erotic that she registers her disorientation. Love seems easier to transfer
across the Atlantic than other concepts. But here *Tristan* casts its shadow once

again, as the erotic emerges as a stand-in for opera and its aesthetics, and for what we can ask of a work, of its media, and of its audience—in general, and in a country where opera might be "a stranger."

The goddess of love arrives in an unfamiliar present, and she questions whether love or its goddess still have a place in it. Perhaps, she fears, our modern priorities have replaced it with gin rummy or skiing:

> Tell me is love still a popular suggestion
> Or merely an obsolete art?
> Forgive me for asking, this simple question
> I'm unfamiliar with this part
> I am a stranger here myself.[2]

In this song, Venus registers her temporal dislocation and laments her own out-of-placeness in 1940s New York. But as the musical continues, Venus soon becomes a symptom of the shift that has made the kind of love she pays tribute to in this song "a stranger here." She is a thoroughgoing unromantic, it turns out, and downright materialist. "Love isn't the dying moan of a distant violin," she says at one point. "It's the triumphant twang of a bedspring."[3] After Rodney tries to whisk her away to idyllic Ozone Heights, she refuses and takes an airplane back to Mount Olympus. She becomes an emancipated woman, and nothing is more poisonous to an opera plot than that.

Although *One Touch of Venus* is resolutely a work of the 1940s, Venus' reemergence in Ozone Heights can be understood as part of Weill's response to the 1920s *Opernkrise*. As Weill observed in 1928, "the humanity music can express has remained the same. But humanity itself has become different, it reacts differently to . . . influences, events and feelings."[4] *One Touch of Venus* harnesses this anxiety about the changes in humanity that opera both reflects and addresses, and turns that anxiety into its central plot point. The idea that the gods made a bad fit for modernity, but that hauling them into it on the opera stage might make for a good angle for persiflage or critique, was a persistent one among Weill's contemporaries. In the twenties, Weill collaborated with the poet Yvan Goll on a cantata called *Der Neue Orpheus*, in which the "new Orpheus" finds his Eurydice slathered in makeup in a Berlin train station.[5] Stefan Wolpe (1902–72), born two years after Weill and mentored by many of the same teachers, turns to the same idea in a "musical grotesque" entitled *Zeus und Elida*, which he completed in 1928, but which was not performed during his lifetime.

While the title sounds like a classical pairing, it is anything but. There is no moon of Jupiter named Elida; the Elida of the title is actually a beauty product. In Wolpe's opera Zeus comes to Potsdamer Platz in central Berlin to find Europa; instead he falls in love with a billboard model advertising Elida, declaring her his new Europa.[6] He subsequently mistakes a prostitute for the Elida model, but she refuses to follow him to Olympus, preferring a cheap flophouse for their tryst. In the end, reversing the gimmick of Weill's musical, Zeus is carried off into a museum and the Elida stand-in goes back to work.

Crammed with modish musical styles (Charleston, tango, foxtrot) in hectic succession, deliberately aping a recitative-aria structure, and rife with allusions to the modern metropolis, *Zeus und Elida* is a statement about musical aesthetics, about the sounds of modernity and the outmodedness of other kinds of sound. Wolpe's narrator explicitly invites the listener to think of Zeus as a Hitler parody. (Wolpe's work is indeed one of the few operas to explicitly invoke Hitler in their libretto[7].) But Zeus' cluelessness in face of the modern city also points to an aesthetic dimension to Wolpe's persiflage. Wolpe did not drag Zeus off Mount Olympus and into the bustle of Weimar-era Berlin streets because he wanted to make a point about classicism and how ill-adapted it was to modern life. He was making a point about a past aesthetic, about operatic practices closer to his day than Zeus on his mountain. His Mount Olympus, the one he thought required confrontation with the traffic and advertisements of the modern metropolis, lay in Vienna and perhaps in Bayreuth—not in Greece.

To be sure, Wolpe's Zeus isn't Richard Wagner. But the erotic gesture that *Zeus und Elida* spoofs, the quest for a beloved object just outside the hero's grasp, is one that opera traditionally depends on. And it is this quest that Wagner and his heirs turned into an aesthetic principle. If Fritz's "distant sound" in Schreker's *Der Ferne Klang* represents the object of a yearning for an aesthetic experience beyond the reified system of commodities and exchange, a true refuge for operatic sublimity, then his student Wolpe unmasks this transcendent erotic object as just a misunderstood billboard.

And *Zeus und Elida* isn't just saying that such a love object has become impossible in 1920s Berlin (where a prostitute doubles for Europa); it's saying that the very quest for it has become an impossibility. The fervor of Fritz's search for the "distant sound" was frustrated again and again by the onstage clamor, but was, in death, finally fulfilled. Not so in *Zeus und Elida*, where the erotic object (Elida, an anagram of "ideal") is but a confusion created by the dizzy raptures of the modern metropolis. Zeus confuses his prostitute with the "Elida" model; he mistakes the brand for the model, and the brand for

Europa. Not just the object is missing here; even the quest has become a series of substitutions and language games.

Wolpe was a student both of Franz Schreker and Ferruccio Busoni, and *Zeus and Elida* is also a young composer's move out of the world that shaped him. It is a move that entails an embrace of extreme fragmentation. (Some of the opera's numbers are less than half a minute long, and the cumulative effect of the stylistic changes is dizzying.) Just like Weill, Wolpe was forced into exile in 1933, and after a sojourn that included Romania, Vienna, and Palestine, eventually settled down in New York City.[8] By the time he got there, however, he had adopted a much more peaceable attitude toward the Zeus of tradition.

For Weill, on the other hand, it was more clearly Wagner on Mount Olympus, and he had a more difficult time leaving the Master there; if *Zeus and Elida* had been Wolpe's definitive exorcism, Weill wrestled with the tradition embodied by Wagner for all of his career. As Stephen Hinton has observed, "the same generation that defined contemporary music and theater as a specific and emphatic negation of Wagner's art had formerly been utterly in thrall to it."[9] In a 1925 article, Weill refers to "that artwork of equal rights between word, music and scene, which through *Tristan* held the world of opera production in its thrall for fifty years."[10] Wagner dominated the young Weill's musical imagination, and haunted the mature Weill as a target of exorcism, or, as Hegel might put it, "determinate negation." Whatever modern music was, it had to be the opposite of Wagner. Even a work as late and seemingly removed from the concerns of the Old World as *One Touch of Venus* thus persists both inside and outside *Tristan*'s shadow.

There was never a sea change in Weill's relationship to Wagner, from unreflected veneration to knee-jerk rejection. Instead, Weill can serve as a case study for Wagner's spectral presence for the generation that most decisively freed itself from his influence. Even Weill's most enthusiastic remarks about Wagner are tempered with a coolness and distance; even his most vicious parodies remain knowledgeable and almost tender in their use of Wagner. Consider the letter a seventeen-year-old Weill wrote to his brother in 1917:

> I think that for me even a passable performance of *Tristan* will always be something special. There is no opera score that contains quite so much; there is no music you can lose yourself in as much, while listening and being waist-deep in it, while rehearsing it and performing it.[11]

While it has the glow of youthful enthusiasm, even in this early statement Weill is far removed from any unthinking Wagner idolatry. The Wagner he conjures here is not a monument to be venerated (let alone a national monument) or to be accepted whole. Wagner is a quarry, to be "waist-deep in." Even the phrase "losing yourself," which, in light of Weill's later association with Brechtian aesthetics, we would not expect to find in later statements by Weill, refers here not to an aesthetic of absorption but to a "losing oneself" in the score—in the logic of the thing rather than in the ritual, the drama, the experience. It helped that Weill encountered *Tristan* most forcefully as a performer—according to a letter to his brother, his first public performance, a piano recital in 1917, included a *Liebestod* transcription.[12] He came to the material as an artisan surveying a new claim.

The fervent adoration evident in this passage may have dimmed over the ensuing decades, but Wagner remained "something special" for Weill. Weill grew up with Wagner's music, but even beyond that he found his musical bearings in the world created by Wagner's heirs. While still a high school student in Dessau (Weill graduated in 1918), the works discussed in the previous chapters were his musical bread and butter. In his letters to his older brother Hans, Weill praised Humperdinck's *Hänsel und Gretel*, for instance. In the same letter he speaks of Siegfried Wagner's *Machwerke*. And even in a work as late as *Street Scene*, premiered in 1947, Weill can casually toss in an allusion to Eugen d'Albert's *Tiefland*.[13]

But if Weill's first musical efforts emerged from the world Wagner made, even before he entered the Berlin *Hochschule für Musik* his relationship to the master of Bayreuth was not without ambiguity. For instance, he follows up his praise of Humperdinck with the qualification "even though Humperdinck works very much based on the Wagnerian model."[14] This is in the same letter in which he rhapsodizes over "even a passable performance of *Tristan*." Wagner is a great quarry, but a bad model—something to be pulled apart, not holistically copied. Or we might say, not a statue to prostrate before, but rather one to kiss to life and drag off to Ozone Park for some much-needed modernization. Of course, his reservations didn't keep Weill from studying with Humperdinck, who had been Siegfried Wagner's teacher, at the Berlin *Hochschule für Musik*.

Weill's stint there proved abortive. World War I wiped out the Weill family fortune, and Kurt had to return to Dessau. When Weill returned to Berlin two years later, this time to study at the *Akademie der Künste*, his mentor was no longer Humperdinck, a man with an ambivalent, though generally positive relationship to the Wagnerian legacy; he now studied with Ferruccio Busoni, whose relationship to that legacy was much more hostile. In his *Versuch einer neuen Ästhetik der Tonkunst*, published in 1917, three years before Weill became his pupil, Busoni had denied that *Tristan* had a shadow at all, or, if it did, that shadow wasn't a very productive place to be:

> Wagner, a Germanic giant, who touched the earthly horizon of orchestral sound, who heightened and yet systematized the form of expression (musical drama, declamation, leitmotif), cannot be outdone, due to the boundaries he set for himself. His category begins and ends with himself.[15]

His pupil, Weill, seems to have followed Busoni's argument. In a 1926 article on "The New Opera" for the journal of the theater union, *Der Neue Weg*, Weill claims that "the musical development of the last few decades has led to the realization that one had to get as far away from Richard Wagner's sphere of influence as possible."[16] Weill thinks the different attempts to accomplish this have been unsuccessful. The only alternative is "a path that, at least for a time, led away from opera"—that is, into absolute music. But now, Weill suggests, we are ready for a "new flowering of opera (as opposed to musical drama)."[17]

Weill's famous collaborator, Bertolt Brecht, would later write in his diary that "when I met Weill, he was a Busoni- and Schreker-pupil, a creator of atonal, psychological operas."[18] In fact, Brecht's self-aggrandizing claim overstates both the latent Wagnerism of the young Weill and understates the Wagnerian legacy in the later Weill. Brecht's factually incorrect assertion that Weill had also been a student of Schreker's underplays the degree to which Weill had always had a more hostile relationship to Wagner and to the "atonal, psychological operas" of his followers. Busoni rejected Wagner specifically because he thought "the poetic, often even the philosophical program" tended to turn the music into mere program music. His operas were not, in Brecht's sense, psychological, and they are—perhaps not coincidentally—fairly unerotic. Being a "Busoni pupil" thus meant not being a very good "Schreker pupil."

Brecht brings up Busoni and Schreker in order to imply a kind of conversion narrative, in which Weill transitioned out of *Tristan*'s shadow with a little help from his friend. But really Weill's half-allergic, half-entranced relationship to the master of Bayreuth predated the composer's encounter with Brecht, and outlasted their collaborations of the 1930s. As Stephen Hinton has argued, both Weill's and his teacher Busoni's musical aesthetics are to be understood as a kind of "determinate negation" of every aspect of Wagnerian musical drama. If Strauss, Schreker, Zemlinsky, and Schmidt had grappled with the long shadow cast by *Tristan* with a mixture of acceptance and rebellion, Weill aimed simply to step outside of that shadow. He and Busoni rejected all that

Tristan stood for. The operatic antecedent they looked to was Mozart ("the opera composer *par excellence*," Weill calls him[19]). The shadow they accepted and struggled with was *Don Giovanni* rather than *Tristan and Isolde*.

This rejection encompassed almost all the historical innovations of Wagner's musical aesthetics. Weill thought that Wagnerian musical drama heightened the autarky and isolation of the opera as form and as institution. In his fragmentary notes for a lecture he drafted while in New York, Weill penciled in a note on how opera would have to evolve: "The opera has to leave its isolation."[20] He agreed with Busoni that Wagner's *durchkomponierte* operas inevitably lapsed into program music, whereas the old number opera was more hospitable to absolute music. In an interview Weill asserted that "music cannot itself be realistic, but instead has to be juxtaposed with a realistic on-stage action." By musical "realism," he meant the tendency of music to "depict action, figures, characters," which the music drama made its linchpin, and which his own works were meant to avoid. "This kind of music," he added, "is the most consistent reaction to Wagner. It means the complete destruction of the concept of music drama."[21] In a 1929 essay in the *Berliner Tageblatt*, Weill identifies the "principle of the number opera" a "reaction against the music drama."[22]

Weill vituperated against the "narcotic, arousing effect" Wagner's operas were meant to have on their audience, foreclosing rather than inviting attention and reflection.[23] He repeatedly insisted that music should not drive operatic action, but rather should erupt from a "moment of stasis" in the stage action.[24] Above all he rejected a style of performance and of singing he, whether fairly or unfairly, seems to have associated with Wagner: a style in which the voice bespeaks a character's deep psychology. When it comes to describing what is wrong with this psychology, Weill's lecture notes seem to give two synoptic answers: Wagner and sex.

> How shall the actor sing?—Opera-Singers, pure voice-acrobates [*sic*] without expression. Sexual effect of a beautiful voice. Music as Opiate. Wagner. All singer voices are alike. No personality.

As this last item on Weill's *cahier des doléances* makes clear, his target was in many respects the "erotic" dimension of Wagner's aesthetic project. The libido-drenched psychology of Wagner's heroes, the erotic valences of Wagner's harmonies and chromaticism, and the "narcotic" effect of the "phantasmagoric" aspects of the Gesamtkunstwerk all pointed in one way or the other to the status of sex in Wagner.

And this dimension pointed to its formal status, not just the way it organized the music, the poem, and the singing, but rather the way it shaped and structured the Gesamtkunstwerk itself. After all, as Cecil Gray so wittily put it, what is the main action that the orchestra performs in *Tristan* that doesn't happen onstage? "If Tristan and Isolde were to behave onstage as they do in the orchestra, the police would soon stop the performance."[25] Character, psychology, expression—in Wagner all of Weill's *bêtes noires* were moved into the spectral realm between the constituent arts. And all of them were infused with the erotic.

But Weill's critique was at once more fundamental than that. He did not view the way in which the erotic was thematized in Wagner's opera as fundamentally retrograde; rather, the fact that it was thematized at all was what made Wagner so noisome. Weill objected to the fact that Wagner conceived of the Gesamtkunstwerk as a carrier of ideas that had nothing to do with music. Weill disliked certain aspects of Wagner's music; Wagner's speculations—about politics, about redemption, about sex—he rejected wholesale, as illegitimate admixtures to the opera form. This was something Busoni had already criticized. In *Versuch einer neuen Ästhetik der Tonkunst*, he writes of Wagner's followers that "instead of architectural or symmetrical formulae, instead of relationships of tonic and dominant, [their music] has tied itself to the poetic, often even the philosophical program as though onto a rail."[26]

In spite of all of his qualms, Weill never fully abandoned his fascination with Wagner. Even decades after declaring that a performance of *Tristan* would "always be something special," in the forties Weill could sneak references to *Tristan und Isolde*, to *Das Rheingold*, and to *Meistersinger* into Broadway musicals like *Lady in the Dark* and *Street Scenes* with a slyness and nonchalance that betrayed that they'd never left his cosmos in the first place. And while parody and pastiche are never far when Weill invokes Wagner, the parody often retains a kernel of the fascination Weill expressed in his letter to his brother. Even in his American exile, it seems, Weill enjoyed losing himself in this music and "being waist-deep in it."

As Weill made clear in a 1929 interview he gave to the *Wiener Allgemeine Zeitung*, the intention behind his now-canonic operas of the twenties was "not to write an opera parody." He added that the *Dreigroschenoper* constituted "the strongest possible detachment" from Wagner, but insisted it was "by no means a rejection."[27] Unlike, say, Hindemith's take on *Tristan und Isolde* in 1921's *Das Nusch-Nuschi*, Weill's confrontations with Wagner were not intended as liquidations, and he seemed uninterested in the political valences of Wagner worship, which had only intensified in the wake of World War I.[28] Weill regarded Wagner as an obstacle to a rejuvenation of the operatic form—itself a thoroughly Wagnerian project, as Weill was well aware.

"I'm a Stranger here myself" represents a grappling with the Wagnerian legacy simply by virtue of the fact that it is a song, because, in a sense, when it arrives onstage it is a stranger there itself. Even before he was forced to leave Germany, Weill composed musical numbers that he called songs, rather than *Lieder* or arias. This was because in German, song has a whiff of the modern, the popular, the louche. Weill's embrace of the form went so far that he and Brecht not only revived the earlier form of the *Singspiel* (which alternated dramatic action and musical numbers), but neologized it as *Songspiel*.

Generically speaking, the song is more particular and more autistic than the aria. The song interrupts the stage action and the stage music of *One Touch of Venus*, negates what comes after it, and then folds up neatly to make room for what comes after. The break into song is precisely that: a break. This fact is emphasized in the lyrics, which are kept in typical Nashian couplets and rhymes unafraid to venture into outright punning ("foible"/"enjoyable"). Each stanza (at the end of the song, even some couplets) is a little nucleus onto itself, and draws on its own rhymes, its own imagery, and its own argument:

> What is your latest foible?
> Is Gin Rummy more exquisite?
> Is skiing more enjoyable?
> For heaven's sake what is it?

It is a musical number consisting of even smaller numbers, each curled up into autistic little balls. Even though the song presents itself as a series of questions, music and lyrics conspire register those questions as a disconnect rather than as a dialogue. Where Tristan and Isolde, Siegfried and Brünnhilde, Guntram and Freihild can dialogue across time and space and thus constitute an erotic geography, Nash's lyrics already foreshadow Rodney and Venus' inablity to find their way to each other, let alone find themselves together in Ozone Heights. Just as on Wolpe's Potsdamer Platz, eroticism in Weill's New York has run out of world and time. Again, the song form helps: the questions here are, all of Venus' protestations to the contrary notwithstanding, essentially rhetorical. "I'm a Stranger Here Myself" is a lament, not an inquiry.

But for all its showy rejection of the Wagnerian conception of the artwork, the song is quite clearly haunted by the strangeness and dislocation of the present. It's hard not to feel sympathy for a goddess of love stranded in a loveless present, which is embarrassed by real feeling and has turned to gin rummy instead. The song's three related strangers—the goddess Venus, true love, and the song itself—are outmoded in the present, but in their outmodedness they indict the present. At the end of the opera, the stage directions tell us, "the creatures of her magic world invade the scene." "Ancient Greece is real, and Ozone Heights the myth."[29]

Much of that is pure parody, of course. But unlike Wolpe's Zeus, who ends up in a museum, where he properly belongs, Weill's Venus deserves better than the loveless present she wakes up in. How could no measure of nostalgia attach to a song with this title, when it is written by a composer who was, in more ways than one, still "a stranger here" himself?[30] "I'm a Stranger Here Myself" is not only a liquidation of past operatic practices, in the way the *Dreigroschenoper* was. It's at least in equal measure a mourning song—mourning for a lost world and for the sense of belonging one felt there, a sense of belonging that has to do above all with love and the erotic.

And here, though negatively, the shadow of *Tristan*'s final scenes becomes visible one last time. For the song doesn't just reject what opera was supposed to sound like; it doesn't just reject the total work of art. The song also rejects Wagner in terms of how it deals with sex. After all, "Victorian views" are not the only ideas about sex that the speaker disagrees with. There is also the kind of view that would see sex as more than "discover[ing] the key to his ignition," more than a matter of "tactics," of "clues," of "diplomatic propositions."

The song is a stranger here itself, if, and only if, "gender is just a term in grammar." It is a song about the possibility of Romanticism, and about the possibility, however unlikely, that love is a deep cosmic force, an author of destinies, an unconscious motor and motivator. In other words, about the possibility of an erotics of the kind Wagner's operas, and those of his followers, trafficked in, and in fact depended on. The text makes this clear. When Venus remarks that "love isn't the dying moan of a distant violin, it's the triumphant twang of a bedspring," she points to the link between "distant sounds" and the erotic in opera, where desire transubstantiates itself unproblematically into music. But no such distance, no such transubstantiation, is offered in *One Touch of Venus*. Instead we get the onstage, the literal, the perfectly imminent creaking of bedsprings.

Ostensibly, the song is a nostalgic celebration of the lost, possibly "obsolete art" of love. But between the lines, Venus lets on that love may never have been what she so busily cracks it up to be. Love may be a stranger in a New York department store in the 1940s, but Venus uses a decidedly modern arsenal of metaphors to lament its disappearance. How wistful are we meant to feel about a love that is compared to the "key to his ignition," and that depends on "my available condition"? And how out of place is this Venus really, given that she seems to know her way around cars, skiing, and gin rummy? The point, it seems, is not that Venus is a department-store mannequin today—in some sense she's always been just that.

Is it an accident that this kind of song relies on this kind of erotics? The lyrics of course aren't Weill's—with Weill, they barely ever are. But the composer had a funny way of gravitating toward lyricists who espoused a similar philosophy. Nash was only the last in a long line of Weill collaborators who treated romantic love with a mixture of wistfulness and cynicism. Bertolt Brecht included in his libretto for the *Dreigroschenoper* the line about the dangers of the "do-you-hear-my-heart-beating text," only to have Polly Peachum fall for that very text a few tableaux later.

Die Sieben Todsünden (1933), Weill's and Brecht's "*Ballet chanté*," chronicles the story of two girls named Anna who prostitute themselves for seven years in various American cities, in lyrics like,

> And we found a man in Boston,
> Who paid well, he was in love.
> And I had a hard time persuading Anna,
> Because she too was in love, just with another,
> And she paid him in love.

Buying and selling, cliché and cupidity—such are the hallmarks of Weill's operatic eroticism. And frequently, whether in the Venus-statue in *One Touch of Venus,* or the dolled-up Eurydice, statements about eros are statements about how eros shapes art—or once shaped art, or was once thought to shape art.

Weill sensed a kinship between the demystification of love undertaken by Brecht, Goll, and Nash on the one hand, and the demystification of the Gesamtkunstwerk he had made his mission on the other. The fact that eroticism and Gesamtkunstwerk were linked has constituted the main thread of this book's argument. It only makes sense, then, that we close with a man who transformed both at once, without any concern whether it might sever their link. Weill not only negated the total work of art; Weill not only negated the narcotic thrall of Wagner's musical eroticism. He also came to realize that the link between the two had to be severed if one wanted to break Wagner's spell, "which through *Tristan* held the world of opera production in its thrall for fifty years."[31] Whether he managed to do so is another matter. "I'm a Stranger Here Myself" suggests that for one night in October 1943, the Imperial Theater on West 45th Street stood in the shadow of the *Festspielhaus* in faraway Bayreuth.

NOTES

INTRODUCTION

1. Kurt Weill, "*Tannhäuser* im Rundfunk," *Musik und musikalisches Theater* (Mainz: Schott, 2000), 219.

2. Richard Wagner, "Metaphysik der Geschlechtsliebe," *Schriften und Dichtungen* 12:289.

3. James Treadwell, "The Urge to Communicate: The Prose Writings as Theory and Practice," in *Cambridge Companion to Wagner*, ed. Thomas S. Grey (Cambridge: Cambridge University Press, 2008), 179.

4. Paul Robinson, *Opera and Ideas* (Ithaca: Cornell University Press, 1985), 3.

5. Lawrence Kramer, *Opera and Modern Culture: Wagner and Strauss* (Berkeley: University of California Press, 2004).

6. Slavoj Žižek, " 'The Wound Is Healed Only by the Spear that Smote You': The Operatic Subject and Its Vicissitudes," in *Opera Through Other Eyes*, ed. David Levin (Palo Alto, CA: Stanford University Press, 1993), 178.

7. Martin Gregor-Dellin, *Richard Wagner* (Munich: Piper, 1980), 392. Wagner believed that chap. 44 of vol. 2 of *The World as Will and Representation* licensed his interpretation.

8. Wagner, "Oper und Drama," in *Sämtliche Schriften und Dichtungen* 4:152.

9. Ibid.

10. Brian Maggee, *Wagner and Philosophy* (London: Allen Lane, 2000), 55.

11. Adrian Daub, *Uncivil Unions: The Metaphysics of Marriage in German Romanticism and Idealism* (Chicago: Chicago University Press, 2012), 287.

12. Denis de Rougemont, *Love in the Western World* (Princeton, NJ: Princeton University Press, 1978).

13. Wagner, "Oper und Drama," in *Sämtliche Schriften und Dichtungen* 4:152.

14. See Frederick Beiser, *Schiller as Philosopher: A Reexamination* (New York: Oxford University Press, 2008).

15. Udo Bermbach, *"Blühendes Leid": Politik und Gesellschaft in Richard Wagners Musikdramen* (Stuttgart, Germany: Metzler, 2003), 35.

16. Dieter Borchmeyer, *Drama and the World of Richard Wagner* (Princeton, NJ: Princeton University Press, 2003), 192.

17. Laurence Dreyfus, *Wagner and the Erotic Impulse* (Cambridge, MA: Harvard University Press, 2010), 71.

18. Cited in Bryan Gilliam, *The Life of Richard Strauss* (New York: Cambridge University Press, 1999), 35.

19. Rudolf Louis, *Der Widerspruch in der Musik* (Leipzig: Breitkopf & Härtel, 1893), vi.

20. Patrick Carnegy, *Wagner and the Art of the Theater* (New Haven, CT: Yale University Press, 2006).

21. Wagner, *Schriften und Dichtungen*, 56.

22. See for example Sanna Pederson, "Defining the Term 'Absolute Music' Historically," *Music & Letters* 90, no. 2 (2009): 242/243.

23. Theodor Uhlig, "Richard Wagner's Schriften über Kunst, Teil III," *Neue Zeitschrift für Musik* 34, nos. 3/4 (1851): 21–34, 33–36.

24. Wagner, *Schriften und Dichtungen* 1:183.

25. Ibid.

26. Pederson, "Defining the Term," 245.

27. Wolfgang Dömling, "Reuniting the Arts: Notes on the History of an Idea," *19th Century Music* 18, no. 1 (Summer 1994): 4.

28. Peter Furth, "Romantik der Entfremdung," in *Phänomenologie der Enttäuschungen: Ideologiekritik Nachtotalitär* (Frankfurt: Fischer, 1991), 44–93.

29. Wagner, *Schriften und Dichtungen* 1:183.

30. John Deathridge, *Wagner Beyond Good and Evil* (Berkeley: University of California Press, 2008), 148.

31. Lawrence Kramer, *Music as Cultural Practice, 1800–1900* (Berkeley: University of California Press, 1990), 163.

32. Michel Poizat, *The Angel's Cry: Beyond the Pleasure Principle in Opera* (Ithaca, New York: Cornell University Press, 1992), 165.

33. Jean-Jacques Nattiez, *Wagner Androgyne: A Study in Interpretation* (Princeton, NJ: Princeton University Press, 1993), 154.

34. Friedrich Kittler, "Weltatem: On Wagner's Media Technology," in David Levin (ed.), *Opera Through Other Eyes* (Stanford, CA: Stanford University Press, 1994), 215–35.

35. Wagner, *Schriften und Dichtungen* 3:117.

36. Wagner, "Das Weibliche im Menschlichen," in *Sämtliche Schriften und Dichtungen* 12:342.

37. Friedrich Nietzsche, "Das Griechische Musikdrama," *Werke KG* 3, no. 2: 516.

38. Gary Tomlinson, *Metaphysical Song- An Essay on Opera* (Princeton, NJ: Princeton University Press, 1999).

39. Leopold Schmidt, "Franz Schmidt, 'Notre Dame,'" *Musikleben der Gegenwart* (Berlin: Max Hesse, 1922), 85.

40. Hermann Häfker, "Kino als Gesamtkunstwerk," in *Geschichte der Filmtheorie* (Frankfurt: Suhrkamp, 2004).

41. Jeremy Tambling, "The Power of Emotion: Wagner and Film," *Wagner and Cinema*, ed. Jeongwon Joe and Sander Gilman (Bloomington: Indiana University Press, 2010), 276.

42. Julius Kapp, *Die Oper der Gegenwart* (Berlin: Max Hesse, 1922), 145.

43. Walter Niemann, *Die Musik der Gegenwart* (Stuttgart, Germany: Deutsche Verlagsanstalt, 1922), 100.

44. Benjamin Goose, "The Opera of the Film? Eugen d'Albert's *Der Golem*," *Cambridge Opera Journal* 19, no. 2 (2007): 139–66.

45. Theodor W. Adorno, *In Search of Wagner* (London: Verso, 2005).

46. J. W. v. Goethe, *Italienische Reise, Werke: Hamburger Ausgabe* 11:78. See also Yvonne Nilges, *Richard Wagners Shakespeare* (Würzburg, Germany: Königshausen & Neumann, 2007), 130.

47. Richard Wagner, "Zukunftsmusik," in *Judaism in Music and Other Essays* (Lincoln: University of Nebraska Press, 1995), 332.

48. Immacolata Amodeo, *Das Openhafte: Eine Studie zum 'gusto melodrammatico' in Italien und Europa* (Bielefeld, Germany: transcript, 2007).

49. Richard Wagner, *Über Schauspieler und Sänger* (Leipzig: Fritzsch, 1872), 7.

50. Houston Stewart Chamberlain, *Richard Wagner* (Munich: Bruckmann, 1904), 482.

51. Richard Wagner, *Über Schauspieler und Sänger* (Leipzig: Fritzsch, 1872), 7.

52. Adolf Weissmann, *Die Musik in der Weltkrise* (Stuttgart, Germany: Deutsche Verlagsanstalt, 1922), 3.

53. Paul Bekker, "Franz Schreker und das Theater," *Anbruch* 5, no. 2 (1924): 51.

54. Paul Bekker, *Wandlungen der Oper* (Zurich: Orell Füssli, 1983), 6.

55. Weissmann, *Die Musik*, 72.

56. Thomas Mann, "Wälsungenblut," in *Frühe Erzählungen* (Frankfurt: Fischer, 2004). 453.

57. Juliet Koss, *Modernism after Wagner* (Minneapolis: University of Minnesota Press, 2010), xiii.

58. Weissmann, *Die Musik*, 143.

CHAPTER ONE

1. Richard Wagner, *Sämtliche Briefe: Band IV: Mai 1851 bis September 1852*, ed. Gertrud Strobel and Werner Wolf (Leipzig: Deutscher Verlag für Musik, 2000), 44.

2. Wagner acknowledged the link in a letter dated May 1851 (Wagner, *Sämtliche Briefe*, *Band IV*, 44).

3. Carl Dahlhaus, *Richard Wagner's Musical Dramas* (Cambridge: Cambridge University Press, 1979), 126–28; *Richard Wagners Musikdramen* (Stuttgart, Germany: Reclam, 1996), 183.

4. Dahlhaus, *Richard Wagner's Musical Dramas*, 127–28; *Richard Wagners Musikdramen*, 183.

5. Julia Kristeva, *Powers of Horror: An Essay in Abjection* (New York: Columbia University Press, 1982), 1–31.

6. Richard Wagner, "Siegfried," in *Sämtliche Schriften und Dichtungen* (Leipzig: Breitkopf & Härtel, 1911), 6:94.

7. Wagner, "Metaphysik der Geschlechtsliebe," in *Sämtliche Schriften und Dichtungen* 12:289. See also Wagner's letter to Mathilde Wesendonck, December 1, 1858 in *Richard Wagner an Mathilde Wesendonck, Tagebuchblätter und Briefe 1853–1871* (Leipzig: Breitkopf &Härtel, 1908), 80.

8. Wagner, "Oper und Drama," in *Sämtliche Schriften und Dichtungen* 4:152.

9. Wagner, "Kunst und Klima," in *Sämtliche Schriften und Dichtungen* 3:219.

10. Slavoj Žižek, *The Sublime Object of Ideology* (London: Verson, 1989), 125. See also Žižek, " 'There is No Sexual Relationship': Wagner as Lacanian," *New German Critique* (1996), 69:14.

11. Stefan Bodo Würffel, "Alberich und Mime: Zwerge, Gecken, Außenseiter," in *"Alles ist nach seiner Art": Figuren in Richard Wagners "Der Ring des Nibelungen,"* ed. Udo Bermbach (Stuttgart, Germany: Metzler, 2001), 120–43.

12. Marc A. Weiner, *Richard Wagner and the Anti-Semitic Imagination* (Lincoln: University of Nebraska Press, 1995), 35–55.

13. Sigmund Freud, "Family Romances," in *The Freud Reader*, ed. Peter Gay (New York: W. W. Norton, 1989), 297–300.

14. Wagner, "Siegfried," in *Sämtliche Schriften und Dichtungen* 6:97.

15. Wagner, "Siegfried," in *Sämtliche Schriften und Dichtungen* 6:106.

16. Theodor W. Adorno, *Die musikalischen Monographien: Gesammelte Schriften*, ed. Rolf Tiedemann (Frankfurt: Suhrkamp Verlag, 1971), 13:103.

17. Dieter Borchmeyer, "Siegfried: Der Held als Opfer," in *"Alles ist nach seiner Art,"* 68–80.

18. Kant's anthropology, for example, distinguishes between "Mutterwitz" and "Schulwitz," BA 24/25, in Immanuel Kant, *Schriften zur Anthropologie, Geschichtsphilosophie, Politik und Pädagogik*, ed. Wilhelm Weischedel (Frankfurt: Suhrkamp, 1964), 425.

19. Wagner, "Deutsche Kunst und Deutsche Politik," in *Sämtliche Schriften und Dichtungen* 8:46.

20. Cosima uses the word when discussing Lawrence Sterne's *Tristram Shandy*. Cosima Wagner, *Die Tagebücher*, ed. Martin Gregor-Dellin and Dietrich Mack (Munich: Piper, 1976), 1:179: "Dem Witz, den einer von sich selbst hat."

21. Wagner, "Siegfried," in *Sämtliche Schriften und Dichtungen* 6:134. Wagner's earlier drafts further emphasized the maternal connection of the *Waldvogel*: One draft has Siegfried saying "Mich dünkt, meine Mutter / singt zu mir!" *Skizzen und Entwürfe zur Ring-Dichtung*, ed. Otto Strobel (Munich: Bruckmann, 1930), 156.

22. Wagner, "Siegfried," in *Sämtliche Schriften und Dichtungen* 6:150.

23. Ibid., 166.

24. Lawrence Kramer, *Opera and Modern Culture* (Berkeley: University of California Press, 2004), 84. Kramer especially emphasizes the link between maternity and the ideology of lineage (in particular, anti-Semitism).

25. Adorno, *Die musikalischen Monographien*, 120.

26. Adorno, *Die musikalischen Monographien*, 103.

27. Wagner, "Siegfried," in *Sämtliche Schriften und Dichtungen* 6:99.

28. Rolf-Peter Horstmann, "Den Verstand zur Vernunft bringen? Hegels Auseinandersetzung mit Kant in der Differenz-Schrift," in *Das Interesse des Denkens: Hegel aus heutiger Sicht*, ed. W. Welsch, K. Vieweg (Munich: Fink, 2003), 89–108.

29. On Wagner's assimilation of the Nibelung's biology in the old Nordic and German sagas, see Würffel, "Alberich und Mime," 125.

30. Abbate's argument focuses on the late Wagner's tendency to compress a variety of types or mythic archetypes into one individual role, presumably in the interest of a Gnostic transcendence of the *principium individuationis*—there is, of course, no such transcendence in the Nibelungs' iterative shape shifting. Carolyn Abbate, *In Search of Opera* (Princeton, NJ: Princeton University Press, 2003), 108.

31. See, for example, *Götterdämmerung*, act 2, scene 1 (*Sämtliche Schriften und Dichtungen* 6:211).

32. For references to this draft, which Wagner worked on during and immediately after his "revolutionary" phase, see Richard Wagner, *Mein Leben* (Munich: List, 1963), 401, 403; *Sämtliche Briefe, Band III: Briefe der Jahre 1849 bis 1851* (Leipzig: VEB Deutscher Verlag für Musik, 1983), 110, 150, 179; Cosima Wagner, *Tagebücher* 1:43; Carl Friedrich Glasenapp, *Das Leben Richard Wagners in sechs Büchern dargestellt* (Leipzig: Breitkopf & Härtel, 1905), 2:319; and Gregor-Dellin, *Richard Wagner*, 254.

33. Wagner, *Sämtliche Schriften und Dichtungen* 11:301.

34. Wagner, "Siegfried," in *Sämtliche Schriften und Dichtungen* 6:128.

35. Max Nordau, *Degeneration* (New York: D. Appleton, 1895), 556; *Entartung* (Berlin: C. Duncker, 1893), 2:555.

36. Wagner, "Der Nibelungen-Mythus," in *Sämtliche Schriften und Dichtungen* 6:139.

37. Wagner, "Siegfried," in *Sämtliche Schriften und Dichtungen* 6:140.

38. Kramer, *Opera and Modern Culture*, 88.

39. Wagner, "Siegfried," in *Sämtliche Schriften und Dichtungen* 6:17.

40. Ibid., 28.

41. Michael P. Steinberg, "Die Walküre and Modern Memory," *University of Toronto Quarterly* 74, no. 2 (2005): 705.

42. Jean-Jacques Nattiez, "The Tetralogy of Richard Wagner: A Mirror of Androgyny and the Total Work of Art," *Diogenes* 52, no. 73 (2005): 78. See also Slavoj Žižek, "Why Is Wagner Worth Saving?" *Journal of Philosophy & Scripture* 2, no. 1 (2004): 28.

43. The fact that *Siegfried* presents the youngster's animus against Mime as something instinctual may well be linked to Gobineau's claim that there is a "mutual repulsion" of different races, which is instinctive both (historically) in the polity and (aesthetically) in the individual. Arthur de Gobineau, *The Inequality of Human Races*, trans. Adrian Collins (New York: Putnam, 1915), 179–80.

44. Judith Butler, *Gender Trouble* (London: Routledge, 1999), xxviii.

45. Žižek, "Why Is Wagner Worth Saving?," 28.

46. Nattiez, "The Tetralogy of Richard Wagner," 80.

47. Linda Hutcheon and Michael Hutcheon, *Opera: The Art of Dying* (Cambridge, MA: Harvard University Press, 2004), 80.

48. Wagner, "Siegfried," in *Sämtliche Schriften und Dichtungen* 6:153.

49. Ibid., 140.

50. Ibid., 153.

51. Ibid., 164.

52. Ibid., 165.

53. Žižek, "Why Is Wagner Worth Saving?," 28.

54. Wagner, "Siegfried," in *Sämtliche Schriften und Dichtungen* 6:164–65.

55. Ibid., 165.

56. Ibid., 94.

57. Ibid., 169.

58. Ibid., 174–75.

59. Ibid., 176: "Erb' und Eigen, ein und all."

60. Dahlhaus, *Richard Wagners Musikdramen*, 183. The translation is my own, since Mary Whittall's more reader-friendly version somewhat obscures the point I am trying to emphasize: "The timelessness of fairy tale, as opposed to the temporal setting of myth, creates a separation between *Siegfried* and *Götterdämmerung* that nothing can bridge." Dahlhaus, *Richard Wagner's Musical Dramas*, 127.

61. Wagner, "Siegfried," in *Sämtliche Schriften und Dichtungen* 6:88.

62. Ibid., 93.

63. Ibid., 93.

64. Wagner, "Das Weibliche im Menschlichen," in *Sämtliche Schriften und Dichtungen* 12:342.

65. Ibid.

66. Wagner, "Siegfried," in *Sämtliche Schriften und Dichtungen* 6:92.

67. Ibid., 89.

68. Abbate, *In Search of Opera*, 122.

69. See Robert Bailey, "The Evolution of the *Ring*," *19th Century Music* 1, no. 1 (1977), 49.

70. G. W. F. Hegel, *Phänomenologie des Geistes* (Berlin: Duncker und Humboldt, 1843), 286–304.

71. Adorno, *Die musikalischen Monographien*, 19.

72. Martin Puchner notes that "Mime is the scapegoat for everything that is suspect about theatrical mimesis." See his *Stage Fright: Modernism, Anti-Theatricality and Drama* (Baltimore, MD: Johns Hopkins University Press, 2002), 49. Weiner connects Wagner's Mime-caricature into outdated operatic (mostly singing) styles. See Weiner's *Wagner and the Anti-Semitic Imagination*, 176–95.

73. Hermann Danuser, "Universalität oder Partikularität? Zur Frage antisemitischer Charakterzeichnung in Wagners Werk," in *Richard Wagner und die Juden*, ed. Dieter Borchmeyer, Ami Maayani, and Susanne Vill (Stuttgart, Germany: Metzler, 1999), 88.

74. Adorno, *Die musikalischen Monographien*, 22.

75. Wagner, "Siegfried," in *Sämtliche Schriften und Dichtungen* 6:92.

76. Weiner, *Richard Wagner*, 176–85.

77. Wagner, "Das Judentum in der Musik," in *Sämtliche Schriften und Dichtungen* 5:71; Richard Wagner, *Stories and Essays*, ed. Charles Osborne (London: Peter Owen, 1973), 28.

78. Danuser, "Universalität oder Partikularität?," 82.

79. Puchner, *Stage Fright*, 50.

80. On the question of Mime's speech and so-called Mauscheln (German spoken in a Yiddish accent), see Weiner, *Richard Wagner and the Anti-Semitic Imagination*, 116.

81. See Borchmeyer, "Siegfried," 78.

82. Mary Ann Smart, *Mimomania: Music and Gesture in Nineteenth-Century Opera* (Berkeley: University of California Press, 2004), 165–66.

83. Dahlhaus, *Richard Wagners Musikdramen*, 184.

84. Dahlhaus, *Richard Wagners Musikdramen*, 185.

85. David J. Levin, "Reading Beckmesser Reading: Antisemitism and Aesthetic Practice in the Mastersingers of Nuremberg," *New German Critique* (1996), 69:129.

86. Abbate, *In Search of Opera*, 122.

87. Puchner, *Stage Fright*, 49.

88. Wagner, "Das Judentum in der Musik," in *Sämtliche Schriften und Dichtungen* 5:71.

89. On the association of endogamy and Jewishness, see Kramer, *Opera and Modern Culture*, 89.

90. Wagner, "Oper und Drama," in *Sämtliche Schriften und Dichtungen* 4:152.

91. Ibid., 151.

92. In describing the plight of the Nibelungs under Alberich's yoke, Mime invokes not only a kind of community (of which we get evidence only in the past tense), who have "wives" (*Weiber*), and turns trinkets (*Tand*), which in Siegfried's vituperation becomes a blistering rebuke, into tokens of love and coupledom (Wagner, *Sämtliche Schriften und Dichtungen* 5:238).

93. Adorno, *Die musikalischen Monographien*, 126.

94. Eve Kosofsky Sedgwick, *Epistemology of the Closet* (Berkeley: University of California Press, 1990), 189–90.

95. See Patrice Chéreau and Pierre Boulez, *Boulez in Bayreuth: The Centenary Ring* (Baarn, Netherlands: Phonogram International, 1981).

96. Philip Kitcher and Richard Schacht, *Finding an Ending: Reflections on Wagner's Ring* (New York: Oxford University Press, 2004), 186ff.

97. Kramer, *Opera and Modern Culture*, 191–92, 198–203.

98. Abbate, *In Search of Opera*, 108.

99. Wagner, "Parsifal," in *Sämtliche Schriften und Dichtungen* 10:346.

100. Friedrich Nietzsche, *Werke in Drei Bänden*, ed. Karl Schlechta (Munich: Hanser, 1954), 2:242.

101. Rudolf Louis, *Die deutsche Musik der Gegenwart* (Munich: Georg Müller, 1909), 85; the English translation is taken from Christopher Hailey, *Franz Schreker: A Cultural Biography* (Cambridge: Cambridge University Press, 1993), 36.

102. Friedrich von Hardenberg (Novalis), *Novalis: Schriften*, ed. Richard Samuel and Paul Kluckhohn (Darmstadt: Wissenschaftliche Buchgesellschaft, 1965), 2:255: "Alle Romane, wo wahre Liebe vorkommt, sind Mährchen—magische Begebenheiten."

103. Kurt Söhnlein, *Erinnerungen an Siegfried Wagner* (Bayreuth, Germany: Schriftenreihe der Siegfried-Wagner-Gesellschaft, 1980), 66.

104. Ernst Rosmer, *Königskinder: Musikmärchen in drei Bildern* (Berlin: Fischer, 1910), 9.

105. Ibid., 40.

106. Ibid., 42.

CHAPTER TWO

1. Joachim Beck, "Die Gezeichneten," *Die Weltbühne* 15, no. 30 (1919): 76.

2. Magali Zibaso, *Franz Schrekers Bühnenwerke* (Saarbrücken, Germany: Pfau, 1999), 130.

3. Hans Severus Ziegler, *Entartete Musik: Eine Abrechnung* (Düsseldorf: Völkischer Verlag, 1939), 12/14.

4. Ibid., 15.

5. Ibid., 17.

6. Ibid., 22.

7. Leopold Schmidt, *Das Musikleben der Gegenwart* (Berlin: Max Hesse, 1922), 81.

8. Richard Batka, *Musikalische Streifzüge* (Leipzig: Diederichs, 1899), 208.

9. Fred K. Prieberg, *Musik im NS-Staat* (Frankfurt: Fischer, 1982), 212.

10. *The Lotus Magazine* 9, no. 4 (Jan. 1918): 194.

11. Anthony Beaumont, *Zemlinsky* (Ithaca, NY: Cornell University Press, 2000), 301.

12. Walter Niemann, *Die Musik der Gegenwart* (Berlin: Schuster und Loeffler, 1913), 263.

13. Oscar Wilde, *The Complete Short Stories* (Oxford: Oxford University Press, 2010), 160.

14. Gundula Kreuzer, *Verdi and the Germans: From Unification to the Third Reich* (Oxford: Oxford University Press, 2010), 134.

15. Sherry D. Lee, "The Other in the Mirror, or, Recognizing the Self: Wilde's and Zemlinsky's Dwarf," *Music and Letters* 91, no. 2 (2010): 211.

16. Wilde, *Complete Short Stories*, 157.

17. Lion Feuchtwanger, *Die häßliche Herzogin* (Berlin: Aufbau Verlag, 1994).

18. Franz Schreker, *Meine Musikdramatische Idee, Anbruch* 1, no. 1 (1919): 7.

19. Paul Bekker, "Wagner Heute," *Anbruch* 15, no. 1 (1933): 3.

20. Paul Bekker, "Franz Schreker und das Theater," *Anbruch* 5, no. 2 (1924): 51.

21. David Levin, "Reading Beckmesser Reading: Antisemitism and Aesthetic Practice in the Mastersingers of Nuremberg," *New German Critique* (1996), 69:129.

22. Franz Schreker, "Wagner Heute," *Anbruch* 15, no. 1 (1933): 12.

23. See chap. 6.

24. Paul Bekker, *Wandlungen der Oper* (Zurich: Orell Füssli, 1983), 6.

25. Ibid., 6.

26. Ibid., 153.

27. Friedrich Nietzsche, *Sämtliche Werke: Kritische Studienausgabe in 15 Bänden* (Munich: Deutscher Taschenbuch Verlag, 1980), 68.

28. Daniel Pick, *Faces of Degeneration: A European Disorder, c. 1848–c. 1918* (Cambridge: Cambridge University Press, 1989).

29. Max Nordau, *Entartung* (Berlin: C. Duncker, 1898).

30. Nietzsche, *Sämtliche Werke*, 69: "Sie kennen mich, mein Herr."

31. Karl Rosenkranz, *Aesthetik des Hässlichen* (Königsberg: Bornträger, 1853), 171.

32. Rosenkranz, *Aesthetik des Hässlichen*, 172.

33. Bekker, *Wandlungen der Oper*, 153.

34. Schreker, "Meine Musikdramatische Idee," 7.

35. Bekker, *Wandlungen der Oper*, 5.

36. Franz Schreker, "Gibt es eine Krise der Oper?" *Anbruch* (1926), 8:209.

37. Richard Batka, *Aus der Opernwelt: Prager Kritiken und Skizzen* (Munich: Callwey, 1907), 167.

38. Leopold Schmitt, *Zur Geschichte der Märchenoper* (Halle: Hendel, 1895), 10.

39. "Zemlinsky über seinen 'Zwerg,'" *Komödie* (Nov. 1923), 12.

40. Niemann, *Die Musik der Gegenwart*, 101.

41. Cited in Christopher Hailey, *Franz Schreker, 1878–1934: A Cultural Biography* (Cambridge: Cambridge University Press, 1993), 36.

42. Paul Bekker, *Franz Schreker: Studie zur Kritik der modernen Oper*, in *Paul Bekker/Franz Schreker: Briefwechsel*, ed. Christopher Hailey (Aachen, Germany: Rimbaud, 1994), 282.

43. Niemann, *Die Musik der Gegenwart*, 102.

44. Bekker, *Franz Schreker*, 282.

45. Rosenkranz, *Aesthetik des Hässlichen*, 164.

46. Ibid., 173.

47. Theodor W. Adorno, *In Search of Wagner* (London: Verso, 2005), 90.

CHAPTER THREE

1. Arthur Schopenhauer, "Ueber die Weiber," *Parerga und Paralipomena* (Leipzig: Brockhaus, 1874), 655.

2. Charles Dowell Youmans, *Richard Strauss's Orchestral Music and the German Intellectual Tradition: The Philosophical Roots of Musical Modernism* (Bloomington: Indiana University Press, 2005), 68–74.

3. Romain Rolland, *Richard Strauss et Romain Rolland*, Cahiers Romain Rolland 3 (Paris: Albin Michel, 1951), 187.

4. As John Deathridge has discussed, at an early stage in Wagner's composition, *Tristan und Isolde* ended in much the same way. In this draft, Isolde cradles the dying Tristan without saying a word; just like Freihild, she is reduced to passive listening—although she is of course not listening to Tristan, but to the music itself. Later drafts of *Tristan* give Isolde a say in the final scene that I call a "dialogue," even though of course Tristan and Isolde never actually duet in the opera's final scene. John Deathridge, "Post-Mortem on Isolde," *New German Critique* 69 (1996): 109.

5. Youmans, *Strauss's Orchestral Music*, 45.

6. On Ritter, see Charles D. Youmans, "The Development of Richard Strauss's Worldview," in *The Richard Strauss Companion*, ed. Mark-Daniel Schmid (Westport, CT: Greenwood, 2003), 76.

7. Quoted in Norman Del Mar, *Richard Strauss* (London: Barrie and Radcliffe, 1962), 1:93.

8. Youmans, *Strauss's Orchestral Music*, 74.

9. Arthur Schopenhauer, *Die Welt als Wille und Vorstellung* (Leipzig: Brockhaus, 1844), 1:449.

10. Ibid., 2:692ff.; 1:444–72.

11. Ibid., 1:470.

12. Ibid., 1:449.

13. Of course, some of the examples Schopenhauer cites for his ascetic "saints" are women, a possibility *Guntram* never seems to entertain—*active* renunciation here is a male business.

14. Julia Kristeva, "Approaching Abjection," in *Powers of Horror* (New York: Columbia University Press, 1982), 1–31.

15. Johann Gottlieb Fichte, "Concerning Human Dignity," *Early Philosophical Writings* (Ithaca, NY: Cornell University Press, 1988), 83–86.

16. Liliane Weissberg, *Geistersprache: Philosophischer und literarischer Diskurs im späten achtzehnten Jahrhundert* (Würzburg, Germany: Königshausen & Neumann, 1990), 34–61.

17. Schopenhauer, "Versuch über das Geistersehen und was damit zusammenhängt," in *Sämmtliche Werke* 7 (Leipzig: Brockhaus, 1871), 324.

18. Schopenhauer, *Die Welt als Wille* 2:27.

19. Otto Weininger, *Geschlecht und Charakter: Eine Prinzipielle Untersuchung* (Vienna: Braumüller, 1907), 240ff.

20. Julia Kristeva, *Speculum of the Other Woman* (Ithaca, NY: Cornell University Press, 1985).

21. William Mann, *Die Opern von Richard Strauss* (Munich: C. H. Beck, 1969), 15.

22. Slavoj Žižek, *Tarrying with the Negative* (Durham, NC: Duke University Press, 1993), 185.

23. Roland Barthes, "The Grain of the Voice," in *The Responsibility of Forms: Critical Essays on Music, Art, and Representation*, trans. Richard Howard (New York: Hill and Wang, 1985), 267–77.

24. Martin Puchner, *Stage Fright: Modernism and Anti-Theatricality and Drama* (Baltimore, MD: Johns Hopkins University Press, 2002), 31–58.

25. Schopenhauer, *Die Welt als Wille* 2:510.

26. Berthold Hoeckner, "Elsa Screams, or The Birth of Music Drama," *Cambridge Opera Journal* 9, no. 2 (1997): 101.

27. On the notated and unnotated screams in Wagner's operas, see Philip Friedheim, "Wagner and the Aesthetics of the Scream," *19th-Century Music* 7, no. 1 (1983): 63–66.

28. Mladen Dolar, *A Voice and Nothing More* (Cambridge, MA: MIT Press, 2007), 105.

29. Aristotle, *De generatione animalium* (Oxford: Oxford University Press, 1992), 5.7.786b.

30. Elisabeth Bronfen, "Kundry's Laughter," *New German Critique* 69 (1996): 147–61.

31. "Die thierische Stimme dient allein dem Ausdrucke des Willens in seinen Erregungen und Bewegungen"; Arthur Schopenhauer, *Parerga und Paralipomena: Kleine philosophische Schriften* (Berlin: Hayn, 1851), 2:699.

32. "Unfähig eines Wortes der Erwiederung."

33. Quoted in Norman Del Mar, *Richard Strauss* (London: Barrie and Radcliffe, 1962), 1:93.

34. Youmans, *Strauss's Orchestral Music*, 68.

35. Schopenhauer's chef d'oeuvre has an exceedingly odd makeup: the first volume was published in 1818 without receiving much attention whatsoever. Therefore, in 1844 Schopenhauer republished this volume with a second volume that comprised the same four "books" as volume 1, each of which commented, clarified, and expanded upon the claims of the first volume. Accordingly, music and opera appear twice in *The World as Will and Representation*, namely in book 3 of volume 1 and in book 3 of volume 2 (*Die Welt als Wille und Vorstellung*), 1:289–302; 2:446–60).

36. Richard Wagner, "Zukunftsmusik," *Schriften und Dichtungen* 7:120.

37. Richard Wagner, Oper und Drama, *Schriften und Dichtungen* 4:215.

38. Schopenhauer, *Die Welt als Wille* 1:576.

39. Puchner, *Stage Fright*, 48.

40. Mary Ann Smart, *Mimomania: Music and Gesture in the Nineteenth Century* (Berkeley: University of California Press, 2004), 167.

41. Friedrich Nietzsche, *Werke in Drei Bänden*, Band 2, ed. Karl Schlechta (Munich: Hanser, 1954), 242.

42. See, for instance, Deathridge, "Post-Mortem on Isolde," 99–105.

43. Georg Lukács, *Die Seele und die Formen* (Berlin: Fleischel, 1911).

44. Richard Wagner, "Beethoven," in *Sämtliche Schriften und Dichtungen* (Leipzig: Breitkopf & Härtel, 1911), 9:70. On Wagner's understanding of the scream, see Friedheim, "Wagner and the Aesthetics of the Scream," 66–67; for two screams that are actually notated in the score of *Lohengrin*, see Hoeckner, "Elsa Screams, or The Birth of Music Drama," 100ff.

45. Schopenhauer, *Parerga und Paralipomena* 2:699.

46. Friedheim, "Wagner and the Aesthetics of the Scream," 68.

47. Catherine Clément, *Opera: The Undoing of Women* (Minneapolis: University of Minnesota Press, 1999).

48. Ryan Minor, "Parsifal's Promise or *Parsifal*'s Reality? On the Politics of Voice Exchange in Wagner's Grail Operas," *Opera Quarterly* 22, no. 2 (2007): 259.

49. Schopenhauer, *Die Welt als Wille und Vorstellung* 1:449.

50. Linda and Michael Hutcheon, "Staging the Female Body," in *Siren Songs: Representations of Gender and Sexuality in Opera*, ed. Mary Ann Smart (Princeton, NJ: Princeton University Press, 2000), 204.

CHAPTER FOUR

1. Theodor W. Adorno, *Versuch über Wagner* (Frankfurt: Suhrkamp, 1974), 82.

2. Paul Bekker, *Franz Schreker: Studie zur Kritik der modernen Oper* (Aachen, Germany: Rimbaud Presse, 1983), 24.

3. Theodor W. Adorno, *In Search of Wagner* (London: Verso, 2005), 91.

4. Wagner, *Schriften und Dichtungen* 1:280: "Wie aus der Ferne längst vergang'ner Zeiten / spricht dieses Mädchens Bild zu mir."

5. Theodor W. Adorno, "Schreker," in *Musikalische Schriften 1–3* (GS 16) (Frankfurt: Suhrkamp, 1974), 370: "Schreker [hat] aus Wagner das Moment der Phantasmagorie herausgelesen, zum Einen und Allen gemacht."

6. Wagner, *Schriften und Dichtungen* 10:339: "Du siehst, mein Sohn / zum Raum wird hier die Zeit."

7. Ibid., 340: "von der mittleren Höhe des Saales vernehmbar."

8. Ibid., 340: "aus der äußersten Höhe der Kuppel."

9. Lawrence Kramer, "Opera, History, and the Sirens," presentation at the annual meeting of the Modern Languages Association, December 29, 2009.

10. See also René Verwer, "Gustav Mahler en het Fernorchester," *Mens en Melodie* 50:220–28.

11. Thomas Schäfer, *Modellfall Mahler: Kompositorische Rezeption in zeitgenössischer Musik* (Munich: Fink, 1999), 215ff.

12. Quoted in Henry-Louis la Grange, *Gustav Mahler* (Oxford: Oxford University Press, 1999), 2:918.

13. Bekker, *Franz Schreker*, 51.

14. Christopher Hailey, *Franz Schreker, 1878–1934: A Cultural Biography* (Cambridge: Cambridge University Press, 1993), 176.

15. Franz Schreker, "Meine Musikdramatische Idee," *Anbruch* 1 (1919), 6–7.

16. This is even a point made by Wagner himself: Richard Wagner, "Das Bühnenweih-festspiel in Bayreuth 1882," in *Schriften und Dichtungen* (Leipzig: Breitkopf & Härtel, 1911), 10:307.

17. Franz Schreker, "Meine Musikdramatische Idee," *Anbruch* (1919), 1:6: "das Problematische der Kunstform Oper überhaupt."

18. Jonathan Crary, *Techniques of the Observer: On Vision and Modernity in the Nineteenth Century* (Cambridge, MA: MIT Press, 1992), 5.

19. Arthur Schopenhauer, "Ueber die Weiber," *Parerga und Paralipomena* (Leipzig: Brockhaus, 1874), 2:655: "ihr Geplapper fortsetzen"; "unter den schönsten Stellen der größten Meisterwerke"

20. Richard Wagner, "Zukunftsmusik," in *Judaism in Music and Other Essays* (Lincoln: University of Nebraska Press, 1995), 332.

21. Jonathan Crary, *Suspensions of Perception: Attention, Spectacle, and Modern Culture* (Cambridge, MA: MIT Press, 2001), 251.

22. See Tom Gunning, "The Cinema of Attractions: Early Film, Its Spectator, and the Avant-Garde," in *Theater and Film: A Comparative Anthology*, ed. Robert Knopf (New Haven, CT: Yale University Press, 2005), 37–45.

23. Martin Gregor-Dellin, *Richard Wagner: Sein Leben, Sein Werk, Sein Jahrhundert* (Munich: Piper, 1980), 506.

24. "Nieder mit der Claque!" In *ÖVZ*, October 12, 1897, pp. 5–6; cited in Sandra McColl, *Music Criticism in Vienna, 1896–97* (Oxford: Oxford University Press, 1996), 79.

25. Wagner, *Schriften und Dichtungen* 9:316.

26. Susan Buck-Morss, *The Dialectics of Seeing: Walter Benjamin and the Arcades Project* (Cambridge, MA: MIT Press, 1991), 80.

27. Susan Buck-Morss, "Aesthetics and Anaesthetics: Walter Benjamin's Artwork Essay Reconsidered," *October* (Autumn 1992), 62:22.

28. Theodor W. Adorno, "Die Naturgeschichte des Theaters," in *Musikalische Schriften 1–3* (GS 16) (Frankfurt, 1974), 309–20; Theodor W. Adorno, "Natural History of the Theatre," in *Quasi una Fantasia: Essays on Modern Music* (London: Verso, 1998), 65–79.

29. We cannot speak of a strictly "Adornian" use of the concept on the one hand and a strictly "Benjaminian" one on the other (one reason why I associated the two variant conceptualizations of phantasmagoria with two particular *texts* rather than their authors). Adorno imports "phantasmagoria" from Benjamin's vocabulary, along with a good many aspects of Benjamin's philosophy. However, Adorno's reception of Benjamin's aesthetics (including concepts such as "aura" and "phantasmagoria") continued over the better part of three decades after Benjamin's early death, changing considerably with time (see Martin Zenck, "Phantas-magorie—Ausdruck—Extrem: Die Auseinandersetzung zwischen Adornos Musikdenken

und Benjamins Kunsttheorie in den dreißiger Jahren," in *Adorno und die Musik*, ed. Otto Kolleritsch (Graz: Universal Edition, 1979), 202–26.

30. Walter Benjamin, *Gesammelte Schriften* (Frankfurt: Suhrkamp, 1982), 7.1: 226.

31. John Dewey, *Art as Experience* (New York: Perigee, 2005), 36–59.

32. Schopenhauer, "Ueber Lärm und Geräusch," *Parerga und Paralipomena*, 2:679.

33. As Jonathan Crary notes, "Schopenhauer is one of the earliest to grasp the link between attention and perceptual disintegration" (*Suspensions of Perception*, p. 55).

34. Benjamin, "On Some Motifs in Baudelaire," *SW* 4:318.

35. Walter Benjamin, *Baudelaire: A Lyric Poet in the Era of High Capitalism* (London: New Left Books, 1973), p. 137.

36. Benjamin, "On Some Motifs in Baudelaire," *SW* 4:318.

37. Adorno, "Die Naturgeschichte des Theaters," 308.

38. Cosima Wagner, *Tagebücher* (Munich: Piper, 1976/77), 1:998.

39. Adorno, "Die Naturgeschichte des Theaters," 309.

40. Fredric Jameson, *Late Marxism: Theodor Adorno or the Persistence of the Dialectic* (London: Verso, 1990), 16.

41. Adorno, *Versuch über Wagner*, 97.

42. Walter Benjamin, *Gesammelte Schriften* 1, no. 2 (Frankfurt am Main: Suhrkamp, 1974), 613–14.

43. Bruno Walter, *Gustav Mahler* (Berlin: S. Fischer, 1957), 30.

44. Theodor W. Adorno, "The Radio Symphony (1941)," in *Essays on Music* (Berkeley: University of California Press, 2002), 257.

45. Adorno, *Versuch über Wagner*, 82.

46. Adorno, *Mahler: Eine musikalische Physiognomik*, GS 13, 157.

47. Hailey, *Franz Schreker*, 176.

48. Adorno, "Schreker," 374.

49. Wagner, *Schriften und Dichtungen* 2:8.

50. Adorno, "Schreker," *Gesammelte Schriften* 16:374.

51. Ibid., 374.

52. Sigmund Freud, *Civilization and Its Discontents*, trans. James Strachey (New York: Norton, 1989), 15.

53. Sigmund Freud, *Beyond the Pleasure Principle*, trans. C. J. M. Hubback (London: International Psycho-Analytical Press, 1922), 74.

54. Adolf Loos, *Trotzdem, 1900–1933* (Innsbruck, Austria: Brenner, 1921), 126.

55. Ibid., 128.

56. Franz Schreker, *Dichtungen für Musik* 1 (Vienna: Universal Edition, 1920), 96.

57. Peter Bevers, "The Seventh Symphony," in *The Mahler Companion*, ed. Donald Mitchell and Andrew Nicholson (Oxford: Oxford University Press, 1999), 385.

58. Hans Heinrich Eggebrecht, *Die Musik Gustav Mahlers* (Munich: Piper, 1982), 50.

59. Susan Buck-Morss, "The Flaneur, the Sandwichman and the Whore: The Politics of Loitering," *New German Critique* (1986), 39:102.

60. Ackbar Abbas, "Cultural Studies in a Postculture," in *Disciplinarity and Dissent in Cultural Studies*, ed. Cary Nelson and Dilip Gaonkar (London: Routledge, 1996), 289–312.

61. "Le fait seul de tourner à droite ou à gauche constituait déjà un acte essentiellement poétique" (M9a,4).

62. "Die Oper als Zentrum," *Gesammelte Schriften* 5, no. 2: 1212; *AP*, 906.

63. Walter Benjamin, *Moskauer Tagebuch* (Frankfurt: Suhrkamp, 1980), 25–26.

64. I am indebted to the Adorno Archives Frankfurt for access to the lecture transcripts (Vo[rlesungen] 3179, p. 153). My translation.

65. This is a connection to which Susan Buck-Morss has pointed already: "The Flaneur, the Sandwichman and the Whore," 105.

66. Adorno, "Radio Voice," in *Current of Music: Elements of a Radio Theory* (Frankfurt: Suhrkamp, 2007).

67. Schreker, *Dichtungen für Musik* 1:68.

CHAPTER FIVE

1. Paul Bekker, *Wandlungen der Oper* (Zurich: Orell Füssli, 1934), 152.

2. Ibid., 153.

3. Richard Batka, *Kranz: Gesammelte Blätter über Musik* (Leipzig: Lauterbach & Kuhn, 1903), 231: "wahrhaft proteusartigen, den Stoffen gemäßen Wandelbarkeit."

4. J. W. von Goethe, *Die Wahlverwandtschaften, Goethe's poetische und prosaische Werke* (Stuttgart: Cotta, 1837), 2:90.

5. Søren Kierkegaard, *Journals and Papers* (Indianapolis: Indiana University Press, 1979), 3:125.

6. Goethe, *Die Wahlverwandtschaften*, 65.

7. Karl Rosenkranz, *Göthe und seine Werke* (Königsberg: Bornträger, 1847), 463.

8. Richard Wagner, "Ueber das Weibliche im Menschlichen," *Schriften und Dichtungen* 12:342: "gänzlich außer ihr liegenden Zwecken."

9. Ibid., 342.

10. Wagner, "Die Walküre," *Schriften und Dichtungen* 6:26: "Unheilig acht ich den Eid, / der unliebende eint; / und mir wahrlich muthe nicht zu, / dass mit Zwang ich halte, was dir nicht haftet."

11. Wagner, *Schriften und Dichtungen* 6:28: "Erfahre so, was von selbst sich fügt, / sei zuvor auch noch nie es geschehn."

12. "Jetzt bist du die Müllerin. / Und die Pacht zahlst du in Liebe. / Das ist doch nur recht und billig."

13. "Schlag ein, mein Junge."

14. "Soll ich? Darf ich? Wird sie mich denn wollen?"

15. Richard Wagner, "Ueber das Weibliche im Menschlichen," 342: "auf Eigenthum und Besitz berechneten."

16. Bekker, *Wandlungen der Oper*, 6.

17. Wilfried Kugel, *Der Unverantwortliche: Das Leben des Hanns Heinz Ewers* (Düsseldorf: Grupello, 1992), 175.

18. "Dies Untier, das dem Hades selbst entstieg / dies Ungeheuer, hinkend, missgestalt."

19. "So viel sah ich, so viel—nur dich erblickt' ich nicht."

20. "Doch will ich weiter leben in der Träume Welt / für dich, geliebter Gatte, für dich allein!"

21. "Mag die Sonne ausbrennen meiner Augen Licht."

22. E. T. A. Hoffmann, *Sämtliche Werke in Sechs Bänden* (Frankfurt: Deutscher Klassiker Verlag, 1985), 3:36: "Nur die Augen schienen ihm gar seltsam starr und tot."

23. "Überhaupt hatten ihre Augen etwas Starres, beinahe möcht ich sagen, keine Sehkraft."

24. Hoffmann, *Sämtliche Werke*, 3:36: "Es schien, als wenn nun erst die Sehkraft entzündet würde; immer lebendiger und lebendiger flammten die Blicke."

25. "Schau ich so anders aus, seit ich sehe?"

26. "Der mir das Licht gab—das mein Glück zerschlug."

27. Richard Wagner, "Jesus von Nazareth: Ein dichterischer Entwurf," *Schriften und Dichtungen* 11:273–324.

28. "Deiner Stimme Klang hült mich ein / wie ein warmer Regen im Mai."

29. Quoted in Kugel, *Der Unverantwortliche*, 175.

30. "Die dichterisch den Verismus zum Kinodrama vergröbern"; "das Kinopublikum unserer Zeit." For a detailed case study on the relationship between film and opera in d'Albert's oeuvre, see Benjamin Goose, "The Opera of the Film? Eugen d'Albert's *Der Golem*," *Cambridge Opera Journal* 19, no. 2 (2007): 139–66.

31. Walter Niemann, *Die Musik der Gegenwart* (Stuttgart, Germany: Deutsche Verlagsanstalt, 1922), 100: "moderne großstädtische Kriegs- und Massenpublikum."

32. Niemann, *Die Musik der Gegenwart*, 101.

33. Richard Batka, *Aus der Opernwelt: Prager Kritiken und Skizzen* (Munich: Callewy, 1907), 163.

34. "Und so fein ist mein Ohr, dass deiner Schritte Rhythmus / leise zittern in meinem Herz."

35. "Mein Ohr trank seiner Stimme Klang."

36. "Der Stierkampf ist aus, Madame."

37. Johann Gottlieb Fichte, *Grundlage des Naturrechts*, in *Werke* (Berlin: Walter de Gruyter, 1971), 3:315.

38. Friedrich Schlegel, *Lucinde, Kritische Friedrich Schlegel Ausgabe* 5:13: "Allegorie auf die Vollendung des Männlichen und Weiblichen zur vollen ganzen Menschheit."

39. Immanuel Kant, *Gesammelte Schriften (Akademieausgabe)*, 6:227.

40. G. W. F. Hegel, *Grundlinien der Philosophie des Rechts* (Berlin: Nicolai, 1821), 168.

41. See also Adrian Daub, *Zwillingshafte Gebärden* (Würzburg, Germany: Königshausen & Neumann, 2009), 15ff.

42. Theodor W. Adorno, *Versuch über Wagner, Gesammelte Schriften* (Frankfurt: Suhrkamp, 1980), 13:27.

43. Adorno, *Versuch über Wagner*, 98.

44. Quoted in Wilhelm Raupp, *Eugen d'Albert: Ein Künstler- und Menschen-Schicksal* (Leipzig: Koehler & Amelang, 1930), 295: "Zwei Kulturwelten stehen sich in diesem Drama gegebüber: das Zeitalter des Rokoko und die Zeit der französischen Revolution. Nur eine Gewalt mag beide zu vereinen: die Liebe. Mit einem feinen Sinn für Humor hat d'Albert Gegensatz und Vereinigung beider Welten zunächst gewissermaßen parodistisch gezeichnet."

45. "Da sind auch musikalisch zwei Welten einander gegenüber gestellt: das Menuett auf der einen, das durchkomponierte Rezitativ auf der anderen Seite."

46. Cited in Raupp, *Eugen d'Albert*, 295: "In [der] musikalischen Sphäre des Menuetts bewegt sich auch im Anfang Alaine, bis ihr (im zweiten Akt) die Liebe zu Marc-Arron auch seine Sprache lehrt, die musikalisch ein strenges, deklmatorisches Pathos kennzeichnet."

47. Ibid., 295.

48. Richard Batka, *Aus der Opernwelt: Prager Kritiken und Skizzen* (Munich: Callwey, 1907), 171.

49. Sophus Michaelis, *Revolutionshochzeit*, trans. Marie Herzfeld (St. Louis: Concordia, 1908), 15: "Deine Heirat ist Symbol."

50. Ibid., 16.

51. Ibid., 15.

CHAPTER SIX

1. Nike Wagner, *Wagner Theater* (Frankfurt: Insel, 1998), 293.

2. Berndt Wilhelm Wessling, *Wieland Wagner, der Enkel: Eine Biographie* (Cologne, Germany: Tonger, 1997), 41.

3. Heinrich Schenker, "Siegfried Wagner," *Die Zukunft* (1896), 14:281.

4. Schenker, "Siegfried Wagner," 281.

5. Brigitte Hamann, *Winifred Wagner: A Life at the Heart of Hitler's Bayreuth* (New York: Houghton Mifflin, 2006), 7.

6. Ibid., 9.

7. Houston Stewart Chamberlain, *Richard Wagner* (London: Dent, 1900), 368.

8. Carl Friedrich Glasenapp, *Siegfried Wagner und seine Kunst* (Leipzig: Breitkopf und Härtel, 1911), ix.

9. Ibid., vi.

10. Siegfried Wagner, *Erinnerungen* (Frankfurt: Peter Lang, 2005), 88.

11. Glasenapp, *Siegfried Wagner*, x.

12. Ibid., xi.

13. Ibid., xii.

14. Nicholas Vaszonyi, *Richard Wagner: Self-Promotion and the Making of a Brand* (Cambridge: Cambridge University Press, 2011).

15. Karl Storck, *Geschichte der Musik*, Zweiter Band (Stuttgart, Germany: Metzler, 1922), 313.

16. Storck, *Geschichte der Musik*, Zweiter Band, 313.

17. Cited in Hamann, *Winifred Wagner*, 6.

18. Richard Strauss and Clemens Krauss, *Briefwechel* (Munich: Beck, 1964), 236.

19. Cited in Hamann, *Winifred Wagner*, 7.

CHAPTER SEVEN

1. Gustave Flaubert, *Madame Bovary: Moeurs de province* (Paris: Charpentier, 1887), 16: "Dont les deux bandeaux noirs semblaient chacun d'un seul morceau."

2. Fyodor Dostoyevsky, *The Karamazov Brothers*, trans. Ignat Avsey (Oxford: Oxford University Press, 1998), 32.

3. Charles Dickens, *Oliver Twist* (New York: Hurd and Houghton, 1867), 98.

4. Cited in Thomas Forrest Kelly, *First Nights at the Opera* (New Haven, CT: Yale University Press, 2004), 269.

5. Wagner, *Schriften und Dichtungen* 5:224: "Verfluchte Lohe, dich lösch' ich aus!"

6. Cited in Kelly, *First Nights*, 269.

7. Carl Dahlhaus, *Richard Wagners Musikdramen* (Stuttgart, Germany: Reclam, 1996), 111.

8. Sven Friedrich, "Loge: Der progressive Konservative," in *"Alles ist nach seiner Art": Figuren in Richard Wagners "Der Ring des Nibelungen,"* ed. Udo Bermbach (Stuttgart, Germany: Metzler, 2001), 182.

9. Wagner, *Schriften und Dichtungen* 5:226: "In Wasser, Erd' und Luft, viel frug ich, forschte bei allen, wo Kraft nur sich rührt und Keime sich regen."

10. Ibid.: "Verlacht nur ward meine fragende List."

11. Wagner, *Schriften und Dichtungen* 5:217: "Doch des Feindes Neid zum Nutz sich fügen, / lehrt nur Schlauheit und List, / wie Loge verschlagen sie übt."

12. Giovanni Verga, *Cavalleria Rusticana and Other Stories* (London: Penguin Classics, 1999), 78.

13. G. W. F. Hegel, *The Phenomenology of Spirit*, trans. A. V. Miller (Oxford: Oxford University Press, 1977), 208.

14. Cesare Lombroso, *Criminal Man*, trans. Nicole Gibson and Nicole Hahn Rafter (Durham, NC: Duke University Press, 2006), 204.

15. David G. Horn, *The Criminal Body: Lombroso and the Anatomy of Deviance* (London: Routledge, 2003), 34.

16. Cesare Lombroso and Guglielmo Ferrero, *Criminal Woman, the Prostitute, and the Normal Woman*, trans. Nicole Hahn Rafter and Mary Gibson (Durham, NC: Duke University Press, 2004), 123–124.

17. Mary Eliza Haweis, *The Art of Beauty* (reprint) (Boston: Adamant Media, 2005), 274.

18. Elizabeth Wilson, *Adorned in Dreams: Fashion and Modernity*, 130.

19. Wilkie Collins, *Armadale: A Novel* (New York: Harper & Brothers, 1902), 288.

20. Galia Ofek, "Sensational Hair: Gender, Genre and Fetishism in the Sensational Decade," in *Victorian Sensations*, ed. Kimberly Harrison and Richard Fantina (Columbus, OH: Ohio State University Press, 2006), 111.

21. Walter Frisch, *German Modernism: Music and the Arts* (Berkeley: University of California Press, 2007).

22. Benjamin Curtis, *Music Makes the Nation: Nationalist Composers and Nation Building in Nineteenth-Century Europe* (Amherst, NY: Cambria Press, 2008), 11.

23. Gerhard Winkler, "Franz Schmidts 'Fredegundis': Bildungsroman einer Femme Fatale," *Frauengestalten in der Oper des 19. und 20. Jahrhunderts*, ed. Carmen Ottner (Vienna: Doblinger, 2003).

24. Quoted in Norbert Tschulik, *Franz Schmidt* (Vienna: Lafite, 1972), 46.

25. Carmen Ottner, " 'Die Verkörperung meiner Rothaarigen Heldin Fredegundis': Franz Schmidts Briefe an Gusti Hasterlik (1916–1921)," in *Musica Conservieta: Festschrift für Gunter Brosche* (Tutzing, Germany: Schneider, 1999), 275–90.

26. Cited in ibid., 282.

27. Cited in ibid., 287.

28. Anne Harrowitz, *Antisemitism, Misogyny and the Logic of Cultural Difference: Cesare Lombroso and Matilde Serao* (Lincoln: University of Nebraska Press, 1993), 108.

29. Otto Weininger, *Geschlecht und Character* (Vienna: Braumüller, 1905), 84: "Je länger das Haar, desto kürzer der Verstand."

30. Felix Dahn, *Fredegundis: Historischer Roman aus der Völkerwanderung* (Leipzig: Breitkopf & Härtel, 1886), 10.

31. Dahn, *Fredegundis*, 13.

32. Cited in Tschulik, *Franz Schmidt*, 46.

33. Cited in Ottner, "Die Verkörperung," 286.

34. Ibid., 286.

35. Winkler, "Franz Schmidts 'Fredegundis,'" 189.

36. Winkler, "Franz Schmidts 'Fredegundis,'" 190.

37. Winkler, "Franz Schmidts 'Fredegundis,'" 190.

38. Janine Ortiz, *"Feuer muss fressen, was Flamme gebar": Franz Schrekers Oper "Irrelohe"* (Vienna: Are Musik, 2008).

39. Gerhart Hauptmann, *Das Friedensfest: Eine Familienkatastrophe* (Berlin: S. Fischer, 1904), 13.

40. Franz Schreker, *Dichtungen für Musik* (Vienna: Universal-Edition, 1921), 165.

41. See Adrian Daub, *"Zwillingshafte Gebärden": Zur kulturellen Wahrnehmung des vierhändigen Klavierspiels im neunzehnten Jahrhundert* (Würzburg, Germany: Königshausen & Neumann, 2009), 111.

42. Cited in Christopher Hailey, *Franz Schreker, 1878–1934: A Cultural Biography* (Cambridge: Cambridge University Press, 1993), 177.

43. Hailey, *Franz Schreker*, 182.

44. Ibid., 182.

45. Schreker, *Dichtungen für Musik*, 170.

46. Ibid., 158.

47. Ibid., 165.

48. Ibid., 166.

49. Ibid., 179.

50. Ibid., 177.

51. Ibid., 166.

52. Ibid., 187.

53. Hailey, *Franz Schreker*, 181.

54. Ortiz, *"Feuer muss fressen,"* 111.

55. Ibid., 110.

56. GS 13, 86: "Das unablässig flackernd nicht von der Stelle sich regt."

57. Adrian Daub, "Adorno's Schreker: Charting the Self-Dissolution of the Distant Sound," *Cambridge Opera Journal* 18, no. 3 (Autumn 2006): 247–71.

58. Erich Käster, *Lärm im Spiegel* (Leipzig: Weller, 1929), 9.

59. Helmut Lethen, *Cool Conduct* (Berkeley: University of California Press, 2002).

60. Cited in Hailey, *Schreker*, 168 (article: "Kompositionsunterricht"); on Schreker and the

New Objectivity, see Ulrike Kienzle, *Das Trauma hinter dem Traum* (Schliengen, Germany: Argus, 1998), 38–40.

61. Carl Dahlhaus, *Schoenberg and the New Music* (Cambridge: Cambridge University Press, 1987), 193.

62. Hailey, *Franz Schreker*, 176.

CODA

1. Stephen Hinton, *Weill's Musical Theater: Stages of Reform* (Berkeley: University of California Press, 2012), 311.

2. Sidney Perelman and Ogden Nash, *A Touch of Venus* (New York: Little Brown, 1944), 25.

3. Ibid., 30.

4. Kurt Weill, "Zeitoper," *Musik und musikalisches Theater: Gesammelte Schriften mit einer Auswahl von Gesprächen und Interviews*, ed. Stephen Hinton and Jürgen Schebera (Mainz: Schott, 2000), 64–67; here, p. 65.

5. Ricarda Wackers, *Dialog der Künste: Die Zusammenarbeit von Kurt Weill und Yvan Goll* (Münster, Germany: Waxmann, 2004), 145ff.

6. Austin Clarkson and Hyesu Shin, "Zeus und Elida: Wolpe's Kunstjazz Opera," *Contemporary Music Review* 27, nos. 2–3 (2008): 251–69.

7. Austin Clarkson, *On the Music of Stefan Wolpe: Essays and Recollections* (Hillsdale, NY: Pendragon Press, 2003), 10.

8. *Contemporary Music Review* 27, no. 2/3 (2008).

9. Hinton, *Weill's Musical Theater*, x.

10. Kurt Weill, "*Tannhäuser* im Rundfunk," *Musik und musikalisches Theater*, 219.

11. Kurt Weill, *Briefe an die Familie (1914–1950)*, ed. Lys Symonette and Elmar Juchem (Stuttgart, Germany: Metzler, 2000), 44 (April 17, 1917).

12. See also Hinton, *Weill's Musical Theater*, xi.

13. Andreas Hauff, "Orientierungsversuche in der Großstadt: Verweise und Bekenntnisse in Kurt Weills *Street Scene*," in *Street Scene: Der urbane Raum im Musiktheater des 20. Jahrhunderts*, ed. Stefan Weiss and Jürgen Schebera (Münster: Waxmann, 2006), 35–55; here, p. 53.

14. Weill, *Briefe an die Familie (1914–1950)*, 44 (April 17, 1917).

15. Feruccio Busoni, *Versuch einer neuen Ästhetik der Tonkunst* (Leipzig: Insel, 1917), 13.

16. Kurt Weill, "Die Neue Oper," *Musik und musikalisches Theater*, 42–45; here, p. 42.

17. Weill, "Die Neue Oper," *Musik und musikalisches Theater* 44.

18. Bertolt Brecht, *Journale* 1 (BBA vol. 26), ed. Marianne Conrad and Werner Hecht (Berlin: Aufbau, 1994), 436 (October 16, 1940); quoted in Hinton, *Weill's Musical Theater*, 37.

19. Weill, "Die Neue Oper," 43.

20. Weill, "Was ist musikalisches Theater?," *Musik und musikalisches Theater*, 144–47; here, p. 147.

21. "Kurt Weill, der Komponist der *Dreigroschenoper*, will den Begriff des Musikdramas zerstören," *Wiener Allgemeine Zeitung* (March 9, 1929), in Kurt Weill, *Musik und musikalisches Theater*, 442–44; here, p. 443.

22. Kurt Weill, "Die Oper: Wohin?," *Musik und musikalisches Theater*, 92–96; here, p. 95.

23. See for example, Kurt Weill, "Das Formproblem der Modernen Oper," *Musik und musikalisches Theater*, 134–36; here, p. 136.

24. See for example, Kurt Weill, *Musik und musikalisches Theater*, 108.

25. Cecil Gray, *A Survey of Contemporary Music* (London: Oxford University Press, 1924), 29.

26. Busoni, *Versuch einer neuen Ästhetik*, 14.

27. "Kurt Weill, der Komponist," 443.

28. Joel Haney, "Slaying the Wagnerian Monster: Hindemith, *Das Nusch-Nuschi*, and Musical Germanness after the Great War," *Journal of Musicology* 25, no. 4 (Fall 2008): 339–93.

29. Perelman and Nash, *One Touch of Venus*, 98.

30. Foster Hirsch, *Kurt Weill on Stage: From Berlin to Broadway* (New York: Knopf, 2002), 219.

31. Kurt Weill, "*Tannhäuser* im Rundfunk," *Musik und musikalisches Theater*, 219.

INDEX

Haweis, Mary Eliza, 173–74
Hegel, Georg Wilhelm Friedrich, 7–8, 12, 47, 50
Henry, Marc, 135, 140
Herbart, Johann Friedrich, 10
heredity, 29, 42–43, 153–54, 157, 166, 174, 182, 183–88
Herwegh, Georg, 3–4, 14
Herzfeld, Marie, 145
heterosexuality, 39
Hindemith, Paul, 57; *Nusch-Nuschi, Das*, 198
Hinton, Stephen, 196
historicism, 128, 149–50, 185
Hoffmann, E.T.A., 137–38
Hofmannsthal, Hugo von, 95
Hölderlin, Friedrich, 7–8
homoeroticism, 42
homosexuality, 147, 153, 163, 166
Humperdinck, Engelbert, 29, 53–54, 74, 128, 152, 195; *Hänsel und Gretel*, 195; *Königskinder*, 54–55
Hutcheon, Linda and Michael, 41, 94

Idealism, German, 2, 6, 14, 36, 134
illusion, 25–27, 62, 70–76, 108–9, 138. *See also* audience
impotence, 32, 47
incest, 8, 38, 51, 159
individuality, 17
infinity, 14
innovation in opera, 5, 12

Jaloux, Edmond, 123
Jameson, Frederic, 109
jazz, 58
Jesus, in opera, 138–40

Kant, Immanuel, 82, 132
Kierkegaard, Søren, 6, 91, 131
Kittler, Friedrich, 16, 118
Klaren, George, 61–65, 69
Klemperer, Otto, 58
Korngold, Julius, 181

Koss, Juliet, 26
Kracauer, Siegfried, 189
Kramer, Lawrence, 5, 99
Krenek, Ernst, 57
Kristeva, Julia, 32, 81, 83

Lacan, Jacques, 152
language, 90–91
Laube, Heinrich, 12
laughter, 48
law, 179–80, 182
Lee, Sherry, 64
Leroux, Gaston, *Phantom of the Opera*, 111–12, 115–16, 118–19
Levin, David, 49
librettists, 11, 54, 61, 73, 94, 95, 103, 129–31, 133, 135–36, 145, 147, 156, 175, 191
Lion, Ferdinand, 130, 145, 148
Liszt, Franz, *Années de Pèlerinage*, 21
Lombroso, Cesare, 173, 178, 184
Loos, Adolf, 118–20
Lothar, Rudolf, 133
Louis, Rudolf, 10, 74
love, 1; autonomy of, 9; commodification of, 15; nuanced, 157–58; as path of salvation, 4, 7, 33; potions, 16; renounced, 79–81, 89, 91; typology of, 33
Lukács, George, 91

Mahler, Gustav, 105, 111; *klagende Lied, Das*, 100; *Seventh Symphony*, 122; *Third Symphony*, 111
Mann, Thomas, 24–26, 39, 67
Marx, Karl, 107, 171
marriage, 3, 28–29, 127–50; loveless, 158, 161; repeated, 131; symbolic, 148
Mascagni, Pietro, *Cavalleria rusticana*, 172
maturation, sexual, 31, 47, 54
Michaelis, Sophus, 145, 148
Milhaud, Darius, 58
mimesis, theatrical, 49
Minor, Ryan, 93
modernism, 26, 58, 60, 150

Wagner, Richard (*cont.*)
  73, 75, 84, 131, 158, 162; *Siegfried Idyll*,
  151–52; *Tannhaüser*, 79, 115; technical
  innovations, 5, 18, 104, 116; *Tristan und
  Isolde*, 1, 4, 8, 9, 15–17, 28, 79, 121, 140–41,
  161, 198; *Walküre, Die*, 24–25, 38, 133–34,
  159, 169, 188. *See also* Gesamtkunstwerk
Wagner, Siegfried, 11, 26, 29, 54, 74, 128,
  151–67; *An Allem ist Hütchen Schuld*,
  159–61, 163, 164; *Friedensengel, Der*, 158,
  163; *Herzog Wildfang*, 163, 166; *Kobold,
  Der*, 163–66; *Liebesopfer, Das (Wernhart)*, 163–64; *Rainulf und Adelasia*,
  161–63; *Schmied von Marienburg*, 163;
  Schwarzschwanenreich, 163; *Sternengebot,
  Das*, 158–59; *Wahnfried Idyll*, 151–52
Walter, Bruno, 111
Warden, Bruno, 175, 179–80
Wedekind, Frank, 95
Weill, Kurt, 2–3, 57, 58; *Dreigroschenoper*,
  198, 01; *Lady in the Dark*, 198; *Neue Or-
  pheus*, 192; *One Touch of Venus*, 191–94,

199–201; *Sieben Todsünden, Die*, 201;
  Street Scenes, 195, 198
Weininger, Otto, 83, 178
Weissman, Adolf, 23–24
Welleminsky, Ignaz, 175, 179–80
Wesendonck, Mathilde and Otto, 4
Wilde, Oscar, *Birthday of the Infanta*, 61–66, 73
Wilson, Elizabeth, 174
Winckelmann, Johann Joachim, 19
Winkler, Gerhard, 181
Wolpe, Stefan, *Zeus und Elida*, 192–93, 200
Wolzogen, Ernst von, 11, 94
Wolzogen, Hans von, 147, 165
women, 112; hair color of, 173; silenced,
  77–78, 84–86, 93, 180; undoing of, 92

Youmans, Charles Dowell, 78

Zemlinsky, Alexander von, 26, 27, 61, 75;
  Zwerg, Der, 61–65, 67–70, 73–74
Ziegler, Hans Severus, 56–58, 76
Žižek, Slavoj, 6, 33, 42